God Does Exist!

Defending the faith using presuppositional apologetics, evidence, and the impossibility of the contrary

By

Michael A. Robinson

Bloomington, IN

Milton Keynes, UK

AuthorHouse™
1663 Liberty Drive, Suite 200
Bloomington, IN 47403
www.authorhouse.com
Phone: 1-800-839-8640

AuthorHouse™ UK Ltd.
500 Avebury Boulevard
Central Milton Keynes, MK9 2BE
www.authorhouse.co.uk
Phone: 08001974150

First published by AuthorHouse 6/8/2006

ISBN: 1-4208-2761-8 (e)
ISBN: 1-4208-2762-6 (sc)

Library of Congress Control Number: 2005901817

Printed in the United States of America
Bloomington, Indiana

This book is printed on acid-free paper.

TABLE OF CONTENTS

DEDICATION

I offer this book to my dear Lord Jesus Christ. This work is given to my Savior, mixed with error and sin, as are all my other works, which amount to nothing without His amazing grace.

INTRODUCTION

THE COMMAND TO WITNESS

One hears silly clichés like, "The truth needs no defense," or "The Bible is a lion; you don't need to defend it; just let it loose, and it will defend itself." These are simplistic and sentimental blatherings of theological neophytes and ecclesiastical cowards. [1]

To know God and make Him known (The Youth With A Mission's purpose statement).

The unchurched population in America would be equivalent to the 11th largest nation in the world. [2]

It has been estimated that probably 95% of American Church members have never led anyone to Christ. Thus the army of Christ has been more than decimated. [3]

---

[1]. Andrew Sandlin, *Keeping Our Sacred Trust* (Vallecito, CA: Chalcedon Foundation, 1999), p. 4.

[2]. George Barna, *Evangelism that Works* (Ventura, CA: Regal Books, 1995), p. 47.

[3]. D. James Kennedy, *Evangelism Explosion* (Wheaton, Illinois: Tyndale House, 1977), p. 4.

Some who demonstrate a passion for accurate doctrine, place a question mark over their love for God by evidencing no active love for the lost. [4]

Therefore go and teach all nations, baptizing them in the name of the Father and of the Son and of the Holy Spirit (Matthew 28:19).

I have become all things to all men, that I might by all means save some (1 Corinthians 9:22).

Preach the Word, be instant in season and out of season, reprove, rebuke, exhort with all long-suffering and doctrine (2 Timothy 4:2).

Therefore those who were scattered went everywhere evangelizing (Acts 8:4).

The authentic Christianity of the Bible is not a safe, smug, cozy, selfish, escapist religion. On the contrary, it is deeply disturbing to our sheltered security. It is an explosive… force, which pulls us out from our narrow self-centeredness and flings us into God's world to witness and serve. [5]

Belief Plus Action

John Stuart Mill set forward a truth that all Christians should affirm when he stated, "One man with a belief is equal to a thousand men with only interest." I do not agree with most of what Mill propagated, but that statement is true. Just look at the Muslim fanatics who will do anything for their false god. Will Christians embrace a more impassioned zeal for the only true God of love and justice? My prayer is that the Lord would dislodge apathy from the church, and we all would become emblazoned followers of the God of grace and truth.

4. Walter Chantry, *Today's Gospel, Authentic or Synthetic* (Carlisle, PA: Banner of Truth, 1985), p. 24.

5. John Stott, *Contemporary Christianity* (Madison, WI: Inter-Varsity Press, 1992), p. 335.

Do you see, do you see,
All the people sinking down?
Don't you care, don't you care,
Are you gonna let them
drown? How can you be so numb,
Not to care if they come? [6]

My Reliance on Other Writers and Apologists

St. Bernard of Clairvaux compared his fellow scholars and students to dwarfs who could not see very far. He added that we could "stand upon the shoulders of giants that great cloud of witnesses, who taught before, so that we may see farther and with greater clarity." I have stood on the shoulders of great scholars and apologists as I have witnessed, debated, and during the writing of this book. I hesitate to mention that I stood on their work and scholarship because I know these pages are far below the academic excellence that mark the work of Cornelius Van Til, Greg Bahnsen, R.C. Sproul, Robert Morey, and John Frame. Yet this book could not have been possible without the sweat and toil of these men and others. My evangelistic application is not invented by me. It is the derivative of Michael Horton, Ray Comfort, and many others. In stating this, I am not trying to portray myself as a man of deep humility. The truth of their greatness and my weakness is self-evident when you compare their books with this book. I am not a scholar, or even a son of a scholar.

A sign stated: "Hire a teenager while he still knows everything." Most of my life, in much of what I was interested in, I thought I had all the answers. I did not have all the answers then, and I still do not have them. But I have enough wisdom in knowing that I do not know it all. I thank God for His good grace and the Holy Spirit who teaches us the truth. I am simply one who has a burning desire to see the gospel preached and defended from sea to sea and pole to pole. My hope is that the following pages will stir up your passion for evangelism, missions, and apologetics.

---

[6]. Melody Green, *No Compromise: The Life Story Of Keith Green* (Eugene, OR: Harvest House, 2000), p. 213.

I want to mention that in the witnessing conversations that follow, and in some of my comments, I have unconsciously borrowed from the thousands of books I have read. I have integrated in my evangelism so many truths gleaned from the works of apologists and scholars, that I cannot trace them all down because I have read almost a book a day for many years. I apologize if I have failed to give credit where credit is due. My desire is not to arrogate the work of others. Yet only a very small part of this book is conceived by me. I have only fashioned and forged the scholarship of others into street level witnessing methods. I will only take credit for any of the philosophical naiveté which dwells between the golden nuggets of truth produced by the great and godly men of letters.

> Beloved, while I was very diligent to write to you concerning our common salvation, I found it necessary to write to you exhorting you to contend earnestly for the faith which was once for all delivered to the saints (Jude 3).

> Sanctify the Lord God in your hearts, and always be ready to give a defense to everyone who asks you a reason for the hope that is in you, with meekness and fear (1 Peter 3:15).

Commanded to Go

All Christians are commanded to defend the gospel. The defense of the gospel, in and of itself, will save no one directly. Romans 1:16 says, "The gospel is the power of God unto salvation." Romans chapter ten, instructs the church that "faith comes by hearing the word of God" as it asks the question, "How can they hear without a preacher?" We are commanded to preach God's word as the means of the salvation of the elect. We should preach the rigor of the law and the comfort of the gospel. And we must pray that God would have mercy on the lost soul, and that the Lord would open the unbeliever's heart. Modernity may hate preaching, yet we are called not just to share the gospel, but to preach it. In Mark 16:15, Jesus said, "Go into all the world and preach the gospel to every creature." He added, "But you shall receive power when the Holy Spirit has come upon you; and you shall be witnesses to Me in Jerusalem, and in all Judea… and to the end of the earth" (Acts 1:8). The Great Commission must be our mission. It is the duty, and privilege of every Christian to obey the commandment to preach the saving gospel to the lost.

> He who continually goes forth weeping, bearing seed for sowing, shall doubtless come again with rejoicing, bringing his sheaves with him (Psalms 126:6).

Frequently, due to fear or slothfulness, we become experts at finding "reasons" why we do not have to witness in the marketplace. We come up with all sorts of "reasons," which are in reality just excuses. Many of Christianity's best and brightest fail to evangelize. They sit around as pedantic cave-dwellers, with their ashen faces that bespeak of men who rarely venture out beyond the narrow illumination of a library lamp. The weeping reaper's attitude, that the Psalmist promotes in Psalms 126, is what must be affirmed and practiced by the church. The main reasons most believers fail to witness in public are fear, indifference, and busyness. I have seen this in both genders and in all age groups and all races. The solution is prayer and obedience. We must ask God to break our hearts for those who do not know Christ. We should schedule time to go out and witness in the public square, on the campus, and in the streets. Many exercise buffs get up everyday at the crack of dawn to do aerobics or to go jogging. They usually make it because they have planned ahead. So we should get serious about the Great Commission and toss out all the excuses and make specific plans to witness regularly. Jesus made it a priority, and we must obey His command. Our attitude should be one of "no compromise." We must put away all excuses.

> Now while Paul waited for them at Athens, his spirit was provoked within him when he saw that the city was given over to idols. Therefore he reasoned in the synagogue with the Jews and with the Gentile worshipers, and in the marketplace daily with those who happened to be there… And he reasoned in the synagogue every Sabbath, and persuaded both Jews and Greeks… And he went into the synagogue and spoke boldly for three months, reasoning and persuading concerning the things of the kingdom of God. When some were hardened and did not believe, but spoke evil of the Way before the multitude, he departed from them and withdrew the disciples, reasoning daily in the school of Tyrannus. And this continued for two years, so that all who dwelt in Asia heard the word of the Lord

Jesus, both Jews and Greeks (Acts 17:16-17, 18:4, 19:8-10).

The passages listed above report that Paul "reasoned" with the lost. The Apostle Paul was an intellectual giant. He debated, argued, and reasoned with the cultured, as well as the religious and the philosophical. Today it seems like many intellectual giants of the church do not witness in the marketplace. Some may climb down from their ivory towers to do a formal debate, but they rarely hit the streets and the public square. I have been a believer for over two decades. And I have noticed most of the Christian witness in the public sphere has been from believers who attend emotionally based churches that often lack intellectual vigor. I have seldom seen Christians witnessing on the university campuses, streets, or marketplaces, who are members of churches that have been blessed with the deepest scholarship and academic excellence. I have had the privilege of rubbing shoulders with members of Reformed churches. The groups that nurtured the Van Til's, the Gerstner's, the Bahnsen's, and the Frame's. I have observed numerous members of the Reformed wing of the church, and I have been overwhelmed at the brightness of their wit, the depth of their theological sophistication, and their vivid, vigorous defense of the faith. But I am often grieved at the lack of passion for personal evangelism in the lives of many who delight in the intellectual quality, brilliance, and penetration of the books authored by the most orthodox scholars.

It breaks my heart to see the believers, who have the best understanding of scripture, leave the work of evangelism to the anti-intellectual churches, as the bright and the brainy remain holed-up in their compounds of abstract academia. This is not my attempt at a scorched earth policy toward theologians and scholars. Many of the ablest scholars have been fervent in their own personal evangelism. Cornelius Van Til would consistently go out in his neighborhood, nursing homes, and Wall Street to witness to children and adults. We should follow in his footsteps as well as Whitefield, Edwards, and M'Cheyne.

Pray Prepare Plan

You may know the *Institutes* like a Sumo wrestler knows the late night menu at Denny's. You may be able to discuss the great doctrines of the word with the sharpest theological minds. You may have read Warfield, Kuyper, Clark, and Frame, but if you never framed an argument for Christ to an unbeliever, you need to repent. It is sin to leave all your theological proficiency in your personal study and in the halls of theological academia. Jesus calls us to care and to put foot and mouth to that concern by preaching the gospel to the unsaved. If you have fear, try the three "P's." Pray for boldness. Prepare for your witness through role playing and training. Plan for your witness as you carve out a specific time to evangelize every month. God is not just looking for wise and sagacious theologians to win the lost; He has enlisted all believers to follow Him in His work of evangelism. An old preacher once said, "God is not looking for ability, but availability." Evangelism training is essential. But we should start witnessing the minute we are saved, while we are being trained, and after we are trained. We should follow Isaiah when he cried to God, "Here I am send me." One of the first things Paul did after his conversion was to go to the synagogues and preach the gospel. The most important reason God doesn't take the Christian straight to heaven upon his conversion is the command that trumpets: "Be my witnesses."

> "You are My witnesses," says the LORD, "and My Servant whom I have chosen, that you may know and believe Me, and understand that I am He. Before Me there was no God formed, nor shall there be after Me. I, even I, am the LORD, and besides Me there is no Savior" (Is. 43:10,11).

Our desire should be for the excellencies of Jesus and a fervent desire to proclaim this to the world. One drop of active and passionate Christianity is worth more than a whole ocean of stiff, indolent, and uncaring ecclesiasticism. The church is not a building. It is a living, breathing organism. It is the body of Christ. A physical body will get sick and eventually die when deprived of exercise and activity. The same is true with the body of Christ. We must have a lively and active faith. Sitting around like gospel sluggards, getting fat off discussions of doctrinal precisions is a good way for a good church to get sick and eventually die. Faith without works is dead. One of the most important works for the church is to declare the truth found in Christ. It may be easier to ignore our evangelism duty, but it is never as rewarding as following in the footsteps of Jesus in preaching the gospel. There have been times that I went out evangelizing when I did not feel like going out. Every time I went, I was glad I went. Most of those times I came back almost walking on air. If you are unsure about stepping out as a witness, go. If you are fearful, go. If you don't feel like going, go! Schedule the day and the time, and go. You will be glad you did, and often you will return with joy and a new spring in your step. Obedience is better than sacrifice. Step out and preach the gospel. Plan it and do it consistently.

My goal for this book is to help stir up the church for evangelism. Yes, I have had the blessing of reading many powerful books authored by Reformed and Presbyterian scholars. Reformed apologists are some of the keenest and wisest in the history of the church. I have noticed that many of those who know the most about God's word have tended to avoid witnessing in the marketplace. I haven't had to say, "Excuse me" for bumping into a Christian scholar and spilling his tracts on the street. I know many of them witness through their books and the internet. That is good and grand. But Jesus said, "Go into all the world and preach the gospel." We must have a passion to hoist King Christ everywhere and as often as possible, by all biblical means necessary. I like how Tom Ertl of Reno, Georgia put it in the letter to the editor for the *Credenda Agenda* in his defense of Charismatics:

> Dear Editors, Your comments on Charismatics… when you used the analogy of their going out to sea with one oar and returning to the shore for the other… Let me suggest a general analogy concerning Presbyterianism… Not only do the Presbyterians have both oars, but they have the most seaworthy ship of all the ports of Christendom. The magnificence of their ships is due to the preciseness and accuracy of the thorough study of the manual. The manual, though difficult to understand by some shipbuilders, has been mastered by many generations of ship building Presbyterians. Their understanding and development of the manual is unparalleled in the history of ship building. One small problem… the good ship Presbyterian is still in dry dock. There is anticipation that one day it may finally be perfected through further study of the manual and set out to sea… However, its builders cannot be rushed… so… the dominion of the sea will be attempted by the multitude of substandard vessels from all the other ports of Christendom. But there is hope… that other ship builders could get a hold of that Presbyterian manual. [7]

[7]. Tom Ertl, *Sharpening Iron* (Credenda Agenda volume 11 Number 3, Moscow Idaho), p. 6.

Schlissel laments, "The favorite pastime of some Reformed people seems to be enforcing quality control standards for other people's navel lint." [8] Schlissel was addressing the pettiness and smallness in the lack of catholicity of some Christians. His point is also appropriate regarding the church's weakness in evangelism. Often we seem to major on the minors. We have a lopsided emphasis on issues that are not core truths. All biblical doctrine is important. We should never despise the thought of precision in our theology. We need to be those who search for truth, delight in truth, and propagate truth. Truth includes minor points in doctrine. We have to cultivate an openness to learn biblical truth and submit to it. This quest is important, but it should not be our total pursuit. Loving God and loving our neighbor are the top two on the chart of duties for the believer. The best way to love our neighbor is to share with him the wonder of our marvelous Savior. We do not sweep the minor issues aside, and just hold hands dancing on a mountain top singing the Coca-Cola song. The church should minor on the minors and major on the majors. Schlissel goes on to close his article, "Too many want to confine the Reformed faith to the Museum of the Holy Proposition rather than to see it lived in a breathing covenant community. Museums, however pretty, testify only to what is past and done. But the word of God is alive and active." [9] Lint inspection should be left to the New Age navel gazers. We have the joy and the delight to love our holy and good God with all our heart, soul, and mind and love our neighbor as ourselves.

We must love God's truth. The treasures in God's word can never be fully mined by any man in one lifetime. The study and digging into the deep things of God are both rewarding and beneficial to our soul. This learning should help launch us into sharing our faith. If we are not out teaching others what we have learned, we become those who are described as "big hat, no cattle." We get big heads that grow and grow into snotty, arrogant, and self-centered gospel slouches.

One of my prayers is that Christians from all traditions will reject elitism, and again get a zingful passion for the lost. Who better than those who are the brightest and best scholars, taking the marketplace,

---

[8]. Steve M. Schlissel, *Covenantal Catholicity* (Vallecito, CA: Chalcedony Report, July/August 2001), p. 24.

[9]. Ibid., p. 25.

and every area of society with the truth of Christ? Jesus not only said that He was the truth, but He also said that He was the way. He is the only way to God. The sharp minds of Christendom must get fired-up and become proactive in proclaiming the saving gospel. Let us again see the church "preach to dying men as dying men." I know that this book is full of rough meanderings that may find real scholars wringing their hands with contempt over some points of philosophy. I agree with Peter Drucker when he said, "I have always known that writing is indecent exposure. By publishing a book one asks to be attacked." I am ready and prepared to receive all the rebukes and philosophical polemics for my street level use of apologetics. I encourage all the bespectacled men of letters to come loaded for bear. But, as you come to bag a callow simpleton, stop along the way and aim your philosophical sights on those in need of the truth found in Jesus.

If you are one of those who breathe only the stuffy air in the ivory towers of scholastic pursuit, I challenge you, today, go and preach the gospel to the unregenerate. Make this a fiery passion that you live out every day. I do not make this challenge to divert one's attention from my lack of academic polish. I desire that my philosophical looseness becomes tighter through the correction of others. "A wise man loves correction." I believe this, and I attempt to live this out. I would count a written rebuke as a blessing. It takes time and concern to write a missive pointing out an author's blunders. I delight in rich and insightful scholarship. The last thing I would propose is the universal intellectual defalcation from the Christian witness. I know that most of American Christianity is extremely weak in its intellectual goals and pursuit. I also know that many Christians, who have bright and beamy minds and strive for intellectual achievement, lack a vigor in their personal evangelism. I want to encourage those who are disinclined to scholarly academic precision to study and make themselves a "workman" approved unto God. Also, I have a passion to see those of keen mind, who believe in the doctrines of grace and are the unmistakable minority status in modern Evangelicalism, embrace an urgency to promote marketplace evangelism.

Son of the Carpenter!
Receive this humble work of mine?

God Centered Evangelism is a wonderful little book on witnessing by Kuiper. In it he exhorts the church with the following: "God commands sovereignly and for that very reason must be obeyed… To apply the foregoing to evangelism, the sovereignty of God comes to vigorous expression in the many missionary commands of the Bible, and in the measure in which one recognizes the divine sovereignty, in that very measure must one be zealous in carrying out those commands." [10]

> Thus it is written, and thus it was necessary for the Christ to suffer and to rise from the dead the third day, and that repentance and remission of sins should be preached in His name to all nations, beginning at Jerusalem. And you are witnesses of these things (Luke 24:46-48).

Hell and Eternity Always Seem to go Together

If you are not fired-up for witnessing, I will give you one of my prime means of motivation: the truth of hell. I ponder the reality of hell and this motivates me to preach the gospel. When I am doleful or tired, I'll reflect on the awful fact of the horrible place called hell. This rekindles my soul for those that do not know Jesus. William Booth wished that all his officers could hang over hell for twenty-four hours prior to their commissioning. He felt that this dreadful experience would stir in them a deeper commitment to evangelism.[11] All true Christians must affirm the sovereignty of God. He controls everything. He knows the beginning from the end. But we must never use God's sovereignty as an excuse not to declare the gospel to those who do not know Christ. God ordains the means as well as the ends. The tool that God uses is the gospel preached because it is the "power of God unto salvation to everyone who believes." I urge you to ponder the reality of hell. Picture the clerk you see twice a week at the Seven-Eleven store, your next door neighbor, your coworkers, or your family members being there forever. Hell is real, and it is forever. Think on the truth of hell. This will motivate anyone who is already saved to proclaim the salvation of God in Christ.

---

[10]. R.B. Kuiper, *God Centered Evangelism* (Carlisle, Penn.: Banner of Truth, 1998), p. 59-60.

[11]. Danny Lehmann, *Bringing Them Back Alive* (Springdale, PA: Whitaker House, 1987), p. 63.

Practice and Prayer

The witnessing and apologetic methods that are taught in this book can be used in witnessing to your family, friends, coworkers, and schoolmates. The best way to mature into an effective witness is practice. We train the people at our church by using role play. One can practice using role play with your family, Christian friends, and fellow church members. Just have one or two people play an atheist or a member of a non-Christian religion. Try having everyone engage in the discussion as if it were real. Do it over and over until you become effective. As you become better at this, you will gain confidence. The two main keys to becoming a competent witness are prayer and practice. Ask God for boldness, and ask Him for opportunity. Petition God to fill you with compassion and mercy for those who do not know the Lord. Start memorizing scriptures that announce the great commission. God's infallible word is Spirit-breathed, sharp, and powerful. Memorizing it presses its truth into the depths of your soul. Christians are indwelt with the Holy Spirit, and He commands us to preach the gospel. Ruminating on Bible verses will inspire you to be a witness or a missionary to the nations.

> And He said to them, "Go into all the world and preach the gospel to every creature" (Mark 16:15).

Anyone can go witnessing. Every believer should go out witnessing. In the Bible we see all ages, genders, and backgrounds sent out to evangelize the lost. All four of my children have gone out witnessing on the streets from Las Vegas (our home) to Montana. They came with us in their baby carriages and started handing out tracts at two years old. Many people on the street will not take a tract from an adult, but will accept one from a cute little child. My daughter Cassie at age three was witnessing in front of the Mormon Temple. She handed out tracts and watched a false religion get dismantled with love and truth. This really strengthens our children's faith. To see that their father really believes what the Bible says, and to observe skeptics getting confounded and called to repentance. I have had the delight of witnessing in the market place to thousands of people, one on one. The imperatives in scripture and my love for the Lord have been the most powerful motivations in my life. God never allowed me to shake the reality of what waits in eternity for the lost. One word stood out in page after page of scripture, "Go!" Early in my Christian walk, I was blessed when I was exposed to the ministry of the late Christian musician Keith

Green. Green was a fiery, passionate witness who called believers to a life of evangelism, missionary work, and a non-compromising walk. He was unsophisticated in theological matters, and I did not agree with all his theological positions, but he helped awaken in me a zeal for evangelism. Steve Camp, Green's disciple, has also impacted my life and impassioned me as a witness. I recommend their music for those who want to get charged-up for witnessing.

I believe all Christians are called to be bold witnesses in the marketplace and in their neighborhoods. A large part of the great commission is the command to be a witness everywhere. This does not mean that this is the only way to express our Christian witness. Scripture mandates that we must press the crown rights of Christ on all areas of life. The church is to influence culture, law, education, and government through our organized witness. This must be a kindhearted, patient, planned, and purposeful victory over the godless world and life view. We are not to abandon one inch of ground to any system that is not based on scripture. There are many fine books and resources that teach how the Christian worldview can change our society. This is not the task of this book. I simply want to inspire the reader to live a life of evangelism and apologetics. This work is written in a simple way so that all believers would understand its contents and use its approach in defending the gospel. My hope is that the following pages will inflame the personal outreach of the new Christian as well as the mature cerebral believer, the simple faithful disciple, and the erudite Reformed scholar.

Speak the Truth

A large amount of this book consists of actual conversations that took place in the marketplace, on the streets and on university campuses. These are real conversations with real people. The dialogues are not invented or twisted to make the Christian speaker look good. The small amount of editing was done to give you the heart of the conversations. You will read much of the raw conversations we had with atheists, New Agers, and others. They are not perfect conversations, and they were not choreographed. This results in some mistakes and errors. Since you cannot hear the actual audio tape recording, some of the dialogues may seem to be rude, highbrowed, and arrogant. I admit, in many conversations, I am bracingly straightforward. Our goal is to represent Christ "with meekness and respect." We take this very seriously, and do not delight in looking as if we are snooty, or that we are poking fun at other people's worldview for sport. The Book of Proverbs exhorts us to "answer a fool according to his folly." When we demonstrate the foolishness of the nonbelievers presuppositions, it may look as though we are thrashing them for pure fun. We are not. We are answering the unbeliever according to the folly of his presuppositions. Give us the benefit of the doubt, as you remember, you cannot see our facial expressions, body language, or hear the grace and patience in our voice. Also, I do not want to inspire any Christians to use this material to bash others for gleeful recreation. Demolishing the unbeliever's worldview and demonstrating the foolishness of unbelief, must be done with humility and respect. Nudge, expose, hint, declare, question, and prod the unbeliever, but "speak the truth in love."

> Speak the truth in love, may you grow up in all things into Him who is the head—Christ (Ephesians 4:15).

We should notice the inclusion of the words "speak" and "the truth" in Ephesians chapter four, verse fifteen. This means we must open our mouths. This command implies we communicate with another person. "Speak the truth in love" is an imperative. We must speak, preach, and defend the gospel and we must do it in love. Love can be tough. Love can declare some unpleasant truths. Love can open someone's eyes to some unhappy facts. Love warns of judgment and offers grace. Jesus spoke harsh words of warning more often than He offered soft and tender words of grace. Shouting at someone who has entered a building that is on fire, is loud and aggressive, but it is a caring act. Paul instructs us that real love "rejoices in the truth." The call is to announce the truth with warnings, love, grace, and righteousness. We must speak. We must not keep it to ourselves.

God commands us to call the nations to Christ. Yes, we are not responsible for anyone's salvation, not even our own. Christians cannot win the world for Christ, only God can. But we must follow and obey our Lord Jesus in the ministry of evangelism and speak the truth in love. I have heard hundreds of Christians declare that we should shine like lights to the lost world, all the while, ignoring the command to preach the gospel. Many teach that we should solely live out our faith as silent loving lights of the Lord. We must never fall into the attitude of Saint Francis of Asissi when asked, "How often should we preach the gospel?" He said, "We preached the gospel all day by doing good works." Good works are just that, good. They bring God glory, and may compel some to ask questions about our faith. But we must never substitute our good works for our preaching witness. God has chosen Christians to be the instruments He uses to bring lost souls to Him. Paul charges Timothy before God to: "Preach the word! Be ready in season and out of season. Convince, rebuke, exhort, with all long-suffering and teaching" (2 Timothy 4:2). Let us obey this command and perform good works.

> Multitudes, multitudes in the valley of decision! For the day of the LORD is near in the valley of decision (Joel 3:14).

Speaking the truth often leads to persecution. I have seen unbelievers get enraged just hearing the name of Jesus. Sometimes they get so rankled that they start shouting like mad men. I have watched an unbeliever attempt to grill me in a public store as she was preaching to me, not to preach at her. I gently exposed her hypocrisy and spoke the truth of Christ to her. She stormed out ranting and raving. The world hates the truth, and even the meekest pagan can lose it within a few seconds of hearing about the claims of Jesus Christ. We must stand up for the truth, even if it angers the world around us.

I have been rebuked by people who hold a wide diversity of worldviews. And I have even seen a lady come storming after us while unleashing a screaming shrill, "I am a Christian. I suppose you, like all Christians teach that Mary Magdalene was a prostitute. You are judgmental and are leading others astray!" She also pressed the idea that we weren't tolerant, and that we were offensive. When she wound down from this spinning diatribe, someone asked her why she was attacking the young man who had given her a gospel tract? This stopped her in her tracks. As she was trying to gather herself together, I asked her why she was so intolerant to my friend? This was more than her ultra-tolerant mind could handle. Stupefied, she cried, "Intolerant, me?" And she stomped off murmuring in a bewildered daze. Often, the best way to stun and get people to see the foolishness of their view is to turn it back on them. This lady wanted to toss us a condemning slur and scamper off. Instead, she and her scornful proposition were called out on the carpet and her false declaration was refuted by the truth. When someone asserts a proposition that contradicts the truth of the Bible, you should turn it back on them. Do what Solomon instructed: "Answer a fool according to his folly." You can do this with every view that is opposed to scripture. Everything that opposes the truth of Christianity will be false, everything. That means we can turn it back on them, and show them how unwise and absurd their view is.

I have also been instructed by some well meaning brothers to not say things that will offend the unbeliever. I understand where my fellow Christians are coming from. Much of the Christian world has become very "seeker friendly." They focus much energy on being "nice." Nice at the right time in the right way is an important aspect of love. But love is not restricted to being nice. Love is kind, but love also rejoices in the truth. Many people erroneously declare that the problem with Christians is they are too aggressive and too harsh. I beg to differ. I agree that there are a few renegade believers that are not patient, gentle, and respectful as they witness to unbelievers. They may number in the thousands. Yet believers who remain silent, or who are overly "seeker friendly," number in the tens of millions in our country. One scholar, I respect immensely, whose intellectual shoes I am not worthy to unlatch, wrote that He did not think that he should enter an unbeliever's space without an invitation. He also discouraged the use of gospel tracts. I believe this is just an excuse that is fueled by fear. We know that when we teach others to wait for the "right moment" to witness to nonbelievers, that hundreds of possible opportunities will be forever gone. Yes, we believe in God's sovereignty, even in our mistakes and laziness. Yet we must fight the attitude that our sinful heart conjures up that supplies excuses for remaining silent. God may not use gospel tracts to bring millions of the lost to the Lord, but I still believe that they are a tool to be used. I know elders, pastors, one evangelist, and one international missionary recruiter that professed that a gospel tract was one of the main instruments that God used to save them. I encourage Christians to carry tracts and hand them out when they buy fast-food, stop for gasoline, see the mailman, and go shopping. I do not practice nor do I teach others to get in people's faces when witnessing. They must approach the unbeliever with respect, patience, love, and truth. But, they must approach them.

The lack of aggressive, compassionate witnessing is a troubling problem. Friendship evangelism and laying back in public waiting for a person to talk to you are legitimate forms of evangelism. The main thing we must do is to talk with unbelievers regularly about the word of God. We should have the attitude of the Indonesian man who I handed a tract. He turned around and pleaded with me to give him more tracts to hand out to his Muslim neighbors in Indonesia. He wouldn't stop asking until I gave him more tracts. I was blessed by his zeal and his concern for his Muslim neighbors.

Patient Witnessing for the Glory of God

We must share our faith with grace and patience, but we are not to deny the Lord who saved us. I try to avoid such persecutions, but if it comes down to putting my faith in the closet or being persecuted, I must follow Jesus and Paul. Most of you will not get arrested, handcuffed, and incarcerated for your faith. But real persecution and hassles will come your way. This is what happened to the apostles and the early Christians who suffered horrendous persecutions, yet they counted it all joy. Our life is not to be one of safety, but one that consists of a faith that risks. The thing we must not adopt is the world's idea that we are not to be confrontational. All Christians have a mandate to confront our culture with the truth of Christ and oppose all things that God opposes. Jesus did it, Paul did it, and all Christians are commanded to do it. We have the promises, the covenants, the gifts, the love, and the grace of God and we should be motivated to share these truths. Today in some states in America, witches have been given tax exemption from the state. More "rights" have been given to sodomites and other perverts than we have for the traditional family. We have had serial liars and adulterers in the White House and in Congress.

We as followers of Jesus need to call our fellow citizens to the holy and righteous God. If you are not part of the solution, then you are part of the problem. Indolence is a sin just as insolence and wickedness are. Read the Bible verses that declare the commandments to be a witness, pray over them, and then schedule a time and a place to obey them.

> And He Himself is the propitiation for our sins, and not for ours only but also for the whole world. Now by this, we know that we know Him, if we keep His commandments. He who says, "I know Him," and does not keep His commandments, is a liar, and the truth is not in him. But whoever keeps His word, truly the love of God is perfected in him. By this we know that we are in Him. He who says he abides in Him ought himself also to walk just as He walked (1 John 2:2-6).

Reaching the world for Christ is something we approach prayerfully and earnestly. We should also pray for others to go witnessing with us. Jesus instructed us to open our eyes and to pray for laborers because the harvest was ripe. The great commission does not command the church to make converts, but to make disciples (Matt. 28:19). This means we must ask the Lord for others to serve with us, and to grow in the knowledge and the grace of God together. I have been blessed over the years with the opportunity to evangelize with many zealous believers. Many of them ministered in a way that wherever they went there was either a "revival or a riot." These believers were kicked off college campuses, thrown out of restaurants and bookstores for lovingly sharing the gospel and warning the lost. I have had some of my most exciting and joyous experiences serving with these men and women of faith. Your duty is to ask the Father to bring you some co-laborers and friends, so you can become a witnessing mentor.

The conversations that are recorded in this book have had some of the names changed for privacy. Some of the conversations were reduced to edit out the parts that were not essential. The main arguments of the dialogues were not changed. They were not edited to make the Christians look like heroes. Frankly, with a trained believer, the unbeliever doesn't have a chance. Like Doug Wilson said at the start of his debate with the atheist Dan Barker, "You have lost the debate before it started." Barker lost the debate because he could not justify the act of debate. He did not have a worldview that supplies the necessary precondition for the logic he used in the debate. Only the Christian worldview can account for logic and debate. Logic is ground on the nature of God, thus when an atheist debates and uses logic, he borrows from the Christian worldview, therefore he has lost the debate. I am no Doug Wilson or Greg Bahnsen. In many conversations that are recorded in this book, I ran through some philosophical stop signs and one-way streets. Please pardon my sophomoric assertions. My goal is to be faithful to God and His revelation in the scriptures. I solicit any suggestions. If you have spotted a theological blunder or a philosophical error, please write me with your corrections.

Another thing I am shooting for is to apologetically train the reader to have confidence enough to go out and witness consistently. One tool I employ for that end is repetition. I repeat the basic apologetic over and over. God uses repetition to teach us many doctrinal truths in the Bible. And it will seem at times I drone on and on and on with the same few points: God is the precondition for the intelligibility of logic, ethics, science, and everything else in our world. My hope is this format does not bore you, but challenges you to defend the truth and win the lost for Christ.

Always Be Ready to Give an Answer

> My appeal is to the Word of God. "What are the reasonings, or opinions, or inferences of men? What is the chaff to the wheat?" says the Lord. Let the Bible decide each question (Bonar: *Truth and Error*).

> Always be ready to give a defense to everyone who asks you a reason for the hope that is in you, with meekness and fear (1 Peter 3:15).

> Beloved... earnestly contend for the faith which was once for all delivered to the saints (Jude 3).

We are called to be a witness for Jesus Christ. We must give an answer to everyone who asks about our faith. The questions about God and the questions about His word are the most important questions we can answer. We are warned in the Bible not to chase down foolish and vain questions like: Do trees make a noise if they fall in an uninhabited forest? What came first, the chicken or the egg? And why do Wintergreen Life Savors sparkle in the dark when you bite into them? We must disregard the folly of this world's inane curiosity and speculations. We must base our life and worldview on God's infallible revelation. This is where we get the answers to the questions of the ages.

We, like Luther, must stand on the word of God. God's revealed truth is contained within its pages, and it has all the answers and solutions we will ever need. Vain philosophy, the speculations of bored and kooky men, will never answer any ultimate questions. Loopy New Age doctrines self-destruct under the scrutiny of intelligent questioning. Vain philosophy raises more questions than it can answer. The Bible alone reveals God's will and way for mankind. I have used, and I hope not abused, the philosophical insights from great Christian thinkers. I attempt to tread this ground carefully and humbly. Bacon's words were often on my mind when he said, "A little philosophy inclines man's mind to atheism, but depth in philosophy brings minds to religion." This book does not attempt to traverse through the shadowy forests of the history of philosophy. I believe that all false worldviews can be easily refuted with simple, but deep scriptural arguments.

One statement that is asserted in this book more that any other: The Christian worldview alone can account for reality and the knowledge of that reality. All other systems of thought cannot account for anything in the world. God's word is the only means to justify all the diverse dynamics in the world. Christianity is not just probably true or hopefully true, it is the only possible foundation for all truth. Only Christianity can provide the necessary precondition for the intelligibility of human experience. It is impossible for Christianity not to be true, for without it nothing can be known. Reason, ethics, meaning, and any predication can be real and can be known, only if the God of the Bible lives. Christianity is not just known, shown, and demonstrated, it is true. The real reality: Deny the God of scripture and nothing is knowable or intelligible. The necessary precondition for truth, science, value, and personhood is the triune God of revelation.

God has graciously given us revelation. He has revealed His nature and character to us through scripture. He has given us all the answers we will ever need in His word. The atheist Ayn Rand was asked by a reporter, "What's wrong with the world?" She replied "Never before has the world been so desperate for answers to critical questions, and never before has the world been so frantically committed to the idea that no answers are possible." The believer has the truth and has God given answers. We have a sure and true confidence that Christ is Lord of all.

A couple notes of caution to the readers: There are some syllogisms employed in the discussion on apologetics. I do not believe that the task of the believer is to construct a rational test, syllogism, equation, experiment, or study to prove the probability of God's existence. That would be futile and unbiblical. I have absolute certainty of God's existence because of the "impossibility of the contrary." The scriptures reveal that God and His word are the precondition to know anything at all. I concur with Augustine, "I believe in order that I may understand." The denial of the triune God would render everything in the Cosmos as meaningless, and such a denial cannot be true because it is self-refuting. For that statement assumes that at least it "has meaning." Without God, we cannot know anything and we cannot make sense out of anything. I have certain knowledge of God because His revealed word renders all knowledge possible. When you come across a syllogism or some evidence in this book, be careful and read the whole context in which it was placed. God is the inescapable truth and because He lives, mankind can reason, have morals, and do science. All men everywhere know that God lives. Atheists attempt to deny this. I advise that you at some point tell them that you know they really do believe in God. They know God exists. Atheists are fulfilling Romans chapter one when it declares that the unbeliever "knows God," but he suppresses this truth in unrighteousness.

A second note of caution: This book will be fairly "intellectual." Many readers will think the content of this book "dummy downs" the issues. I would exhort you to go pick up some books by Bahnsen, Van Til, Frame, and Plantiga. This book is written for the "average" Christian. Those of you that might not have done well in school, you hated it. You did not excel in school: Physical science meant studying the offensive line of the football team; chemistry was something that happened when you met a good looking girl. Much of the Church shies away from intellectual stretching and learning. If that is you, this book will assist you in developing a robust intellectual aspect of your faith. Jesus instructed us to "love God with all our heart, soul, and mind." Our mind is very important. Part of our duty as believers is to grow in the knowledge of our religion.

Warning: Read This

I want to alert you to read the quotes I put at the head of the chapters. Some of these quips come from unbelievers and inconsistent Christians. Many are from the pens of brilliant Christian thinkers. I challenge you to do some thinking, and use the Bible as your standard for discerning whether the quote is true or absurd. You will also notice that the main theme of this book is asserted in an almost uninterrupted manner. My hope is that it will not smother you, but will inculcate you with the simple scriptural way to defend and preach the gospel. I may not be the clearest or most persuasive apologist you read, but my sincere desire is to equip you to step out and exalt Christ in your world. Please remember, I have listed diverse quotes, many from loony theologians and wacked-out skeptics. If you are puzzled over a quote, there is good reason. Vain philosophy is just that: vain, puzzling, and absurd.

The apologetic method I employ comes from Dr. Cornelius Van Til, Dr. Greg Bahnsen, and their numerous disciples. The vocabulary, the phrases, and the arguments are from their work and not my own. Without their previous scholarship over ninety-percent of this book could not be written. Though I did not meet him, Bahnsen taught and inspired me more than almost any other man. I thank God for his ministry.

> The grass withers, the flower fades, but the word of our God stands forever (Isaiah 40:8).

CHAPTER I

ONCE UPON AN *A PRIORI*

We have to wonder if the atheism resides in the theory or the theorist. [1]

Fundamental propositions, or propositions not deducible from deeper ones, can be established only by showing the complete congruity of all the results reached through the assumption of them. [2]

For three billion years, more or less, the evolution of species proceeded ponderously along a hit-or-miss fashion, until... a sufficiently intelligent species evolved. Then the intelligence took a hand, and evolution was never the same again. The key to evolution is randomness. [3]

Authority and reason have their separate rights: a moment ago one had all the advantage; here the other is queen in her turn. [4]

---

1. John P. Koster, Jr., *The Atheist Syndrome* (Brentwood, TN: Wolgemuth & Hyatt, 1989), p. 25.
2. Herbert Spencer, *First Principles* (N.Y.: D. Appleton, 1900), p. 495.
3. Isaac Asimov, *Science Past - Science Future* (N.Y.: Ace Books, 1975), p. 207.
4. Blaise Pascal, *Concerning the Vacuum* (Chi., IL: Univ. of Chicago, 1982), p. 357.

Our generation is overwhelmingly naturalistic. There is an almost complete commitment to the concept of natural causes in a closed system. [5]

It is difficult to know how, by analogical inference, we arrive at the conclusion that there is a cosmic Creator and not just a cosmic architect.[6]

It is true that we assume the existence of an explanation for anything we encounter. [7]

All my false preconceptions get in my way, and these preconceptions surely please Satan, for they turn me from the Creator to the tempter who is much more "reasonable." [8]

There is a constant need in our civilization to prefer illusions over reality, a need to deny our perceptions. [9]

To become a Christian does not mean to renounce reason; on the contrary, it enables a man to become truly rational... Augustine... at the very heart of his thinking is the conviction that Christian faith alone enables a man to be rational... a man must believe in order that he may understand. [10]

---

[5]. Francis Schaeffer, *True Spirituality* (Wheaton, IL: Tyndale House, 1971), p. 60.

[6]. Michael Martin, Atheism: *A Philosophical Justification* (Philadelphia, PA: Temple University Press, 1990), p. 130.

[7]. B.C. Johnson, *The Atheist Debater's Handbook* (Amherst, NY: Prometheus Books, 1981), p. 61.

[8]. Madeleine L'Engle, *The Genesis Trilogy* (Colorado Springs, CO: Waterbrook Press, 1997), p. 30.

[9]. John Saul, *Voltaire's Bastards: The Dictatorship of Reason in the West* (New York, NY: Random House, 1992), p. 11.

[10]. John Heaney, *Faith, Reason, and the Gospels* (Westminster, Maryland: Newman), p. 80-81.

Learned men scorn to submit their reason to divine revelation (Jonathan Edwards).

Now, though Mr. Locke supposes sensation and reflection to be the only two springs of all ideas… yet abstraction is certainly a different act of the mind. [11]

It is that knowledge or rudiment of knowledge concerning God, which may be obtained by the contemplation of His creatures; which knowledge may be truly termed divine in respect to the object, and natural in respect to the light. The bounds of that knowledge are, that it sufficeth to convince atheism. [12]

For in it the righteousness of God is revealed from faith to faith, as it is written, "The just shall live by faith." For the wrath of God is revealed from Heaven against all ungodliness and unrighteousness of men, who suppress the truth in unrighteousness, because the thing which may be known of God is clearly revealed within them, for God revealed it to them. For the unseen things of Him from the creation of the world are clearly seen, being realized by the things that are made, even His eternal power and Godhead, for them to be without excuse. Because, knowing God, they did not glorify Him as God, neither were thankful. But they became vain in their imaginations, and their foolish heart was darkened. Professing to be wise, they became fools (Romans 1:17-22).

Explaining and proving that the Christ had to suffer and rise from the dead. "This Jesus I am proclaiming to you is the Christ" (Acts 17:3).

---

[11]. Isaac Watts, *Logic* (Morgan, PA: Soli Deo Gloria Publications, First Printed 1724, Reprinted 1996), p. 81.

[12]. Francis Bacon, *The Advancement of Learning* (London, England: Dent & Sons, 1957), p. 88.

Apologetics: Defending the Faith Biblically

Most believers and nonbelievers fail to understand that there is no neutrality in discussing worldviews. How a man sees the world and interprets reality is determined by the presuppositions he holds. Everyone has presuppositions. All atheists, agnostics, religious people, and Christians have presuppositions. Presuppositions are the lens in which we interpret the world. They are the basic assumptions we take for granted. These basic assumptions are the preconceived ideas that are rarely challenged. We all have them. Presuppositions determine what you believe and the way you look at life. Most people are unconscious of them. Nonbelievers have their foundational assumptions about life and the world. They live most of their life employing basic principals that are inconsistent with their unbelieving worldview. Much of how they live is consistent with the Christian worldview. Nonbelievers do this because they take their presuppositions for granted. They rarely think about them or follow them to their logical conclusion. The job of concerned Christians is to make the nonbeliever aware of their assumed biases. We should try to open up their eyes to acknowledge the inclinations that the nonbeliever brings to the knowledge enterprise. We want to help them be tough minded and to answer the question: How do we know what we know? Schlissel gives us this amusing illustration regarding presuppositions:

> Presuppositions can function like preferences or tastes, as when you approach a buffet. As you scan the buffet table, without even thinking, you reflexively eliminate what is distasteful to you. You don't even register, say the pickled carrots. You move on to consider with your eyes only that which your appetite tells you is in the running, and you choose from that. Your preferences and tastes have functioned as a filter, as a presupposition… Yes, your tooshie, like a presupposition, is always with you; it is behind and under everything you do. Yet you do your lifelong best to keep it hidden and protected. Romans 1:28: "They did not think it worthwhile to retain the knowledge of God." They suppressed God's self-disclosure like passing pickled carrots - neither held any interest for them, being out of synch with their tastes, their presuppositions. [13]

---

[13]. Steve M. Schlissel, *The Revisionists' Tooshies* (Vallecito, CA: Chalcedon Report, September 2000), p. 23.

> Every human experience is interpreted by the explaining person... It is always interpreted within the framework by which that person comprehends what is real. [14]

The Christian must understand that all thinking people have presuppositions. The Islamic fundamentalist has the presupposition that they should imitate the bloodthirsty Muhammad and religiously murder anyone who disagrees with Islam. Evolutionists have the presupposition that life came from non-life and a human is nothing more than a supped-up monkey. Atheistic materialists assume that the only thing that exists is the physical universe: no spirits, no angels, no demons, and no God. We must demonstrate the error of the nonbeliever's presuppositions. This is what biblical apologetics is concerned with. We demolish everything that opposes God's word. We must preach the law and the gospel to them and urge them to repent.

Essential Definitions

The following list of definitions is needed for the remainder of the book. If you are not familiar with apologetics and its terminology, you will want to put a bookmark on this page and refer to it until you are fluent with the vocabulary.

- **Apologetics:** The study and application of defending the faith. See 1 Peter 3:15; Jude 3; Acts Chapters 17 through 20.

- ***A Priori* Argument:** An argument prior to or independent of observation and experience, which is fully and universally independent of all experience, discernment, and discovery by the five senses.

- **Empiricism:** The notion that truth is found through the use of the five senses. Observation and measurement are the means to discover reality. Truth is discovered by the senses: what we can see, feel, observe, and measure.

[14]. John Spong, *Rescuing the Bible from Fundamentalism* (San Francisco, CA: Harper Collins, 1991), p. 25.

• **Epistemology:** The study of how we know what we know; that which is the nature and basis of knowledge; the accounting and justifying of knowledge claims and the sources and scope of knowledge.

• **Ethics:** The rules of what humans ought to do, the standard of morality and behavior.

• **Laws of Logic:** Abstract, non-concrete laws of thought and reason that are nonmaterial, universal, timeless, obligatory, and absolute. All rational communication and thinking assume the laws of logic. The most well-known law is the law of non-contradiction; "A" cannot be "A" and "Non-A" at the same time in the same way. A man cannot be his own father. The laws of logic reflect the nature and mind of God, thus they have ontological grounding and cannot be reduced to human convention, opinion or psychology.

• **Law of Non-Contradiction** (also known as the Law of Contradiction): A law of logic that is defined as "A" cannot be "A" and "Non-A" at the same time in the same sense. A tall man cannot be a non-man. The law of non-contradiction is an unavoidable and a necessary principal of all rational thought and communication. If the law is denied, then rational thinking is impossible. To deny the law, one must use the law in attempting to deny it. Those who deny the law are participating in a self-refuting effort.

• **Materialism:** The philosophical theory that asserts that only matter exists and only matter is real. There is nothing beyond the physical world of matter and motion.

• **Naturalism:** A system of thought that asserts that what is ultimately real is only that which belongs to nature and the natural. Matter, energy, and particles in motion are all reality. Nature is all there is.

• **Pragmatism:** The belief that truth is whatever works. If it works best, it is true. Pragmatism asserts that truth is found in the methodologies that work best; it is concerned primarily with what is the most expedient and profitable.

• **Presupposition:** A preeminent belief held to be true and taken as a pre-commitment. It is the belief that is held at the most foundational level of one's grid or web of beliefs. The lens in which one interprets reality that is taken for granted and assumed in making a statement or a theory. It is one's starting point, primary and fundamental assumption, and metaphysical foundation. Everyone has presuppositions: primary belief patterns that color all one's thought and outlook. Reason, logic, and morality are only consistent with Christian presuppositions.

• **Rationalism:** The belief that truth is found by the right use of reason and logic.

• **Relativism:** The notion that there is no ultimate truth and there are no moral absolutes. What is true or good for me may not be good or true for you.

• **Worldview:** An overall perspective of life. One sees and defines the world through its presuppositions. It is the grid that one uses to evaluate reality.

The Place of Apologetics

> The part that Apologetics has to play in the Christianizing the world is rather a primary part, and it is a conquering part... Christianity... stands out among all religions... as distinctively "the Apologetic religion." [15]

One of the most important definitions in this book is the word presupposition. We all have presuppositions. Presuppositions are beliefs that are held at the most foundational level of one's grid or web of beliefs.

---

[15]. B.B. Warfield, *Selected Shorter Writings of B.B. Warfield II* (Nutley, NJ: P & R, 1973), p. 99-100.

Russell's words, in his book *A History of Western Philosophy*, are very helpful in understanding rational pre-commitments: "If you always wore blue spectacles, you could be sure of seeing everything blue." One's presuppositions are the intellectual glasses we have on when we view human experience. I will illustrate this truth with the story of the big black spider who declared that he could snag all the flies in Mexico in his new web. After a week and hundreds of flies getting caught in his web, he announced that there were no more flies in Mexico. But many friends of the spider told him that they saw many other flies buzzing around. The proud big black spider replied, "They are bees or beetles. They cannot be flies because my web has caught every fly in Mexico. If my web did not snag them, they cannot be flies." The spider is the nonbeliever who believes only in what he can see or what he can rationally understand. The web is his mind and his five senses. But God alone is a being large enough to snag all the flies with His web. He alone can see everything and understand everything. There is nothing that God cannot know or understand. That is the reason we must use His web as our starting point and our lens to look out to the world. My web is too small to understand and account for everything in reality. Your web is too small to understand your world. We must build our worldview on the presupposition that God and His word are the precondition for the intelligibility of our world. Without God's web we cannot account for logic, ethics, science, induction, and even ourselves. Our web is too small, and the world is too big.

Christianity Is The Foundation For Reason

> For the wrath of God is revealed from heaven against all ungodliness and unrighteousness of men, who suppress the truth in unrighteousness (Romans 1:18).

Most non-believing men and women of high standing have never given a serious study of Jesus of Nazareth, yet they spew out of their mouths that Jesus was just a good man, just a good moral teacher. These are grand stand critics. Not only are they criticizing a game for which they themselves do not play, but they have not even taken the effort to acquaint themselves with the rules. They are clouds without water. They assert with all personal authority that Christianity is unreasonable. That faith is a blind commitment that attempts to bridge the gap between belief and certainty. Paschal forcibly stated, "Those who do not love truth excuse themselves on the grounds that it is disputed and that many people deny it."

Some atheists are skilled debaters. They are like a "good lawyer with a bad case." Good lawyers can dazzle with clever arguments and shout the loudest. They can win the debate, although, their argument is the weakest. So the truth must be proclaimed on the housetops. Christians have the truth, and we can learn to share it with great zeal and clarity. As you read this book, you will discover that you do not have to learn to marshal volumes of evidence; you do not have to learn to be a "good lawyer." You will learn to demonstrate that without having Christ and God's word, as the metaphysical pre-commitment, the atheist cannot make sense out of anything. He cannot account for the universe, mankind, history, or science. He will be left to repent or remain speechless. God is the foundation and source of all meaning, purpose, and rationality. God alone is the one who makes rationality and argument possible. Without God, the unbeliever cannot account for anything in the universe. We can demonstrate that the Lord is the source of all law, order, logic, mathematics, truth, goodness, beauty, science, and philosophy. The atheist, in reality, has no argument. God must live or we could not argue at all.

Many atheists and skeptics declare that Christianity is opposed to reason. They tell us that faith is unreasonable, and it is just an illusionary subjective experience. Freud asserted that people of faith are fearful of reason when it scrutinizes religion. He said, "Where questions of religion are concerned, people are guilty of every possible kind of insincerity and intellectual misdemeanor." I do not doubt that some believers, in every generation, have been insecure and dishonest about the claims of their religion. Yet, when I have spoken with skeptics, scoffers, atheists, and agnostics, not only do I find all of them insincere and suppressing the truth, but they are guilty of intellectual felonies, high crimes, and capital offenses. These intellectual outlaws not only despise the scrutiny of reason and revelation, but they generally cower and run when the heat of logic and truth bear on their worldview. In hundreds of individual conversations with anti-theists, I have seen only a couple dozen who would discuss the truth of worldviews for longer than ten minutes. I have seen hundreds of them snap, snarl, and scream for me to leave when their view of life is challenged. They get rankled quickly, although I speak the truth in love, grace and patience. The skeptic is suppressing the truth in unrighteousness, and a full-orbed biblical defense of the faith lifts that suppression. Then the unbeliever gets real uncomfortable, in a hurry. They, at that point, want to flee as fast as possible.

Not only do atheists despise reasoning, they cannot even make reason, reasonable. They can be reasonable, but they cannot tell us where reason comes from, and why one should be reasonable. They cannot account for or justify human reason. Atheists, when asked why reason is useful, will say, "It's just that way." Thus the atheist lives on blind faith. So force the skeptic to justify the reason one should be a rational person; when pressed, they can only say, "It is just that way!" They live in blind and unreasonable faith. In like manner, the atheist cannot account for his counting. He can count, but he cannot justify his counting. There are a great many other things in life that the skeptic takes for granted and cannot justify. He cannot account for his unchanging personhood, motion, mathematics, morality or logic. The non-Christian cannot explain anything. They have no ultimate answers for any part of reality, period. The unbeliever is living in a world that he cannot explain inasmuch as he suppresses the truth in unrighteousness. He despises biblical morality and desires sin. He is an intellectual criminal because he is a moral criminal first.

Jesus the Logos

> In the beginning was the Word, and the Word was with God, and the Word was God (John 1:1).

Christians are not to be fearful of reason and logic. R.C. Sproul correctly asserted: "The Christian faith affirms logic not as a law above God but as an aspect built into the Creation which flows from His own character." Jesus is the great logos, and logic is an element of His being and nature. We are the only group of people who can account for reason. It comes from the nature of God. The true and living God is a reasonable God. Reason cannot be held over of His head, but reason is a reflection of His nature, and we must embrace it in submission to God's revelation in the Bible. Christians should base their worldview on God's word and His character. Logic has no physical content. The abstract application of reason also has no material content. Logic is essential and a precondition for any intelligent communication. Logic was not invented by philosophers. Logic is the foundational instrument necessary for all discourse, debate, science, mathematics, and learning. Without using logic, one cannot even deny that logic is mandatory for communication. The precondition for the laws of logic is the God of the Bible. Without the sovereign, nonphysical, non-temporal, transcendent, logical, and universal God Almighty, one cannot justify or account for transcendent, nonphysical, non-temporal, universal, and abstract logic. God is the precondition for logic. Logic is the precondition for knowledge, discourse, and argumentation. Logic is absolutely necessary for the intelligibility of life and God is absolutely necessary for logic. Thus God is, and has to be.

Nonbelievers cannot account for logic or morality. They must use the laws of logic, but logic has no physical form or concrete properties. They are abstract, universal, nonmaterial laws, hence they do not possess size, weight or shape. They have no biological properties or chemical elements to them. You cannot trip over the laws of logic or pick them up on sale at Walmart. The materialistic atheist can give no ultimate grounding and no absolute foundation for the absolute laws of logic. The laws of logic are universal and transcend the material world. Yet there can be nothing transcendent or universal in the atheist's worldview. Atheism is rationally untenable on its own grounds. An atheist cannot argue against Christianity without assuming Christian thought because he depends upon logic to assert this claim. Christianity is logical and true because it rests upon the foundation of the transcendent living God. Only Christianity can provide the necessary precondition for rational thought and logic. We must ground our use of logic on God and His word. He is our final and ultimate universal authority who reigns in sovereign glory. Christian theism is absolutely necessary. It is impossible for it not to be true. It is inescapable. That is the reason I will repeat the basic simple argument: Christianity must be true to reason or argue about anything. I will declare this repeatedly in this book. I employ this redundancy so that the reader will discover how easy it is to use biblical apologetics, and how completely effective it is in defending the truth. My desire is to challenge you to use this format and for you to engage in role-play witnessing with your Christian friends, until you gain confidence and proficiency.

> In whom (Christ) are hidden all the treasures of wisdom and knowledge (Colossians 2:3).

The ancient Greek architects had three qualities for building a right building: *firmitas, utilitas, and venustas*; namely: firmness, usefulness, and beauty. God is the only foundation in which we should build a firm, useful, and beautiful worldview. Only Christianity can give us these three traits and more. It provides the prior foundation to justify and utilize all elements of the physical, the abstract, and the spiritual. What are the obligatory preconditions for the intelligibility of mankind's experience? What has to be true to make sense out of our world, our experience, and all the various dynamics we take for granted in our day to day life? Christianity is the only answer, and even more devastating: Christianity alone can ask the question and justify it. The unbeliever is left with his mouth stopped up. He must remain silent or rely on the Christian worldview. God is the precondition for the use of morality, freedom, equality, science, and logic. Without God, one cannot account for reason and the rational use of thought.

When unbelievers use reason, they presuppose and rely on God, even as they are attempting to disprove God. The denial of God presupposes that God lives. Without presupposing the God of the Bible, one cannot rationally assert anything. As Van Til demonstrated, the atheist is like the little child on her father's lap that slaps her dad in the face, but in order for her to slap her father, she must sit on his lap. And the atheist, as he attempts to refute the existence of God, must rest on the presupposition that God lives. God must be his presupposition forasmuch as he uses logic and reason to attempt to slap the Lord. Yet as an atheist, he cannot account for reason. When he attacks God using logical thought and right reason, he borrows from the Christian worldview, which alone can account for reason. So anti-theism presupposes theism. Attacking the existence of God, with rational thought, actually depends on that which they are attempting to disprove. The atheist tries to prove that only the physical world is there, all the while using nonphysical reason. All intellectual warring against the Lord presupposes His existence. We do not have to prove that God exists, everything in the universe shouts His existence. We should allow the anti-theist to keep talking, and demonstrate that for his ranting to be rational, he must presuppose that God lives.

God is King; Reason is His Servant

"Let us reason together," Says the LORD (Isaiah 1:18).

The atheist borrows from the Christian worldview when he uses and applies reason. Atheists testify that they adore reason and logic. That is the rationale behind Robert Ingersoll assertion: "Upon every brain reason should be enthroned as king." Skeptics do not want to bow to God, so they will bow down to an idol, such as human reason. This creates a big problem for them: Deny God and you cannot account for reason. A great example of this is what happened in the debate between evangelist Ray Comfort and atheist Ron Barrier. Mr. Barrier accidentally picked up Comfort's glasses while making his case for atheism. Comfort in his response said to the crowd, "If you are an atheist, you are wearing someone else's glasses." That is what all atheists and unbelievers do: They borrow from the Christian worldview whenever they use reason or morality. These are nonphysical dynamics that the atheist cannot justify, only the Christian can. Remember, he only believes that the physical world exists, reality consists of matter and motion and nothing more. Atheists, when they use and apply logic or morality, are borrowing our glasses. The job of the Christian is to take the glasses off their head and let them know, without Christianity, they cannot see anything at all. C.S. Lewis' notion that I believe in God as I believe in the Sun; not so much that I see the Sun, it's more like without the Sun, I cannot see anything at all. The only lens that can make sense of the world and give us vision is God's revealed word.

God Is The Precondition For Knowledge

I heard of a man who woke up one night at the sound of his car being taken. He ran down stairs, and it was not being stolen; it was being towed. He stopped the tow truck driver and wanted to know why he was taking his car. The tow truck driver told him that they were filming a movie on the street, and they needed the space. The owner of the car wanted to know how he would have found his car after it had been towed and parked in an unknown location. The tow truck driver told him that he would put a note on the car. That of course would not have done the befuddled owner any good. For the car would have been lost, and a note on a lost car is also lost. And that is the problem with the unsaved person. He is lost, and he cannot use his own reason or experience to find his way to truth. He is lost, and his autonomous reason is lost with him. The only way he can find the truth is through an objective unchanging source. That is God. God is there, and He is immutable.

The biblical God is the precondition for true self-knowledge and the intelligibility of the world. Without God, man is lost holding his own note. Only through God and His revelation can a man be found and have an objective basis for truth. God is the absolute and transcendental necessity for the intelligibility of all human experience. He is the precondition for the grounding and understanding of knowledge. If you do not presuppose the truth of God in Christ, you cannot make sense out of the cosmos and all reality. Christianity is true not because it makes better sense, but it alone supplies the foundation for logic. It is true because without it you cannot make sense of anything, anywhere, at any time. All other religions, philosophies, and worldviews lack the transcendentally required precondition for the intelligibility for logic, ethics, and truth. The truth is so powerful and frequently offensive that we do not have to be pugilists, we should simply declare the truth of God in Christ as Lord and Savior.

Jesus said to him, "I am… the truth" (John 14:6).

There is true truth. Every scientist or philosopher that is searching for truth, must begin with God and His revelation in Christ. Science is involved with more than rocks, slime, and stars. The concept of truth, beauty, justice, ethics, and reason lay beyond the world of concrete nature. These abstractions cannot be explained in terms of the material world alone. Even the material dynamic within our world cannot be explained solely by physical terms. The physical world is made up of organized energy. The materialist cannot explain what energy is and why it "self-organized." The believer can declare God's thoughts after Him, and He has revealed that all power comes from Him. He organized it for His glory and the delight of mankind. The materialist is always going to be at a loss for words when you ask him for foundational answers. He has none. He cannot account for anything in the physical or nonphysical world. His worldview is self-defeating, backward, and destructive to science. Whenever they discover something that will benefit the world, they have breached their worldview, and in that discovery they have borrowed from the Christian worldview. Ultimate and full fledged materialism contradicts true science and inhibits the motivation for progress.

Empiricism Cannot Account for Knowledge

Many people say that they cannot believe anything unless they can see it for themselves. This is a form of empiricism. Many hold to empiricism as their worldview. They declare that unless something can be tested empirically, using the five senses, it is not true. The main problem with those types of statements is that they cannot be tested by sight or the other four senses. Thus they are self-refuting statements. The theory self-destructs under its own assertions. Another problem surfaces because our senses are not perfectly accurate. They are fairly reliable, but cannot be fully trusted. Augustine pointed out that a straight oar appears bent when it is in the water. Many of us, as we drive our car, during a hot day, see mirages on the road up ahead. If an elephant is a mile up the road and I put my thumb in front of my eyes, the beast seems to be no larger than my thumb. In Las Vegas, there are dozens of magicians who make a good living from tricking the empirical senses of their audiences. The hand is quicker than the eye. Our eyes and other senses can deceive us. We cannot base our world and life view on them, nobody can. Skeptics who claim that they only believe in what they can see, do not and cannot follow that philosophy consistently. Their use of logic, induction, and mathematics is not intelligible by the senses alone. These are nonmaterial entities that the material-only claimant utilizes everyday. God must be presupposed to understand this world.

The notion that all truth is ascertained using the senses cannot even justify two plus two is always four and that all animals die. For they cannot be in all places simultaneously where two plus two occur, and they have not witnessed the death of all animals. The believer can trust the basic reliability of the senses because an infallible God, who knows all things exhaustively, has told us that we can. The reason good scientists repeat their tests and experiments over and over, sometimes hundreds of times, is due to the unreliability of the senses. Men of science and industry have built instruments and machines to help bypass the inconsistency and unreliability of the senses to further science.

Man's five senses are partially unreliable because humans are not perfect and infallible. They do not have the divine ability to possess universal knowledge. Certain knowledge requires a man to depend on a being who is perfect, infallible, and has exhaustive knowledge: God. The five senses can only provide awareness and information of some attributes of an object. Numerous people claim that they only believe what they can see. Well, in one way, under their non-Christian worldview, they cannot see any object. Human eyesight cannot give direct and immediate awareness and understanding of any object. Eyesight can provide information on some aspects and attributes of any given object. But God can see all the millions of atoms, and He can fully understand the protons and electrons with exhaustive knowledge. He has exact and exhaustive knowledge of the color, texture, size, weight, density, and complete physical makeup of all objects in the universe. No human can have exhaustive and perfect knowledge of even one of those attributes. Yet he wants to trust his eyesight and senses above God, who alone can understand all things.

The senses are generally reliable. We can know this because of God's revelation in the Bible. We must have a transcendent source that "sees" everything and reveals to us that the senses are basically dependable. The problem comes when one rejects God's word and constructs a worldview based on our senses alone. Our senses can routinely deceive us. Professional illusionists get paid good money to fool our eyesight. Conversations between husbands and wives can quickly reveal how unreliable the sense of hearing can be. Many taste-tests studies have demonstrated the sense of taste is not always reliable. Surgical medical teams leave clamps, sponges, and other tools inside 1,500 patients nationwide each year. These are highly trained teams with large potential lawsuits looming over them, and yet their senses fail them at times. One cannot construct a reliable worldview based exclusively on the senses as many scientists attempt to do. It is impossible for them to avoid the truth of God in view of the fact that all their theories, notes, and scientific conclusions utilize logic. Logic is nonphysical and invariant, therefore presupposes the God of scripture. Empiricism fails, as a worldview, every time you stub your toe or trip over a rock. Our senses are normally reliable, but we cannot build a worldview on their reliability. God is the precondition for an intelligible worldview. This includes the basic trustworthiness of our five senses.

Rationalism Cannot Account for Knowledge

> According to rationalism, thought is thought of thinking. Only that can be known for certain. Once some more specific content is specified, certainty disappears. Thus the consistent rationalist will deny that there is anything, ultimately, except "pure thought," "pure being," etc. Everything else is illusion. But what is "pure thought" that is not a thought of something? Does that idea have any meaning at all? It is a pure blank. The knowledge of which rationalism boasts turns out to be a knowledge of… nothing! [16]

Many others declare that they cannot believe anything unless it is based on reason. They try to make the world intelligible through rationalism. Everything must bow down to human reason. There are many problems to this. The first one is the question: Why? This problem comes to light if they assert that one *should* base his life on rationalism. This forces him to jump over into ethics, which pure rationalism is silent about. Another difficulty

[16]. John Frame, *The Doctrine of The Knowledge of God* (Phillipsburg, NJ: P & R, 1987), p. 61.

with rationalism is the mind functions as untrustworthy as our empirical senses. Rationalism as a worldview discovers the truth about nothing. Our rational capabilities must be built on the foundation of scripture and the person of God.

Another interesting fact: The mind can conceive and mathematically prove that perfection exists. Mathematically, one can propose a perfect circle, a perfect line, and a perfect square. Yet nowhere in our entire physical universe can you find a perfect line, circle, or square. Thus the physical universe could not have produced the notion of perfection. Perfection is based on God's perfect nature. Therefore in mathematical theory and geometry, when one studies or discusses perfection, one presupposes God. The perfect holy God is the precondition for perfection. Without God, one cannot account for perfection. How can one fully trust the mind if it can assert perfection, yet no one can find perfection in the physical universe? Comfort brings this out with his intelligence test he uses in witnessing. He exposes the imperfection of our use of reason and the use of our senses in the following test:

> (Take the test quickly, have someone else read the questions to you and read the question one time only. Do not look over the test before you take it. Record your answers on paper.)
>
> 1. How many animals did Moses take into the ark?
> 2. What is the name of the RAISED PRINT that deaf people use?
> 3. Is it possible to end a sentence with the word "THE?"
> 4. Spell the word "shop." What do you do when you come to a green light?
> 5. It is noon. You look at the clock. The big hand is on the three, the little hand is on the five: What time is it?
> 6. Spell the word "silk." What do cows drink?
> 7. Listen carefully: You are the driver of a train; there are thirty people on board. At the first stop, 10 people get off. At the next stop, 5 people get on. Now for the question: What is the name of the train driver? [17]

---

[17]. Ray Comfort, *The Ten Commandments* (Bellflower, CA: Living Waters,1993), p. 192.

Most people get the majority of the questions wrong. The answers are at the back of this chapter. The questions are actually really simple, but our minds cannot always be trusted. They are not perfectly dependable, and we cannot make sense out of the world using reason alone. We must rely on God alone. He, exclusively, is perfect and infallible. The world is real, and our real human mind can know its real nature because God has given us our mind, and He has revealed to mankind that the world can be known. Our minds are not infallible and that is one of the major problems with rationalism. Hence there is no reason to trust autonomous reason.

Modernity Despises Evangelism

The whole idea of evangelism is not only out of favor in modernity, it is despised and called intolerant. Asserting that Christ is the only way to God is not tolerated in our secular culture. It also declares conservative Christianity demands that an intellectual straitjacket be strapped on society. A bondage that will infringe on the personal rights and liberties of "free" individuals. The thought of converting one to Christ is asserted by the liberal media as arrogant and egotistical. This attitude has infected the Church, as the modern church has fallen into deep indifference. When a Christian actively pushes the claims of Christ in the market place, he is immediately confronted by angry infidels and professing Christians. Both passionately claim that the evangelist is unloving and intolerant. I have received hundreds of encouragements from previously unknown Christian well wishers on the streets. I have also received many more negative and sometimes hostile rebukes from Christian men and women. Their main beef: They think pressing the moral law of God on the unbeliever is too harsh. Jesus and the Apostles were much less tolerant than we are, and they pronounced many more unpleasant truths to the nonbelievers. Due to the fact of our delicate culture, we should try to be as soft, patient, and gentle as possible, without compromising the message, but most often it is the message that upsets those who rebuke us. This just demonstrates how far our culture has bought into a false tolerance. We are called to follow Jesus and proclaim the truth of God to a mostly unreceptive world. We do this knowing that we are not in a popularity contest, but in a war. A war that God will win as He uses us to share the love, grace, and truth of God's word. Plug your ears to the world's concept of tolerance, trust Christ, and press His unique claims upon the unbeliever.

Stott makes the case this way, "To cultivate a mind so broad that it can accommodate every opinion, however false or evil, without ever detecting anything to reject, is not a virtue; it is the vice of the feeble minded and amoral." The teachings of Jesus are clearly and radically intolerant. Jesus is the only way. He is THE truth. The modern evangelical's abeyance of the immoderate and unique claims of Christ is devastating to the health and growth of the Church Universal. We are never to attempt to force conversions, or fence someone in so we can preach to them. We do not need to be foaming at the mouth wild-eyed fanatics. We have the Holy Spirit dwelling in our hearts by faith, and we have a sovereign God. Beating someone into submission, intellectually or physically, is sin. It demonstrates a lack of trust in God's sovereign work in the hearts of the lost. God elects His people, we do not. His grace is sufficient.

We are not to sit back at home watching the *Twilight Zone* marathon and neglect our witnessing duty. I find most believers do not have to worry about being too aggressive. Most have to concern themselves more with actually going out and witnessing occasionally. Van Til in his landmark book *The Defense Of The Faith* put it well when he said, "The natural man must be blasted out of his hideouts… the Reformed apologist throws down the gauntlet and challenges his opponent to a duel of life and death from the start." We should be aggressive with truth, love, and kindness. One can be zealous and effective in our witness without being bombastic and rude. When you have the truth, it is easy to fall into the error of vituperating against the unbeliever, or puffing out your apologetic chest with your pithy philosophical comments. Christians must be respectful and kind. We should love others as ourselves. There is no place in the Christian witness for pride and ungodly churlishness.

The Lover of Wisdom

This book will have more philosophy in it than most evangelism books. If you have not been exposed to much philosophy, do not worry, I will not drown you in a bottomless plunge into vain philosophy. The definition of the Greek word for philosophy is: a lover of wisdom. Christians are to petition God for wisdom, search the scriptures for wisdom, and study to become wise unto salvation. God's word reveals the true philosophy. All other schools of thought are vain, and we must cast down vain imaginations and take all thoughts captive. Paul instructs us not to embrace the "vain" philosophy of non-Christian thought. Scores of people in the modern church falsely believe that Paul annuls all philosophy. The imperative is against a particular type of philosophy: Vain philosophy is what God disallows. All philosophy that is not based on God's revelation is empty, barren, and vain, and the Bible prohibits it. Philosophy that is derived from biblical revelation can expose bad arguments and will bring forth light through good arguments.

> Therefore he reasoned in the synagogue with the Jews and with the Gentile worshipers, and in the marketplace daily with those who happened to be there (Acts 17:17).

The Christian apologist is never to put God in the dock. There is no external standard that can judge God or His word. Historical, archeological, mathematical, and other evidences are not to judge the Bible's truthfulness as the word of God. A man cannot certify or rubber stamp the Bible as a revelation from God. It is impossible for the Bible not to be the word of God. God must be true for anything in this life to be intelligible. God is the requirement for evidences, and the law of non-contradiction. No external authority is to be used to verify the Bible as a revelation from God. Mankind cannot be the authority. Evidences cannot be the authority. Only God can be the ultimate authority. To make sense of this world, we must start with God and His revealed word. There is nothing that we can use independently of God's authority. The laws of logic, historical evidences, archeological finds, tests, and experiments all presuppose the triune God. We do not need to verify or test scripture. It has authority, and without it we cannot make sense out of any element or concept in the world. God is, and He does not need to be justified. Lost mankind needs justification.

There is Proof, Proof, Nothing but Proof

Yes, the Bible reveals to humanity that the Earth hangs on nothing (Job 26:7) and is a sphere (Isaiah 40:22). Scripture declared this thousands of years before telescopes and modern science discovered those facts. God's word teaches us the proper function of the water cycle (Job 38:12-14), the existence of ocean currents (Psalms 8:8), the solar cycle, and the expansion of the universe (Isaiah 40:22) centuries before modern science found these truths. These evidential facts are consistent with the authority of the Bible. These and other evidences do not give the Bible authority; it is endued with it because it is God's word. All science, testing, and examination presuppose God and His word. Testing utilizes a number of dynamics such as logic and induction. A materialistic worldview cannot justify the existence or the use of the laws of reason. They are nonphysical and abstract dynamics that can only come from the nature of the one true God. We have certain knowledge that the God of scripture lives. We do not think He probably exists. Our faith is not just reasonable or plausible. It is impossible for the true and living God not to exist because without Him, we cannot know anything at all. He is the precondition for all knowledge. God must be presupposed as the basis of every element of mankind's experience, knowledge, and value.

God is the Foundation of all Reality

Ponder the following syllogism:

1. The God of scripture is the foundation of all reality or reality is unintelligible.

2. Reality is intelligible.

3. Therefore, God is the foundation of reality.

The consequence of affirming that God does not exist is to assert that the world is unintelligible and unknowable. That proposition is impossible because it is self-refuting. If the world is unintelligible and unknowable, then that statement also would be unintelligible and unknowable, hence it would be self-voiding and false. This consequence leads to the truth that God is the ground and foundation of knowledge. Unless Christianity is true, we can know nothing of reality. If we can know nothing of reality, we cannot know that proposition. Unless the God of revelation is and has spoken, human knowledge has no intelligible basis. Harry Blaimires commented, "The Old and New Testament… No one can pretend it isn't there. Everyone who is concerned with the meaning of life, and the destiny of the human race will have to take it into account." [18] God's word declares that life must revolve around Him. We must have no other gods before Him. All men have a destiny that will find its consummation at the judgment seat of Christ. Self-deceivers can pretend that God does not

[18]. Harry Blaimires, *On Christian Truth* (Ann Arbor, MI: Servant Books, 1983), p. 129.

exist, but God lives. Those, who pretend He has not spoken, live a life that is contradictory and confusing. Their life will end one day and they will give an account for their life. This truth must consistently remain in front of our eyes. We should live and move before the face of God. This is our duty and our joy.

There are many professional skeptics and scoffers in our culture who marshal their full-bore nastiness to defend atheism. These men stroke their tobacco stained beards, and try to act sagacious, as they employ their acerbic wit to attack God. They are truth "falsifiers." They become experts at wishful thinking and self-deception. They have elaborate arguments that instruct the blind how to stay in the dark, while professing to make them wise.

My Unfavorite Martin

Michael Martin pontificates that "belief in the incarnation is clearly unjustified. Not only is the evidence for the incarnation lacking, but it is incoherent and conceptually problematic." [19] That statement lacks evidence and is more than problematic. The anti-theistic Martin cannot even account for the reality of evidence or the discovery of apparent problems. He must stand on the Christian worldview to discuss evidence and problems. Only Christianity can have a justified basis for the evaluation of evidence and the intelligent identification of problems. Martin's "case" is unintelligible because his assertion disqualifies itself. Thus his atheism is self-defeating like all systems that reject God's word. Atheism proclaims physicalism, that all reality is composed only of physical material. Yet that proclamation is not made up of anything physical or material. The atheist's view cannot support or justify itself. Atheism is a nonphysical system that teaches that the nonphysical does not exist. But the anti-theist's critiques of theism are not physical in and of themselves. It pops its own philosophical balloon. Proposing any philosophy, including the concept that only the physical world exists, is a nonphysical exercise. When one propagates anything, he is affirming that God lives through his use of nonphysical assertions and critiques. To claim to be a physicalist, one is actually assenting to anti-physicalism.

---

[19]. Michael Martin, *The Case Against Christianity* (Philadelphia, PA, 1991), p. 156.

God Completes all that He Begins

> Thus says the LORD, the King of Israel, and his Redeemer, the LORD of hosts: "I am the First and I am the Last; besides Me, there is no God. And who can proclaim as I do? Then let him declare it and set it in order for Me… Let them show these to them. Do not fear, nor be afraid; have I not told you from that time, and declared it? You are My witnesses. Is there a God besides Me? Indeed there is no other Rock; I know not one. I have declared the former things from the beginning; they went forth from My mouth, and I caused them to hear it. Suddenly I did them, and they came to pass … Even from the beginning I have declared it to you; before it came to pass I proclaimed it to you… You have heard... all this. And will you not declare it?… Come near to Me, hear this: I have not spoken in secret from the beginning; from the time that it was, I was there. And now the Lord GOD and His Spirit have sent Me. Thus says the LORD, your Redeemer, the Holy One of Israel: I am the LORD your God, who teaches you to profit, who leads you by the way you should go. Oh, that you had heeded My commandments! Then your peace would have been like a river, and your righteousness like the waves of the sea… Declare, proclaim this, utter it to the end of the earth…" (Isaiah 44:6-8 and 48:3-20).

Another area of "proof" is the messianic prophecies that were fulfilled by Jesus Christ. The Tenach (Old Testament) foretold the coming of the Messiah in exact detail. The text was written centuries before the coming of Jesus, and it predicted over three hundred prophecies about Him. No other founder of any religion can provide a similar prophetic record of his life written down centuries before his birth. Joseph Smith, Mary Baker Eddy, David Koresh, Muhammad, and Buddha cannot supply a widely transmitted, preexisting written record that accurately predicted the details of their life.

The three hundred clear prophecies of the coming Messiah were predicted and predestined by God. The Lord forecasted events and historical facts about the coming of Jesus prior to His birth. All these predictions came true in the birth, life, death, and resurrection of Jesus of Nazareth. No other leader or prophet had predictive material written about their life recorded before they were born. Jesus had over three hundred predictions about His life that were fulfilled in exact detail.

Christ's virgin birth was predicted about seven hundred years before He was born in Isaiah 7:14: "So the Lord Himself shall give you a sign. Behold, the virgin will conceive and shall bring forth a son, and they shall call His name Emmanuel." His place of birth was forecasted in Micah 5:2: "And you, Bethlehem... out of you He shall come forth to Me, to become Ruler in Israel, He whose goings forth have been... from eternity." The exact date of His entry in Jerusalem was predicted by Daniel in chapter nine. God prophesied the Palm Sunday event recorded in Zechariah 9:9: "Rejoice greatly, O daughter of Zion! Shout, O daughter of Jerusalem! Behold, your King is coming to you; He is just and having salvation, lowly and riding on a donkey, a colt, the foal of a donkey."

Christ's death on the cross was foretold before that form of execution was even invented by Persia. Psalms 22:1-16 announces the crucifixion hundreds of years before it happened: "My God, my God, why have You forsaken me... But I am a worm, and no man; a reproach of men, and despised by the people. All who see me laugh me to scorn; they shoot out the lip; they shake the head, saying, He trusted on the LORD; let Him deliver him; let Him rescue him, since He delights in him! I am poured out like water, and all my bones are spread apart; my heart is like wax; it is melted in the midst of my bowels and You have brought me into the dust of death. For dogs have circled around me; the band of spoilers have hemmed me in, they have pierced my hands and my feet." This evidence is overwhelming. But the truth is even more certain and compelling than compiling great blocks of evidence to prove the facts of Christianity. The argument for Jesus Christ is certain. Without God, one cannot provide the necessary preconditions for truth and certainty.

The Certain Argument

> But our God is in heaven; He does whatever He pleases (Psalms 115:3).

The simple biblical argument is: Without God one cannot account for anything. God is the precondition for logic, morality, mathematics, and everything else in the cosmos. This is the certain argument that is absolutely true. This truth will be hammered and hammered throughout this book, so when you are finished, you will know it inside and out. The truth is simple and it is powerful. You must understand that the unbeliever needs to hear it echo and reecho. When you are talking with a skeptic be unremitting with this apologetic.

The great thing about employing the "argument from the impossibility of the contrary" is that it grows in power when the unbeliever attacks it. The argument grows in force because the unbeliever must use logic to make his intellectual challenge. Logic requires God. Only Christianity supplies the necessary preconditions for logic. Thus every time an unbeliever rationally attacks God he is demonstrating that God lives. Without God, he cannot make any rational assertion. The old science-fiction movie that has a huge electric monster on the loose illustrates this point. The monster in this thriller grows larger and stronger every time someone uses a weapon in attempting to kill it. The monster is ready to take over America, and the President orders the army to hit it with an atomic bomb. The troops launch the bomb and as the mushroom cloud slowly starts to dissipate, when the smoke clears they are stunned by the horror of horrors: the energy monster survived. Not only does the monster survive, he now is ten times larger. The energy monster absorbed the massive energy from the bomb. It did not get weaker, but grew in size and strength. Similarly, the unbeliever will attempt to fire intellectual weapons at the "argument from the impossibility of the contrary." Nevertheless, all their attacks will only be consumed by the truth, while the defense of the truth grows stronger and larger. There is nothing a skeptic can assert without ultimately relying on theism, since God alone provides the preconditions for the laws of logic. Thus the unbeliever's argument will always presuppose God because the unbeliever cannot supply the preconditions for the nonphysical laws of logic. The triune God is the preexisting foundation for all debate. Deny God and one cannot debate anything.

> Whom God raised up, having loosed the pains of death, because it was not possible that He should be held by it... Therefore let all the house of Israel know assuredly that God has made this Jesus whom you crucified, both Lord and Christ (Acts 2:24 & 36).

Answers To The Test:

1. None. Noah was on the ark, not Moses.
2. Deaf people do not use raised print.
3. The question is an example of one.
4. Go.
5. Noon.
6. Water.
7. You are the driver of the train.

CHAPTER TWO

CHRISTIANITY AND EVIDENCE: GRACE AND TRUTH

Any logical argument against the existence of God affirms the existence of God. All atheists and agnostics assume the laws of logic, but cannot account for them. A physical world cannot produce nonphysical laws of logic. If there is such a thing as proof then there is logic, thus there is a God. [1]

A Faith which goes on believing despite the evidence is not a faith worth having. The biblical idea of faith is trust in God because of what God has said and done. [2]

Faith is the great cop-out, the great excuse to evade the need to think and evaluate evidence. Faith is belief despite, even perhaps because of, the lack of evidence.[3]

---

[1]. Dr. Greg Bahnsen, *Bahnsen and Gordon Stein Debate 1985* (Irvine, CA: Covenant Media Cassette Tape).

[2]. Colin Brown, *Philosophy and the Christian Faith* (Downers Grove, IL: I.V. Press, 1968) p. 284.

[3]. Richard Dawkins, *Servant Magazine* (Winter 2000), p. 8.

I have declared the former things from the beginning; They went forth from My mouth, and I caused them to hear it. Suddenly I did them, and they came to pass... Even from the beginning I have declared it to you; Before it came to pass I proclaimed it to you (Isaiah 48:3-5).

To whom He also presented Himself alive after His suffering by many infallible proofs, being seen by them during forty days and speaking of the things pertaining to the kingdom of God (Acts 1:3).

For the law was given through Moses, but grace and truth came through Jesus Christ (John 1:17).

For the wrath of God is revealed from heaven against all ungodliness and unrighteousness of men, who suppress the truth in unrighteousness, because what may be known of God is manifest in them, for God has shown it to them (Romans 1:18).

The Overwhelming Evidence for Theism

"Present your case," says the LORD, "Bring forth your strong reasons," says the King of Jacob. "Let them bring forth and show us what will happen; let them show the former things, what they were, that we may consider them, and know the latter end of them; or declare to us things to come. Show the things that are to come hereafter, that we may know that you are gods; yes, do good or do evil, that we may be dismayed and see it together" (Isaiah 41:21-23).

Remember this, and show yourselves men; recall to mind, O you transgressors. Remember the former things of old, for I am God, and there is no other; I am God, and there is none like Me, declaring the end from the beginning, and from ancient times things that are not yet done, saying, "My counsel shall stand, and I will do all My pleasure" (Isaiah 46:8-10).

There is overwhelming evidence that God exists. But the evidence alone will not convert a pagan into a saint. The bare facts of the three hundred-plus messianic prophecies of Christ are astounding and convincing to me as a Christian. I love the evidence that God has given us. The prophecies that foretold the birth, life, and death of Jesus are found in Genesis 3:15, 49:10; Psalms 2:6-7, Psalms 22; Micah 5:2; Daniel 9:25; Zechariah 9:9, 12:10; Isaiah 7:14, 9:6, 53:1-8; and many other passages. These were written down before the birth of Christ as recorded in the Dead Sea Scrolls and the ancient Jewish Targums. There are over three hundred predictions of the coming Messiah and they were all fulfilled by Jesus.

Peter Stoner calculated the odds as ten to the one hundred and fifty-seventh power that forty-eight of these predictions could be fulfilled by blind chance in the life of Jesus. In the Probability Theory, it is agreed that odds smaller than ten to the fiftieth power are the same as zero. And ten to the one hundred and fifty-seventh power is much larger than that. Hence the predicted life of Jesus was ordained by God Almighty. There are lots of self-styled prophets and claimants bouncing around in our world today. The tabloids have prophecies and predictions that they share with the world for a fee. Recently, the *National Enquire* forecasted fifty-five prophecies. None of them came true. But we incorrectly use these failures to validate the prophecies in the Bible. Just because one source gives false prophecies, does not mean that the biblical prophecies prove the claims of Christ. The messianic prophecies are wonderful "proof" built upon the Christian worldview. The accuracy and specific detail of the events that the Bible forecasted are astonishing to the believer. They are not vague generalities. The messianic prophecies are bold, startling, detailed, and specific. But a sharp skeptic will not affirm them as proof.

> All things must be fulfilled which were written in the Law of Moses, the Prophets, and the Psalms concerning Me (Luke 24:44).

The historical and biblical testimony concerning the resurrection of Christ is convincing to me and other believers as well. Those outside the faith have a different set of presuppositions, and this leads to problems when you employ biblical proof. The scriptures do not instruct us to press the *prima facie* evidence, but to placard the *a priori* necessity of the truth of Christianity. The job of the Christian isn't to demonstrate the probability that God exists through displaying the brute evidence. It is to cast down all imaginations that rise up against God. We tear down all the unbelievers folly and lift up the truth of Christ. The faithful witnessing approach uses the argument from the impossibility of the contrary. God is the precondition for all argument, proof, evidence, and reason. It is impossible for God not to exist forasmuch as He is the precondition for all intelligent exchanges. The nonphysical, universal, timeless, and unchanging God alone provides the necessary preconditions for the use of nonphysical, universal, timeless, invariant laws of logic. To argue at all, you must presuppose that God lives. We demonstrate that it is impossible for Jesus not to be Lord of all, and we cast down all foolish thought that rises up against Christ and His word. We do this with grace, love and patience, knowing that salvation is of the Lord.

Many evidential apologists have blessed me and have enhanced my faith. These are the Christian scholars who focus on the evidence of the reliability of the scriptures and the Christian faith. This is the faith I already had by God's grace. The truth of God's existence is not probable, it is impossible for Him not to exist. God's existence is the absolute precondition for all our questions and doubts. We utilize logic in our questions as well as in our doubts, thereby affirming that God lives. Christianity is the only worldview that provides human reason a foundation for its proper function. Non-Christian systems of thought cannot furnish a foundation for the law of non-contradiction, thus those systems of thought can only offer self-contradictory worldviews. Unless one believes in the triune God, one cannot account for human experience. God is the precondition for all argument, proof, evidence, and reason. It is impossible for God not to exist for He is the precondition for all intelligent thought. All human thought requires the employment and assumption of the universal and invariant laws of logic. Only the transcendent, nonphysical, and unchanging Almighty God provides the necessary preconditions for the use of nonphysical, universal, and unchanging laws of logic. To argue at all, you must presuppose that the true and living God exists.

Ask Questions

The contrary of Christianity is impossible inasmuch as all other worldviews fall into absurdity, since they are self-contradictory. They lead to conclusions that are contradictory on their own assumptions. A very important strategy, in your defense of the faith, is to ask the nonbeliever some questions. In their answers, they will soon contradict their own worldview. The primary question you must ask: What will supply the preconditions to make reality intelligible? Without God, nothing comports and nothing can make sense. This is the biblical truth. The true and living God is the precondition for the intelligibility of reality and the understanding of all human experiences. As we defend the faith, we must be faithful to scripture. We are not to swap "evidence" with the non-Christian. We should graciously attack their assumed starting points in all that they postulate. We must use the truth from the word of God to dislodge the unbeliever from their self-deceptions and delusions. We do this by demonstrating the self-defeating nature of their presuppositions.

The Evidence is Glorious

Evidence is wonderful. The Christian faith has tons of evidence that supports its claims. In reality, there is nothing but evidence for the God of the Bible. Every star and every atom declares the majesty of God. We see evidence of God's finger prints in every corner of the universe. Mankind discovers the proof and affirms the facts that the Bible records and announces. The greatest miracle is the resurrection of Jesus. Jesus Christ is alive! He is the only religious leader in history to rise from the dead. He is the only one who promised a resurrection, and He kept His promise. You can visit the tombs of all the deceased religious leaders and find their remains still in the grave. The great grandson of Gandhi took the revered man's ashes to the Ganges river as thousands of onlookers sang and chanted. He opened the copper urn and dropped Gandhi's ashes in the river. This proved Gandhi died, and stayed dead. Recently in Israel, the Muslims and the Jewish people have fought over the control of the tomb of Abraham, Isaac, and Jacob. You can visit their occupied graves just as you can the heterodox leaders: Mary Baker Eddy, Joseph Smith, and Muhammad. All these allotheists died and stayed dead; their occupied sarcophaguses attest to this. However Jesus is alive. His grave is empty, no bones about it.

Jesus thundered, "All power on earth and heaven has been given to me." No force could keep Him down. The Romans killed Him. He was put into a cave tomb, and a huge boulder was rolled at a downward angle in front of the cave. Then they pasted Caesar's seal on the crypt and posted Roman guards to protect the tomb. They were only trying to prevent the inevitable. Jesus had all the power to rise, and nobody could stop Him. Can you imagine, after the resurrection, what the men thought who had Jesus executed, as they are walked down the street and saw the risen Jesus.

What do you say when you see Him on the sidewalk? They must have been stunned. God used this, and the preaching of the Apostles to win many of Christ's enemies to salvation. The Book of Acts reports in chapter six verse seven: "Then the word of God spread, and the number of the disciples multiplied greatly in Jerusalem, and a great many of the priests were obedient to the faith." Even many Pharisees came to believe in Jesus (Acts 15:5).

Men do not die willingly if they know they have been deceived. The followers of Jim Jones, the people who knew that he was a kook and a fraud, tried to escape Jonestown. Once they knew Jones was an impostor, and that he whipped up a batch of poison Kool-Aid, they ran and hid in the jungle. Many others tried to escape and were shot. They knew Jones was a charlatan and they did not want to die for him. However the Apostles and hundreds of others in the first century died for Jesus because they knew Jesus was alive.

The first century followers of Christ died believing that He was perfect and sinless. Many of them spent day and night with Him for over three years. And they believed He was sinless. If you spent sixty minutes with any other human, you would soon find out that they were not perfect. You would not lay down your life declaring that they were sinless. You would not die for what you know is a lie. Koresh understood this problem since he was a cunning deceiver. Knowing that his followers would observe him sinning every day, he devised a crafty way to avoid the problem of claiming to be the Messiah as a sinner. Koresh called himself the "sinful Messiah." The antithesis to Koresh is Jesus. He had all His friends and enemies confess that He did not sin. The disciples, His betrayer, His religious enemies, and His Roman enemies, were all in agreement on one subject: Jesus never sinned. No one could accuse Jesus of sin. Jesus is alive as the sinless Messiah. That is a fact. It is not a brute fact that stands by itself and awaits the judgment of man. It is true, and it is impossible for it not to be true.

Love Presupposes God

> Love suffers long and is kind; love does not envy; love does not parade itself, is not puffed up; does not behave rudely, does not seek its own, is not provoked, thinks no evil; does not rejoice in iniquity, but rejoices in the

> truth; bears all things, believes all things, hopes all things, endures all things. Love never fails. But whether there are prophecies, they will fail; whether there are tongues, they will cease; whether there is knowledge, it will vanish away (1 Corinthians 13:4-8).
>
> God is love (1 John 4:8).

One thing is very clear, the skeptic and the nonbeliever cannot account for or justify anything. They cannot tell the informed believer, under the scrutiny of truthful investigation, where anything comes from, and why one should affirm any notion. Only the Christian worldview can account for logic, ethics, identity, motion, induction, and even love. Ask the atheist: "What is love? Is it a pat on the head, or a hug and a kiss for his wife?" No. A man can hate his wife and still give her a hug and a kiss. Love is more than a touch or an agitating flux of hormones and neurotransmitters in the brain. Love is grounded in the nature of God. The one and true God is the Father, Son, and Holy Spirit. Throughout eternity, the Father loved the Son and the Holy Spirit. The Spirit loved the Father and the Son, as the Son also loved the Father and the Spirit. Only the one eternal God in three persons can tell us where love came from and what love is. No other religion can justify or ultimately explain love because their god or gods, are not eternally coexisting as infinite, immutable, and loving persons in one being. The Father, Son, and Holy Spirit have eternal, unchanging love among the Godhead. Yahweh alone is God and He alone can be the eternal ground for love. The love and the fellowship among the persons in the Godhead are the pattern, and the source of human love and interpersonal communication. We love others because it is the perennial aspect of bearing the image of God. "There are three persons in the Godhead, the Father, the Son, and the Holy Spirit, and these three are one God, the same in substance, equal in power and glory."

Only Christianity can Account for Love

Your job, as a witness, is to ask the person you are engaging: Where did love come from and what is love? Is love just a physical action? If a woman pinches the cheeks of her grandchild and kisses her husband when he goes to work, is that love? No. A woman could do that, all the while, plotting to murder them. The non-Christian cannot give an answer that is grounded on unchanging truth. The nonbeliever will not have any ultimate answers. Asking questions is one of the best tools you have as a witness. Jesus witnessed frequently by asking questions. The Bible records (Luke 2:46-47) that He was teaching the Rabbi's in the temple by "asking them questions and they were astonished at His answers." Asking questions will bring to the surface the foolish presuppositions of the unbeliever. If you read this book a few times, and listen to Bahnsen and Sproul tapes every day, you still may get stumped. Getting stuck, and stammering to respond to a skeptic can be a frightful moment. Asking questions is a great way to prevent getting stupefied or trapped. If you do not know the answer to their question, admit it, and go on. Turn it around on them and remind them that they cannot even account for questioning, but you can. Then ask them more questions, and if you know the contents of this book, you will immediately see the folly and weakness of the unbeliever. The skeptic has no ultimate answers. You do. Bear upon them this weakness, and then trumpet the law before them. Only Christianity can account for love. Love comes to us through the triune God. God's nature is the ultimate and objective basis of love. Real love is objective and eternal because it is an eternal attribute of the eternal God. God presupposes love, and love presupposes God. Christians can justify love, and we should share that love. We must be charitable in word and deed. Too often we leave out the "word." Some generations of Christians were encouraged to "talk the talk, and walk the walk." In our generation, it seems that we are more willing to support charities while remaining a silent witness. Giving to the poor is good, and this is our duty. Yet charity, without evangelism, is just "picking the lint off a corpse."

The only True and Living God

> "You are My witnesses," says the LORD, "And My servant whom I have chosen, that you may know and believe Me, and understand that I am He. Before Me there was no God formed, nor shall there be after Me. I, even I, am the LORD, and besides Me there is no Savior" (Isaiah 43:10,11).

The only true God is the Father, the Son, and the Holy Spirit: one God in three persons. There is no other God in whom we must believe. He is the only God who lives and the only God who is necessary.

Encounter at Denny's, Salt Lake City, Utah

The following is a summary of a conversation that a group of friends and I had with a professed Satanist:

Satanist: I don't believe in God; I believe in the Devil.

Mike: Do you have any evidence for this belief?

Satanist: I have seen his power.

Mike: How is that proof? People from all types of religions claim to feel power. These are contradictory religions that disagree with one another. This cannot be evidence because they all feel that their religion is true, yet they all disagree with each other.

Satanist: OK, I don't have any evidence, but neither do you.

Mike: Actually, Christianity has tons of evidence. The Holy Bible predicted the coming of Jesus through 333 prophecies that were written before He was born. The odds on all these coming true by chance are higher than the number of electrons in the universe. This is just a smidgen of the evidence of Christ and His claims. Yet the God of the Bible is not to be tried or evaluated by mere men. Any evaluation or discussion of evidence presupposes that God lives!

Satanist: What?

Mike: Do you believe there is such a thing as evidence?

Satanist: Of course, but how does that prove God?

Mike: It's not so much that it proves God, as if He's in the dock, but God is the precondition for there to be evidence. Do you use logic when you look at evidence?

Satanist: Yes.

Mike: Is logic physical? Can you go down the street and buy some logic and reason at K-Mart's blue light special?

Satanist: No.

Mike: You are correct, you can't. The laws of logic are abstract, nonphysical, nonmaterial, fixed, invariable, and universal. A physical changing reality, our world, could not produce logic and reason.

Satanist: That doesn't make any sense.

Mike: Remember, Christianity has tremendous evidence for its dogma; everything that exists is evidence for the Triune God. You not only do not have any evidence or reasons for your faith; you cannot account for reason without the God of the Bible. A person who asserts that only the physical world exists cannot account for his use of nonphysical logic in his reasoning. Logic is not physical. It is transcendent, universal, and abstract. Only the Christian worldview can supply the necessary preconditions of the nonmaterial, unchanging, and universal laws of logic. The laws of logic cannot be found in a glove box or a cookie jar. You can't purchase a set of laws of logic on sale at the swap-meet. They are not concrete, hard and physical. Only the transcendent, timeless, unchanging, universal, and nonphysical God can provide the necessary preconditions for transcendent, universal, timeless, unchanging, and nonphysical logic. This demonstrates that it is impossible for the atheistic scientist to be correct in declaring nothing exists except the physical world. For even that declaration is nonphysical, hence it is false. It is impossible for God not to exist.

Satanist: I don't buy it.

Mike: Whether you acknowledge the truth of Christ or not, you stand on the Christian worldview every time you use logic or have an intelligent conversation. Keep in mind, every time you look at the Denny's menu, talk to your friends or add up your lunch bill, you are declaring that God lives! Every time you disagree and debate a subject, as you use logic, you are affirming the Christian faith.

Satanist: No, I don't believe in Jesus.

Mike: Yes you do; you just haven't put your trust in Him. You are suppressing the truth so you can live the way you desire. Remember, you cannot account for an intelligent dialogue or the law of non-contradiction. Yet you depend on these dynamics every day of your life. Despite your verbal disagreement with Christianity, you are standing on its truths. You have broken God's law, the Ten Commandments, and you will perish in your sins. Your only hope is to flee to Christ. Jesus alone died on the cross and rose again in power.

Satanist: I'm not going to listen to you.

Mike: I pray you change your mind. What is waiting for you without Christ is eternal horror and pain. You will not party in hell with your friends. You will not escape God even in Hades. The Bible says in Psalms 139 that God's wrathful presence is there, unmediated and unending. Repent and trust Christ.

Satanist: We are done.

Mike: Don't forget, all the while you are denying God, you are borrowing from His worldview.

Be a Gracious Witness

I have observed that in witnessing to hard core or aggressive people, you must cordially lead the conversation. Do not let the pagan take control of the dialogue through dozens of unrelated questions. You ask them a few questions about Christ. If they purport unbelief, ask them whether they used logic in their objections. Then ask them where does logic come from? These questions put them on the defensive. No matter how smart they are, they will not have any real objective answers. You then give them the biblical answers. After you have torn down their vain imaginations, and have demonstrated that all reality presupposes God, give them the law and the gospel. Show them that they have broken God's law and they need the Savior. We must always keep in mind that unbelievers are actively suppressing the truth in unrighteousness.

> For the iniquity of his covetousness I was angry and struck him; I hid and was angry, and he went on backsliding in the way of his heart (Isaiah 57:17).

Most of the questions that unbelievers ask are not sincere inquires, but excuses that they hoist to justify their sinful lifestyle. Anyone can be a skeptic and ask fatuous questions. There is a story in the Talmud where one Rabbi rules on the ownership of a wild bird. Rabbi Eliezer, who serves as the community's judge, adjudicates the dispute. He says, "If the bird is found within fifty cubits of a man's land, the bird is his property. If it is found outside the fifty cubits limits, it belongs to the person who discovers it." After this ruling, Rabbi Jeremiah attempts to stultify Eliezer with the question, "If one foot of the bird is discovered in the limit of the fifty cubits and another foot is on the other side, outside the fifty cubits, what is the law?" The Talmud goes on to say, "It was for that question that Rabbi Jeremiah was thrown out of the house of study." People can ask an endless number of questions, and frequently they really do not want the answers. Their questions are calculated to lead the evangelist down a limitless number of rabbit trails. There comes a time that you stop the hike and warn them of the wrath of God. I do not recommend that you throw them out, but often you must cut to the chase and press the law and the gospel on their lost souls for their own good.

It is easy to ask imprudent questions and be a dime store skeptic. It is a lot more challenging to be tough-minded. Most of the world does not like to evaluate their own worldview and ask the difficult questions. The tenacity of the unbeliever's self-deception is extraordinary. They suppress the truth with herculean strength in view of the fact that they know God exists, but they do not want to be intellectually honest. Error begets error, and deception begets deception. The more they suppress the truth, the more they embrace lies and inconsistencies. They are quick to adapt loopy esoteric beliefs and practices in an attempt to fortify their disbelief in God. We must turn it around on the unbeliever and bear the challenging problems of unbelief down on them.

It is comforting to know, not only is there incredible evidence for Christianity, but everything in existence is evidence for God. As God's word proclaims, every flower is evidence for God's existence. It is not so much that we have to prove theism, but we are called to realize all proof presupposes the God of the Bible.

Witnessing One Sunday Night

On a night that our church went out witnessing and passing out gospel tracts, a friend named Nathan was talking with an atheist. Recorded below is their conversation.

Atheist: I just try to live my life pure, like the American Indians.

Nathan: How do you know that they lived a pure life?

Atheist: (He was fumbling his words trying to find and answer.) Uh, um…

Nathan: Who defines purity?

Atheist: I don't know.

Nathan: Then how do you know you are living a pure life? (God is the only one who defines purity, thus he could not give an account for his so-called "purity").

Atheist: (He could not give an answer.) I only believe in what I have seen.

Nathan: Have you seen the whole solar system?

Atheist: No.

Nathan: Then how do you know that all the planets that are reportedly out there, exist?

Atheist: Did you know that Adam and Eve did not really exist?

Nathan: How do you know that they did not exist? Were you around at the time to see whether they were there or not? After all, you said you believe only in things that you have seen.

(He then walked away because he could not give an account for his worldview.)

The nonbeliever will make many claims that contradict his worldview (i.e. universal truths, absolute morality, laws of logic, etc.). Universal claims of knowledge cannot comport with an atheistic worldview because atheism fails to provide them. The great thing about the apologetic of Van Til is that it can refute all non-Christian worldviews. It is incredibly powerful because it is derived from the Bible. Christianity is the only worldview that supplies human reason a base for proper function. No non-Christian system of thought can furnish a foundation for the law of non-contradiction, hence those systems of thought can only offer a self-opposing worldview. Unless one believes in God's revealed word, you can consistently and logically believe in nothing else. God is the precondition for all argument, proof, evidence, and reason. It is impossible for God not to exist. He is the precondition for all intelligent communication since all human communication requires the use of the laws of logic. The nonphysical, universal, timeless, and unchanging God alone provides the necessary preconditions for the use of nonphysical, universal, timeless, and unchanging laws of logic. To argue at all, you must presuppose that God lives. Non-believing thought cannot supply the necessary preconditions for the laws of logic. Hence it results in futility because of the internal contradictions it is entangled in. Thus the contrary of Christianity is impossible because it falls into absurdity. It is self-contradictory. All non-Christian worldviews lead to conclusions that are incongruous with their premises. The most important thing in your defense of the faith is to ask the nonbeliever some questions. In their answers, they will soon contradict their worldview. The primary question you should ask: What will supply the preconditions that make reality intelligible? The logical reality is, without God, nothing can make sense. The true and living God is the precondition for the intelligibility of reality and the understanding of all human experiences.

CHAPTER THREE

ATHEISM: I DON'T LIKE GOD

If a man walked down the railway track, saw a train racing toward him, closed his eyes, and said, "I believe it's a marshmallow train," would it change reality? What he believes doesn't matter. What matters is that if he doesn't get off the track, he will be a marshmallow. [1]

A young Atheist cannot guard his faith too carefully. Dangers lie in wait for him on every side. [2]

Atheism is too simple. If the whole universe has no meaning, we should never have found out that it has no meaning. [3]

I was at this time living, like so many atheists or anti-theists, in a whirl of contradictions. I maintained that God did not exist. I was also very angry with God for

---

1. Ray Comfort, *Hell's Best Kept Secret* (Springdale, PA: Whitaker House, 1989), p. 120.
2. C.S. Lewis, *Surprised by Joy* (NY: Harcourt, Brace & Co.,1955), p. 211.
3. C.S. Lewis: *Martindale and Root, Editors, The Quotable Lewis* (Wheaton, IL: Tyndale House, 1989), p. 60.

> not existing. I was equally angry with Him for creating a world. [4]
>
> The conception of God is necessary for the intelligible interpretation of any fact. [5]
>
> Solidity... is perfectly incomprehensible alone... Our modern philosophy, therefore, leaves us no just nor satisfactory idea of solidity; nor consequently of matter. [6]
>
> The only thing that exists is matter (a basic belief of materialism).
>
> But you be watchful in all things, endure afflictions, do the work of an evangelist, fulfill your ministry (2 Timothy 4:5).
>
> For the wrath of God is revealed from heaven against all ungodliness and unrighteousness of men, who suppress the truth in unrighteousness, because what may be known of God is manifest in them, for God has shown it to them. For since the creation of the world His invisible attributes are clearly seen, being understood by the things that are made, even His eternal power and Godhead, so that they are without excuse, because, although they knew God, they did not glorify Him as God nor were thankful, but became futile in their thoughts, and their foolish hearts were darkened. Professing to be wise, they became fools (Romans 1:18-22).

Darkened Hearts

Atheists hate God. They could not hate God if God did not exist. This is the reason Madalyn Murray O'Hair, on the night of her consecration to the faith of atheism, shook her fists at the sky and declared to heaven, "I

---

4. Ibid., Lewis, p. 60.

5. Greg Bahnsen, *Van Til's Apologetic* (Phillipsburg, NJ: P & R, 1998), p. 494.

6. David Hume, *A Treatise of Human Nature* (Oxford, UK: Oxford Press, 2000), p. 150-151.

do not believe in you." If God did not exist, who was she shaking her fist at? The famous nineteenth century skeptic Ingersoll delivered a speech that attempted to prove that God did not exist. He rambled on and on with his reasons why he did not believe in God. At the end of the lecture, he challenged God to strike him dead if He exists. Nothing happened and Ingersoll left with great satisfaction. After he left an atheist asked a Christian, "Didn't Ingersoll prove something tonight?" Her reply was memorable. "Yes, he did," she answered, "He proved that God isn't taking orders from an atheist tonight." Of course, a couple years later, God did honor his request, when Ingersoll died like every man. The triune God does live. Atheists lash out at God and thus become fools. Scoffers have been known to call God an "egomaniac" because He requires worship. God is not frazzled by the truth suppressing hi-jinks of the atheists. The Bible announces: "The fool says in his heart there is no God." It is nonsense to say that God doesn't exist. If there is no God, we are all just molecules in motion, and we have no sense and no mind; we are just the random firing of chemicals in the brain. If our minds are composed of only physical matter, then our thoughts are, as Doug Wilson wittily quipped in his debate with atheist Dan Barker, just "brain gas." In that debate, Wilson went on to use an illustration of two soda-pop cans. If our minds are just the result of chemical reactions, then in the debate over pop cans, God's existence can just as rightly be settled by shaking the two soda-pop cans simultaneously. Labeling one can "Atheism" and the other can "Theism"; after shaking the cans, the one that "fizzes the most wins" the debate. If our minds were simply the fluctuations of proteins, neurotransmitters, and other brain biochemicals, then an intellectual debate is equivalent to the chemical reactions that occur when one shakes up a couple cans of soda. This is foolishness. God does live. Because He lives, we can debate, and we can also account for the nonphysical logic that is utilized in a debate.

The Atheist Syndrome and Wishful Thinking

The fact is atheists hate God. They know He exists, and they want to malign and defy Him. Koster, in his provocative book *The Atheist Syndrome*, convincingly demonstrates that most of the famous atheists had difficult or non-existing relationships with their earthly fathers. Thus they attempted to take their hurt and frustration out on their heavenly Father by actively disbelieving in His existence. Koster documents that the ranting and ravings of atheists such as Nietzsche, Freud, Huxley, Darwin, Ingersoll, Darrow, Hitler, and others were the consequence of an unhealthy relationship or lack of a relationship with their earthly father that fueled their wishful thinking. He goes on to establish that this led to mental illness in many of them, hence the "Atheist Syndrome." He brings this point to our attention with the following:

> Materialists and atheists will, of course, be offended if we suggest that their heroes were actually insane, and their attack on God... was a deranged fantasy and not an explanation of scientific knowledge. But... Darwin, Thomas Huxley, Friedrich Nietzsche, and Sigmund Freud - had many hallmarks of mental illness stamped on their personality. In point of fact, a careful study of their biographies in light of improved scientific knowledge may reveal not only that each man was mentally ill, but that each man suffered the same form of mental illness. It was this mental illness that led each of them to pervert science into an attack on God. [7]

Koster goes on to present how atheist Shelley rebelled against God because he was "tormented and beaten in a religiously oriented school." Huxley and Freud revolted against the Almighty because they were "son-victims" and they actually relieved their symptoms of mental illness by "raving against Christianity." Huxley called his sedition against the Holy "crib-biting" and this raving produced physical and mental wellness and improved digestion. For Huxley raging war against God cheered him up and improved his health. Koster reports how Freud, so diseased that his flesh was putrefying and rotting away, the stench from the decaying and noxious flesh repelled even his faithful dog, yet he kept his pen in hand to "hammer away on his final book, *Moses and Monotheism*." A book that assaults the foundations of the biblical faith. Vitz, in his book *The Faith of the Fatherless*, demonstrates that once Freud and numerous other atheists as children were "disappointed in or loses respect for his earthly father, belief in a heavenly father is impossible."[8] He goes on to reveal, from Nietzsche to Russell, that all these famous atheists had very troubled relationships with their fathers or had no father in their life at all. Hume's father died when he was two years-old, Russell's when he was four, Sartre's father at age one, Camus' father died when he was one year-old, and Schopenhauer's father

---

7. John P. Koster, Jr., *The Atheist Syndrome* (Brentwood, TN: Wolgemuth & Hyatt, 1989), p. 12.

8. Paul Vitz, *Faith of the Fatherless* (Dallas, TX: Spence, 1999), p. 16.

died when the boy was a young teen. H.G. Wells, O'Hair, Stalin, and Freud all had difficult and troubling relationships with their earthly fathers. This led them to reject their heavenly Father because of their moral corruption, self-deception, and psychological instability. The two books listed above are fascinating and open up the emotional windows of those who actively and aggressively reject God and suppress His truth.

Atheists: Crypto-Theists

> He is the image of the invisible God, the firstborn over all creation. For by Him all things were created that are in heaven and that are on earth, visible and invisible, whether thrones or dominions or principalities or powers. All things were created through Him and for Him. And He is before all things, and in Him all things consist (Colossians 1:15-17).

Anti-theist's believe in God. They know He exists. The ungodly do not know God in a saving way, in a covenant relationship. They know Him through His attributes of providence, righteousness, justice, and goodness. They just don't like Him. They really don't like Him. Not liking someone does not prove that they do not exist. Not liking someone presupposes that this someone does, in fact, exist. It is not so much that one cannot prove that God does not exist or that we can prove that God does exist, both these assertions are true, but God is not on trial. We do not have to go around proving God exists. The true and living God lives, and everything we think, do, or say, presupposes the truth that God lives. Without God, one cannot make sense of anything, even the very question of God's existence. He has to exist, or we could not ponder that question or any other question. Everything around us can only be justified if God lives. All atheists know that God exists because the atheist has to rest upon the Christian worldview to deny God's existence. The atheist uses logic, morality, and other nonphysical truths to pronounce that God doesn't exist. When he does this, he affirms Christianity, even as he attempts to refute it. The atheist cannot furnish the necessary preconditions for logic, reason, and the concept of truth. The non-theist claims he doesn't have enough evidence to believe in God. There is evidence all around him, nothing but evidence. Anyone, who just opens his eyes, believes in right and wrong, knows that God dwells in eternity. It's like the old folk slogan: "It doesn't take a doctor of veterinary medicine to know when a dead skunk is on the road." Only with God, as our foundation for life, can we make sense out of the world. To allege that God does not exist, requires God to exist to make the allegation. Bahnsen demonstrates that in the following illustration:

> A person that argues that air doesn't exist, will, all the while breathe the air, while he is arguing; yet if what he said were true, he couldn't breathe at all. The theory that air doesn't exist - would mean that, you wouldn't be breathing. He could say you must be wrong about that - because I'm arguing that air doesn't exist, and I am breathing. In reality, continuing to breathe disproves his theory, because he cannot account for his breathing. If he were right that air doesn't exist, it would be impossible to breathe. [9]

Obviously, the atheist suppresses the truth in unrighteousness, so the job of the believer is to hold over him the reality that he cannot account for the laws of logic, ethics, and the pursuit of truth. When you ask the atheist, "Where does logic come from?" He will not have an ultimate answer. The laws of logic are not physical or material; they do not consist of atoms and molecules. The atheist is attempting to demonstrate that only physical substances exist in the universe, so when he uses nonphysical, universal logic, he is refuting his own position.

God is the Transcendental Necessity

The sovereign ruling God of scripture, speaking the universe into existence, sustaining and providentially controlling all things in the universe, is the only presupposition that can justify induction and the uniformity of the physical world. Therefore God is the precondition for science and the investigation of the natural world. The true and living God must subsist to account for the intricate, distinct, and interconnection of the particulars in the united cosmos. That is the reason Anslem said, "I believe in order that I may understand." Van Til uses this illustration:

> We cannot prove the existence of the beams underneath the floor if by proof you mean that they must be ascertainable

[9]. Dr. Greg Bahnsen, *Covenant Media Tape* (Irvine, CA: Covenant Media).

> in a way that we can see the chairs and the tables of the room. But the very idea of the floor as a support for the tables and chairs requires the idea of beams underneath. But there would be no floor if no beams were underneath. Thus there is absolute certain proof for the existence of God... Even non-Christians presuppose its truth while they verbally reject it. They need to presuppose the truth of Christianity to account for their own accomplishments. [10]

No one can make sense of anything in the world without presupposing the existence of God. When one attempts to construct a worldview on anything but Christianity, one will find, under philosophical scrutiny, he cannot justify or account for anything in the cosmos. The person who denies the existence of God uses logic and reason to articulate his disbelief. Yet he cannot justify the use of the necessary, non-material, non-concrete, and universal laws of logic. God is inescapable. When anyone attempts to escape the truth that God exists, he falls in a trap he cannot get out of. This point is well made in Van Til's fantastic illustration of a man made of water, who is trying to climb out of the watery ocean by means of a ladder that is made of water. He cannot get out of the water for he has nothing to stand on. And without God, one cannot make sense of anything. The atheist has nothing to stand on, and nothing to grip or climb.

Encounter at Border's Books

The following is a conversation that Tony Rogers had with an atheist at Border's Bookstore:

> Tony: Do you believe in God?
>
> Atheist: No!
>
> Tony: Why not?
>
> Atheist: I just don't see how it is possible for one person or being to do that sort of thing (create the universe).

---

[10]. Cornelius Van Til, *The Defense of Faith* (Phillipsburg, NJ: P & R, 1955), p. 120.

Tony: Does it seem more credible to you that no person or being did it?

Atheist: Well, I would have to know how He did it before I could believe that sort of thing.

Tony: How then do you believe the world came into existence? Or do you believe it has just always been there?

Atheist: Well, I think there was an explosion or something.

Tony: What was it that exploded, and what brought about this turn of events, so that it exploded then and not before the actual explosion?

Atheist: Well, I'm not sure.

Tony: Do you think you are being consistent? Earlier you attempted to be very rigorous in seeking to rationally systematize reality and justify your beliefs, which would allow you to reject God. Now, when pressed for an explanation on your approach to the creation of the cosmos, you resort to an irrational approach: nobody knows, or can know.

Atheist: Now that you mention it, I do see a problem.

Tony: Your problem results from a sinful attempt to know something independently of God and His revelation. God exists, and He knows the answer to these cosmological problems. You don't. We are not left with skepticism because God has revealed Himself.

A person, who embraces any worldview except for Christianity, cannot account for anything in the cosmos. The skeptic who declares: "We can't know anything," ask him whether, "He knows that?" His statement is self-disputing. All propositions and opinions that do not stand on the Christian worldview are self-defeating.

Opportunity at Cedar City

The conversation that follows was with a woman who claimed that she was a hardened atheist. I will let the dialogue speak for itself:

Mike: Hello, do you have some time to chat?

Linda: I just spoke with your friend and it would be a waste of time. I'm an atheist!

Mike: I don't think it would be a waste of time. I believe God would want me to tell you some things.

Linda: (She then went on and asked a range of questions on subjects from evolution to the Mormon church).

Mike: The Bible tells us that we all have broken God's law and have sinned. Everyone is a sinner. This is easily empirically verified by reading the newspapers, or in our daily observation of people on the freeway. The morning headlines place before us the evil actions of mankind everyday. We all have sinned and that includes you and I. However, heaven is a perfect place, and God is holy, righteous, and perfect. Nothing imperfect will enter heaven, so how can an imperfect man or woman get to heaven?

Linda: I don't know.

Mike: This illustration may help: A young lady went speeding and a police officer pulled her over and issued her a ticket. Her father was the judge in that town. On the day she appeared in his court, he heard her case and pronounced her guilty. His judgment decreed that she must pay a hundred dollar fine. She didn't have enough money. She was convicted, and she had no means to pay the penalty. After he banged his gavel, the judge took off his robe and paid the fine himself. He was just and merciful. And that is what God did for us. Jesus, the judge of the universe, came down from heaven, took off His

> heavenly robes, and paid the fine for guilty sinners on the cross. When you come to Christ in faith, you repent and trust in His death and resurrection, He then washes away all your sins, failings, and mistakes. He then imputes His perfect, righteous record into your account. You can now go to heaven based on who Jesus is and what He did for you.
>
> (She then started crying and weeping very hard. I encouraged her and shared with her the love of God, and that He came not to condemn sinners, but to forgive them. As she was sobbing, almost uncontrollably, she professed faith in Jesus and prayed through tears to trust Him and follow Him.)
>
> Mike: No one has done more for you or cared more about you, than the Lord Jesus. He has your heart, and He owns your soul. Trust Him, live for him, join a good biblical church, and keep praying. Here is a copy of the Gospel of John for you to read. Read your Bible everyday for strength and growth. Let me have your phone number and address and I will give it to a local church, and they will invite you to a Sunday service.

We have the profound blessing to tell others about our wonderful Savior. We do this not just to win an argument, though we must cast down all vain assertions, but we proclaim Christ to win souls. Herman Dooyeweerd said we need to have a "dialogue that seeks to convince rather than repel." We marshal all our scripture and arguments to compel the sinner to come to Jesus. The world cannot escape its metaphysical dependence on God. And we should try to open their eyes to that truth with gentleness and patience.

> Only the transcendent revelation of God can provide the necessary preconditions for logic, science, morality, etc., in which case those who oppose the faith are reduced to utter foolishness and intellectually have nowhere to stand in objecting to Christian truth claims. [11]

---

[11]. Ibid., Greg Bahnsen, *Van Til's Apologetic*, p. 676.

A Free Falling Atheist

The next conversation inscripted below is one that I had with an aggressive atheist. The outline of this conversation can be utilized in witnessing to many types of skeptics. The main thing you must keep in mind is to stick to the point that you are making. Do not let the atheist change the subject. Stick to one point. Follow it all the way through, until the atheist receives Christ or leaves.

Mike: Hello, can I ask you a question?

Atheist: I'm busy, but go ahead.

Mike: Are you a Christian?

Atheist: No way, I do not believe in God or in other fairy tales.

Mike: What do you believe in?

Atheist: I believe in evolution! I believe in science and in reason.

Mike: Why?

Atheist: Because it is true.

Mike: How do you know that?

Atheist: Well, I have seen pictures of fossils and geological columns that prove evolution is true.

Mike: Do you believe it is logical to believe in evolution?

Atheist: Of course. Only Neanderthals don't.

Mike: You said evolution is logical, where does logic come from?

Atheist: What do you mean?

Mike: You state that you believe in evolution, and you must also believe that only the physical reality exists. My question to you is, if only the physical reality exists, where do the nonphysical, abstract, universal laws of logic come from? Can you buy them off the rack at Sears or pick them off the field down the street?

Atheist: Uh, no.

Mike: There's your problem. Atheism cannot supply the foundation for logic. Every time you use logic, even when you attempt to prove that God doesn't exist, you are actually presupposing that God exists. Without God, you cannot prove anything or understand anything because you use logic in those pursuits. The precondition for logic is God.

Atheist: Well, I don't believe in God and I use logic all the time.

Mike: That's my point, all men everywhere are dependent on God in their use of logic and reason. You, as an atheist, cannot justify your use of nonphysical logic.

Atheist: That's fine, but…

Mike: Let me ask you another question. Do you believe that it is wrong to murder little children, and that it is wrong to burn down all the Amazon rain forests?

Atheist: Of course, it's wrong.

Mike: Why?

Atheist: It's wrong and you know it is.

Mike: Yes I do, but why is it wrong according to your worldview of evolution and the survival of the fittest? If a child is brutally murdered in your worldview; the little kid is just a non-survivor, just some physical matter that became unanimated. To affirm moral laws one must presuppose the God of the Bible. God must be, or there can be no foundation for moral laws that are binding to everyone. Do you have a foundation for saying that something is right or wrong?

Atheist: I guess not.

Mike: Do you want to repent and turn to Christ?

Atheist: No, not today. You gave me many things to research.

Mike: Maybe we can get together later. Here take this tract and an invitation to the church I attend.

Atheist: Thanks.

A Fictional Confrontation

One night when my soul was craving a little brain candy, I turned on the tube and I had the unfortunate opportunity to watch the politically correct television show *Politically Incorrect* with Bill Mahr. He had a guest who declared that Christianity was repressive. The guest also stated that slavery was evil and repressive, and Christianity was responsible for the “horror of slavery.” The following is a short conversation I would like to have had with him based on the point of view that he expressed on the T.V. show:

Recriminator: Christianity is repressive. The testimony of history demonstrates that everywhere Christianity goes it coerces and forces cultures to abandon their view of the world and replace it with Christianity’s. And in that cultural conversion process, often they persecuted and committed genocide to bring about their goals of cultural reformation.

Mike: In my scanning of history I do not see it this way. I would like to ask you a question. If one walks into McDonald’s and claims to be a hamburger, does his proclamation put him on the McDonald's menu? Does it make him a hamburger simply because he says he is?

Recriminator: No, that's silly. What's your point?

Mike: If some evil people perpetrated crimes on humanity and claimed to be Christians, by definition they were not Christians. A Christian is a person regenerated by God, and he follows Jesus. He must be lawful, loving, and truthful. If one claims to be a follower of Jesus and doesn't follow him, his claim is vain.

Recriminator: Well, we know that many thousands of Christians practiced slavery. They abused, imprisoned, and tortured these African slaves.

Mike: Is it evil to do that?

Recriminator: Yes, it's wicked.

Mike: On what standard do you pronounce that repression and torture are wicked?

Recriminator: It is inhumane.

Mike: By what standard is it inhumane?

Recriminator: Everyone knows it's wrong to repress and torture.

Mike: How do you know that? A review of history, and the reading of the daily newspaper seem to contradict that statement. By what standard do you identify anything as evil?

Recriminator: Most of humanity believes that it's evil.

Mike: How do you know that? And what if, like in Hitler's Germany, the people elect to participate in mass atrocities? By your standard of the people's will, you cannot say they were evil.

Recriminator: There can never be an objective, unchanging standard.

Mike: If that is what you believe, you can never proclaim anything is morally wrong, unless it's the people's will. The people's mood changes, and without an objective standard, all manner of evil and wickedness can flourish.

Recriminator: Well, you have exposed the weakness in my standard. But nobody else has one. It's like all things are relative. If you are so intelligent, what's your standard? How can it not evolve or change over time? How can it stop from being molded to the people's will?

Mike: My standard is God's word, the Bible. God's holy law is unchanging, perfect, and objectively true. It is an immutable standard. Nine men in black robes do not decide what is right or wrong. The people, whether Nazi's or Turks, do not decide what is morally good or evil. God's law is the standard. It doesn't change inasmuch as it reflects God's unchanging nature. Is it wrong to murder? God's word says, "Yes." Is it wrong to rape and abuse? "Yes," says God's infallible word. I have an objective, unchanging, perfect rule. Mankind can know what is good, honorable, and virtuous. This standard doesn't rely on the feelings and changing beliefs of the people. God's word transcends our world and our culture because it comes from a transcendent God, who does not change. With our God and His word, one has an absolute standard. Laws can change. Atrocities could be legalized and adopted by the nations. There must be an objective, unchanging standard. There is. It is the Bible.

The person, who asserts a system of ethics without the God of the Bible and His law, has no foundation or justification for morals. Without God, murdering someone would just be the displacement of the atoms of the murder victim to another form. The victim is just a non-survivor. There is nothing wrong with adding water to dirt and making mud, or raking leaves and tossing them into a fire. The atoms of the dirt and the leaves just take on different forms. The body of the murder victim, if only made up of physical atoms, would just be changed into another form. Dirt, leaves, and a human body are, under the materialist worldview, all the same. God is the precondition for right and wrong, for justice and injustice. The famous atheist and libertine, Russell, in his unconvincing book *Why I'm Not A Christian*, mused: "The world I should wish to see would be one freed from the virulence of group hostilities and capable of realizing happiness for all." The question I would ask the former atheist (he died in 1972 - death makes one an instant theist) is: "Why? Why should the world pursue that?" The atheist has no justification for asserting or affirming any morals, any "oughts." The believer should witness to them by just asking, "Why?" At some point, the non-theist will have to shut down due to the fact that they have no ultimate answers for anything, including ethical imperatives. Our job is to expose this problem, and demonstrate that only the Christian worldview can justify morality.

Personal Identity Presupposes God

> Then God said, "Let Us make man in Our image, according to Our likeness" (Genesis 1:26).

> If the world were not as scripture says it is, if the natural man's knowledge were not actually rooted in the creation and providence of God, then there would be no knowledge… The non-Christians have made and now make discoveries about the state of the universe simply because the universe is what Christ says it is. The unbelieving scientist borrows or steals the Christian principal of creation and providence every time he says that an "explanation" is possible, for he knows he cannot account for "explanation" on his own. [12]

The nonbeliever cannot account for the intelligibility of anything, even his own personal identity. When someone says I am "Ernie," and he means he is the same "Ernie," as the person that is in his high school yearbook named "Ernie," he is borrowing from the Christian worldview. Only Christianity can give us a reason to be certain we are who we are. Our physical body changes every moment and everyday. Human beings

[12]. Ibid., Bahnsen, p. 696.

lose one-sixtieth of an ounce of respiratory moisture and sweat every minute. There is a net loss every second. This means humans physically change every moment, hence under a physical-only worldview, I am not the same person I was a second ago. The skin replaces itself once a month. The stomach lining is replaced every five days. The cells in the liver are replaced every six weeks, and the skeleton about every three months. The body of every human being constantly changes. The cells of a human body are in a constant state of flux, and are always being modified. In one year, the average person has ninety-eight percent of his atoms exchanged for new ones. In seven years time, every atom in a person's body has been replaced by new ones. Thus the person is a new and completely different being, within the worldview of the materialist atheist (faster if you visit the dentist frequently).

The atheist affirms that only the physical world exists. He claims that nothing spiritual or nonmaterial exists. This means that after seven years, everyone is a different person. So the atheist cannot account for personal identity. By his standard of a physical-only world, everyone is a different person after seven years because every physical atom has been swapped for new ones. Would a car, over the course of twenty years, which had every mechanical part replaced with new ones, be the same car? No. The car does not have a soul. If we consist of only physical matter, and are devoid of a soul like the car, under the atheist physical-only view, after our bodily atoms were completely exchanged for new ones, we would be different people. The atheist, under his worldview, is not married to the woman he married nine years ago. They are totally different physically, due to the complete exchange of bodily atoms after seven years. If he has a child over the age of seven, by the atheist's standard, the kid is not the same child that was born to them. Therefore, if he wanted to be consistent in his worldview, he should throw away all his baby pictures and their wedding album. Every molecule in his body has changed. And under a material-only world, he is a different person. He will not do that because he is basing much of his life on the Christian worldview. The atheist husband still hugs his wife without being unfaithful to her, since Christianity is true. He will still take his kid to the park and buy him a balloon. But he will not buy the unknown kid who is next to him a balloon. The atheist knows that his child is the same child who was born to him years before. He lives much of his life on the Christian worldview.

A Boat and a Bob

A man named Bob builds a fishing boat and names it Dolly Mae. A couple years afterward, he replaces all the wood because the color is fading. He throws the wood in a pile on his side yard. Later, Bob replaces all the nails and metal binders with new ones. He tosses them in the side yard with the wood. His friend sees the wood and the nails, and asks Bob whether he can have them to build a canoe. Bob lets him have them, and he builds a canoe with all the wood, nails, and metal from the boat. Which vessel should be named Dolly Mae? This paradox exposes the problem that atheists have with human identity. The first boat has none of its original parts, the canoe has them all, but with a different shape. Hence neither vehicle is the original. They both have changed. The first has changed in its physical parts, and the second in shape and design. In a physical-only view of life, humans that lose body parts to disease or accidents are not the same people they were before the loss of their physical parts.

The Christian professes that man is made in God's image. We all have what scholars have called *sensus deitatis*, a sense of God or deity. We know who we are by looking at God and His revelation. God's word announces who we are, our unchanging personal identity. Humans have a personal identity that transcends the physical world. Christians can hold their ten year-old child's hand and hug their grandparents, and remain consistent within their own worldview. When the unregenerate performs these types of caring actions towards his loved ones, he is being inconsistent with his presuppositions.

The atheist knows that men have souls, although they deny this obvious truth, they live as if it is true. If personal identity did not have a nonphysical aspect, anyone who had lost a couple limbs in an accident, had their skin burned off in a fire, or lost a couple organs, would not be the same person. Their identity would change in a materialist's worldview. Suppose a man lost all his skin due to a chemical accident. That same man had to replace his kidneys due to a reaction with his medication. He got so depressed, he drank in excess, and had to receive a new liver. One day, he is so despondent that he hurls himself over his third story window and loses all his limbs. New technology puts new working limbs on him, to go with all his new organs and his new skin.

With almost all his physical body exchanged, is he still his mother's son? Is he still his wife's husband? Is he still the father of his little girl? Is he still the same man? The answer is yes to all those questions. Yes because he has a spirit, and he is a soul. He is made up of more than his physical body. He is a human being created in the image of God. This is another reason that the anti-theist cannot live consistently within his worldview. He has to borrow from the Christian worldview because Christianity is true, and is the basis of all truth. Unless God is presupposed, there is no objective unchanging reason to value all men and women. On the atheist worldview, a human is just a bi-pedal blob of water and protein. There is no moral reason for the world to esteem a human being as anything more important than a bumble bee. Nevertheless, we see atheists affirming the dignity and value of man. When they do this they are living outside their worldview. For the non-theist there is nothing in the world, including the world itself that can be justified. There is no accounting for value, truth, or science without the God revealed in scripture. God has spoken. He has revealed Himself. This is the reason we value humanity, and we can make sense out of this world. Christianity must be true because it alone makes the world intelligible, and knowledge possible. We are called to challenge our culture with the truth. There can be no truce. Our duty is to confront our world as merciful conquerors, and lift our swords to proclaim the law and love of God to everyone.

Do the Crime and Do the Time?

Rejecting the notion of man having a spirit has applications for our penal system as well. According to the atheist's worldview, the only thing that exists is the material world. If this is true, the state after seven years, should let all the murderers out of prison. Remember, under an atheist worldview they have had all their atoms exchanged for new ones. Therefore they are now different people according to the belief of atheism: They are totally different people, physically, so he is not kissing the woman he married. He should not buy his nine-year old son an ice cream over the kid next to him at the counter. To live consistently, within a physical-only philosophy, is ridiculous and confusing. We sip champagne on our tenth anniversary with our spouses, and we buy birthday presents for our twelve year-old daughter because the Christian worldview is true. It is impossible for it not to be.

> In Christ are hidden all the treasures of wisdom and knowledge (Colossians 2:3).

In a consistent atheist world, one cannot ever say, "I believe there is no God." You cannot say, "I," because in consistent atheism, there is no "I." As an atheist you cannot even make an assertion. Only a Christian can account for self-identity and justify personal assertions. It is not just that Christianity makes better sense in describing human experience, but Christianity is the precondition to make sense out of any item in the world. Without it, one cannot account for one's personhood or the universe one lives in. One has no ultimate authority to assert that he understands anything in the entire cosmos. We are not to employ slick arguments to verify that God lives. But God is the ultimate reference point, and He is the judge of all things. His word is foundational, necessary, and self-authenticating. What God says was, or is, or will be. We do not have to scramble around trying to prove God with ingenious arguments that can dazzle men. God is the foundation for all meaning, purpose, morals, and rationality. God alone is the one who makes any rational argument possible and reasonable. He is the source of all truth, order, logic, mathematics, goodness, beauty, and philosophy. The problem with the lost is not the lack of a good convincing argument or the lack of evidence: The problem is a wicked heart. We are not to attempt to authenticate or verify God. We should proclaim that He lives and without Him, you cannot know anything at all. There is absolute and certain proof that God lives. Bahnsen put it so well when he stated:

> The Christian offers the self-attesting Christ to the world as the only foundation upon which a man must stand to give any "reasons" for anything at all. The whole notion of "giving reasons" is completely destroyed by any ontology other than the Christian one. The Christian claims that only after accepting the biblical scheme of things will any man be able to understand and account for his own rationality. [13]

I Do not Exist!

There are those who claim that they, themselves, do not exist. This is impossible because in stating that "I" do not exist, I must employ the word "I," and presuppose this "I." A man's personal identity is a necessary

[13]. Ibid., Bahnsen, p. 696-697.

precondition to assert that "he" does not exist. Just as logic is a necessary precondition, but it is not sufficient to explain the world, personal identity is necessary, yet not sufficient. Thus personal being is undeniable. To deny your existence, presupposes your existence. The problem for the unbeliever is he cannot account for personal identity. The same line of argument can be applied to the person who claims that others do not exist. When they proclaim, "You do not exist!" You ask them, "Who does not exist?" They must say, "You" or just shut up. Thus they refute themselves. If they reject Christ, then with the closing of their mouth you have done your apologetic duty.

There is but One God

> And God said to Moses, "I AM WHO I AM." And He said, "Thus you shall say to the children of Israel, 'I AM has sent me to you'" (Exodus 3:14).

An atheist, who asserts that the physical world alone exists, devoid of all spiritual and abstract entities, cannot justify his use of nonphysical logic in his reasoning. Logic is abstract and not physical. It is transcendent, universal, and nonmaterial. Only the Christian worldview can supply the necessary preconditions for the nonmaterial, unchanging, and universal laws of logic. The laws of logic cannot be found in a box or a closet. You cannot purchase a set of the laws of logic on sale at a store. They are not concrete and physical. Only the transcendent, unchanging, universal, and nonphysical God can provide the necessary preconditions for transcendent, universal, unchanging, and nonphysical logic. This demonstrates that it is impossible for the atheistic scientist to be correct in declaring nothing exists except the physical world. Even that declaration is nonphysical, hence it is false. It is impossible for God not to exist.

We should learn how to declare God's word in fullness. We should demonstrate that the unbeliever's worldview collapses under its own weight, and the atheist cannot justify or account for the rational world. I reiterate this throughout the book, until you can anticipate my words because humanity has a strong propensity for self-deception. The unbeliever will deny all the evidence for theism, as he deceives himself, so that he may sleep better at night. Our duty is to wake them up out of their self-deception. The Gallup poll of February, 2002 (six months after Muslims blew up the World Trade Center and murdered 3000 people) was a survey of the Muslim world. Most of the Muslims polled, the great majority, believed that the act of the planes crashing into the Towers was morally justified. Most of the Muslim countries did not believe that Muslim Arabs flew the planes into the buildings. The massive Muslim denial toward the truth of the wickedness of these crimes, and their continued deception in believing that Muslims did not participate in these atrocities, illustrates the human trait of self-deception. Humans willingly and tenaciously desire to hold onto what they know is false, just to make themselves feel better. Very few people want to examine difficult truths about themselves and their false god. Our job is to declare the person of God, as we demonstrate that without God, the unbeliever cannot make sense out of any thought, word, and deed in the heavens and the earth.

Gods Made in the Image of Man

The false gods in other religions cannot help anyone. They do not exist for they are made in the image of man. The only God who is not contingent is the true and living God of the Bible. The Mormon gods, the Hindu gods, the Islamic god, and the Sikh god do not have necessary existence. There are worlds one could think of where these gods would not exist. They are not necessary in all possible worlds. They are not logically and ontologically necessary beings. Only the triune God of scripture is the precondition for the intelligibility of this world, and any world one could imagine. He is necessary. He is not contingent. The entire cosmos is dependent upon God. Yahweh is necessary; it would be impossible for the Lord God not to exist. The Almighty is all sufficient, all knowing, and all powerful in His sovereignty. God is not dependent on anything, in any world. The world is completely dependent on Him. All existence, all opinions, and all debate, presuppose the Lord God who spoke from the burning bush and declared to Moses and future generations: "I AM THAT I AM."

CHAPTER FOUR

AGNOSTICISM: IGNORANCE ISN'T BLISS

You're worried about being lost, Palmer. You're worried about not being central, not the reason the universe was created. There's plenty of order in the universe. Gravitation, electromagnetism, quantum mechanics... they all involve laws. [1]

Dare to know (Kant).

Who can possibly do justice to the intellectual brilliance displayed by philosophers and heretics in defending their errors and incorrect opinions? (Augustine).

The knowledge of God is inherent in man. It is there by virtue of his creation in the image of God. [2]

Agnosticism is completely self-contradictory. And it is self-contradictory not only upon the assumption of the truth of theism, but it is self-contradictory upon its

[1]. Carl Sagan, *Contact* (NY: Simon & Schuster, 1985), p. 251.

[2]. Cornelius Van Til, *The Defense of Faith* (Phillipsburg, NJ: P & R, 1955), p. 152.

> own assumptions. Agnosticism wants to hold that it is reasonable to refrain from thorough epistemological speculations because they cannot lead to anything. But, to assume this attitude, Agnosticism has itself made the most tremendous intellectual assertion that could be made about ultimate things. In the second place, agnosticism is epistemologically self-contradictory on its own assumptions because its claim to make no assertion about ultimate reality rests upon a most comprehensive assertion about ultimate reality. [3]

There are a few denominations of agnostics. Some proclaim: "Nobody can know anything about God." Of course that is wrong because they know that about God. The agnostic that proposes we cannot know anything about God, says something very important about God. He is unknowable. This is an exception to their own arbitrary claim. Not only do they have no philosophical or logical basis to make such a claim, the claim self-destructs and implodes from within. The agnostic, though attempting to confess ignorance of theology, has a rather elaborate theology. His assertion that we can know nothing about God is to build a vast theological system. This system asserts that we can't know that God is omnipotent, omnipresent, loving, just, and sovereign. Agnostics must also know that God has not revealed Himself to humanity. This implies God is either too weak in power or too indifferent in His care for His creatures. This is to claim a lot about God. As you can see the agnostic has quite a theological system.

Open but Unconvinced

Another type of agnostic is the one who admits he doesn't know whether God exists, but others might. The word agnostic is not a label that I would desire to be named. The word comes from the Greek word that means: ignorant, without knowledge. In one sense I can see this term is fitting. Anyone, who tries to hoodwink others into believing their claim that they do not know whether God exists, is pretty ignorant and self-deceived. The Bible clearly teaches that they do know that God is, and they actively suppress that knowledge. This will be evident as you read some of the conversations I submit later.

---

3. Greg Bahnsen, *Van Til's Apologetic* (Phillipsburg, NJ: P & R, 1998), p. 479-480.

Self-Deception

The agnostic is self-deceived. He knows that God exists, but he doesn't like Him. Hell, judgment, and all that noxious stuff is not for him. He lives on wishful thinking. He deceives himself by suppressing the truth in unrighteousness. He is like the real-life guy, in the summer of 2001, who used what Coast Guard, Cmdr. Dee Norton described as "poor judgment." This deceived man strapped on homemade "water-walking shoes" and decided to walk on the Pacific Ocean from California to Hawaii, a distance of more than two thousand miles. The amazing thing was, he got about ten miles before his shoes started taking in too much water. He radioed for help and was rescued. This man should be enshrined in the Self-Deceived Hall of Fame. He actually believed he could cross the high seas by walking across the Pacific Ocean with extra large "shoes." This seems absolutely crazy. However, the unbeliever has more reasons to trust God than a man has for realizing he could not step-walk across the deep blue sea.

As we go about proclaiming the gospel, we should remind ourselves of the great disposition of the unregenerate man to deceive himself. Man's propensity to fall for and embrace self-deception found its height following the wicked acts committed on September 11, 2001. The great majority of Muslims, in over twenty countries, did not believe that other Muslims flew the planes into the Twin Towers and the Pentagon. They said they did not see any "smoking gun" and that it was all a "Jewish plot." Months later, the "smoking gun" of the Bin Laden tapes were released. These showed him bragging about his murderous acts on 9-11. However, the great majority of the Muslims polled believed the wicked acts were not committed by Muslims. The self-deception goes even farther when the same *USA Today's* opinion poll revealed that most of the Islamic world did not believe that the terrorism committed against America on September eleventh was "morally wrong." This duplicity should send shivers down the backs of world leaders. Yes, the Islamic world is the Michael Jordan of self-deception, but all unregenerate men have a similar capacity and desire to deceive themselves. Often, you just do not want to believe the bad news even if the bad news is there. This is the reason so many can live under the nurture, the warmth, and the glow of God's benevolent common grace and assert that He does not exist. The Christian does not have to live under the dark umbrella of self-deception. He has certainty. Unless

Christianity is presupposed, there is no proof for anything. Christianity is the very foundation for proof, and the discovery of truth.

When you confront the non-theist with the truth, frequently, they will behave like the "little boy who is mad at his parents for punishing him, and hides under his blanket, and declares that his mom and dad do not exist." Reality is his parents exist whether he likes it or not. He can attempt to deceive and lie to himself, in a futile ploy to make himself feel better. As Dr. Greg Bahnsen has illustrated, the unbeliever is doing the same thing. He is mad at God for being God. He is angry about the coming judgment of his personal sins. So he hides under his blanket of unbelief, hoping that God isn't there. Others hope that God will just go away. So every day, the unbeliever has to try really hard to convince himself that the triune God does not exist. Nonetheless, if one is hiding, or rebelling in the open, God still dwells in majesty.

An Encounter at UNLV

Mike: Hello, do you have a moment to take a survey?

Phil: No. I'm late for class.

Mike: Can I walk you to your car?

Phil: Fine.

Mike: Are you an agnostic or a theist?

Phil: I'm an atheist.

Mike: So you don't believe in God?

Phil: Well, not really. Uh, I, well, I actually do believe in God.

Mike: Were you raised Christian, Muslim, or Roman Catholic?

Phil: I was raised by two of those you listed. I was born and raised in Africa. My father is a Muslim and my mother a Catholic. I went to Catholic schools because those were the only schools in my area. I do not believe in any of those religions. I have investigated religions and found all of them lacking.

Mike: I'm sure you know the main difference between Christianity and Islam is the person of Christ. Christianity asserts that Jesus is God's Son and Islam denies this.

Phil: Yes.

Mike: Have you heard of the evidence for the resurrection of Christ?

Phil: Yes, but, hum, we had missionaries from Europe teach us in school.

Mike: You then realize that the resurrection was first proclaimed in Jerusalem, the very town of Christ's death and burial. That there were Roman guards securing the grave of Christ. After three days the tomb was empty, and the followers of Jesus announced that Jesus had risen from the dead. All the disciples, except Judas, died or were persecuted for believing and proclaiming that Christ rose on the third day. Extra-biblical writers of that generation recount the resurrection of Christ, including Josephus. Muhammad stayed dead. Jesus rose. Can you see the contrast?

Phil: Um.

Mike: Let me give you the argument from the impossibility of the contrary. The God of the Bible is the foundation and the precondition for all reason, logic, and morality. Without the God of the Bible you cannot account for rationality, logic, or ethics. Everyone that is going to school here is using reason and logic in their studies. Yet, if they say that God doesn't exist, they cannot account for reason and logic. They cannot tell us where the logic they use for studying came from, or the reasoning they use in trying to assert that God doesn't exist. For them to make a logical assertion, they have to stand on Christian assumptions. Reason and logic are laws, and they are not physical or material. You can't go down the street and buy them on sale. The laws of logic are abstract, transcendent, universal and nonphysical. The laws of logic are always true. "A" can't be "A" and "non-A" at the same time in the same way, always. If the Christian worldview is not true, then logic is impossible. Only Christianity supplies the foundation necessary for logic, science, and mathematics. No non-Christian system of thought can furnish a foundation for the law of non-contradiction, thus those false systems of thought are self-contradictory. The true and living Creator is the precondition for all knowledge, proof, math, evidence, and logic. The nonphysical, transcendent, and immutable God supplies the necessary preconditions for the use of nonphysical, transcendent, universal, and immutable laws of reason. Thus the contrary of Christianity is impossible because all other worldviews fall into absurdity since they are self-refuting.

Phil: OK.

Mike: The laws of logic come from God. Since we use logic, we affirm God, even when we are attempting to deny Him. Logic presupposes the God of the Bible. God's nature is the only way to account for the laws of logic. Now, there is another matter to ponder: you have made mistakes and I have made mistakes. We have all sinned and have broken God's law.

Phil: Yes.

Mike: What religion has an answer to the sin problem? You have admitted that you have sinned, so have I. The problem for us is: God is Holy and perfect; Heaven is perfect and we aren't. How does one who is not perfect get into a perfect heaven?

Phil: Um.

Mike: In all the world's religions, the only answer for the remission of sins is Christ's atoning work on the cross.

Phil: Um.

Mike: Christ died on the cross to remove the believer's sins so that we could make it to heaven by grace alone. Do you follow me?

Phil: Yes, I follow you. Jesus died to be merciful, and to take care of God's justice.

(At this point we made it to his truck. The providence of God was clearly displayed because he discovered that he had lost his keys. This gave me an opportunity to walk him back and expound more on the person and work of Christ. It was a long walk in both directions. I first asked him whether he needed any assistance to find his keys. I gave him some gospel tracts and a church invitation. Then I started where I had left off.)

Mike: So, the infinite justice of God…

Phil: Um.

Mike: If God is just, how can He be merciful?

Phil: Um.

Mike: In other words, you wouldn't want an earthly judge in our world to be merciful with the exclusion of justice. Suppose a judge had in his court: rapists, murderers, and thieves, you wouldn't want that judge to say, "I'm going to be merciful today, you guys are all forgiven. Just go." You would be outraged. Muslims, Jewish people, and other people would say that men make it to heaven because God forgives them. If you ask them, on what basis does God forgive them, they would say, He is merciful. But if He is merciful without justice, then He is not really good, honorable, and just. If a civil judge freed a courtroom full of rapists and murderers because he said he wanted to be merciful, society would be outraged. They would say he is unjust, evil, and morally corrupt. If one says God forgives everyone based solely on His mercy, one has a God who is evil, unrighteous, and unjust.

Phil: OK.

Mike: Only Christianity solves the dilemma of applying justice and mercy on the sinner. God has been merciful to us by sending His Son to die for us on the cross, satisfying God's justice. He paid the price for the believer's sins. The penalty was paid on the cross. God acted in mercy, and carried out perfect justice. Non-Christian religions have a god who gives mercy, but doesn't execute justice. And God is infinitely more just than any judge in the entire world. So the dilemma is, how does a world religion solve the problem of the tension between mercy and justice? A god who says, "I forgive you on an account of nothing," is not a good, holy or just god. The God of the Bible is holy, just, good, and merciful, Him alone.

Phil: Um.

Mike: A god, like Allah, who forgives without executing justice is a capricious and arbitrary god.

Phil: You can't know what God will do.

Mike: I'm saying, if that is your god, he's capricious and arbitrary. You can say he does that, but that is your god. That can be your proposition, you can say that, but then, the nature of the god you are proclaiming is a god who is arbitrary and capricious. Only the biblical God is merciful and not arbitrary. He sent His Son, an eternal perfect being, to pay an eternal price. And all the sins of those who come to Him are forgiven. Do you follow me?

Phil: Yes, I follow you.

Mike: There is no other world religion that has answers to those problems, only Christianity supplies the answers.

Christ offers justification. When you put your faith in Him alone, God declares you forensically righteous. Your sins are removed and God imputes the righteousness of Christ.

Phil: What is the main thing you are trying to tell me?

Mike: God is sovereignly in control of the whole world, and for some reason, He set up this time for you and me to talk for a moment. He even arranged for you to lose your keys, so you would come to understand that you are a sinner. We have all sinned against God's law, and I'm here to say that Christ is the only solution to the problem of God being merciful and just to sinners. If you turn and trust Him, He will forgive you.

Phil: He will forgive me?

Mike: Yes, because of what He did on the cross.

Phil: So you are telling me, that God is merciful.

Mike: Yes. You see He is merciful and just. He met the requirements of justice and mercy at the cross. Only the Christian God has done that. He alone is the true and living God. He is calling you to turn from sin and believe in Jesus Christ. It's been good talking with you.

Phil: Yes, it has.

Mike: Let's get together again some time.

Phil: OK. Take care.

Mike: You too.

Man's Purpose

Therefore, whether you eat or drink, or whatever you do, do all to the glory of God (1 Corinthians 10:31).

The person of God gives man purpose. Hope, faith, and meaning come from God and His revealed will. The Westminster Catechism sums up the Bible and instructs us that our purpose is to "glorify God and enjoy Him forever." The man who refuses to believe in God cannot find any ultimate purpose or meaning. In the agnostic worldview, everything is heading for oblivion since there is no personal God. The second law of thermodynamics guarantees that the whole universe is heading for a cosmic heat death. The universe is running down like a clock. And the sun, the stars, and the galaxies will be extinguished, in a death by distilled energy. In the distant future, there will be a total burnout of the entire universe. All the schemes, fancies, and accomplishments of mankind will be like "cosmic snowmen," who melt at the coming of the summer, melting into nothingness. The moon, the planets, the quasars, and all the solar systems will be snuffed out, and with them will go all the accomplishments and intents of mankind. The law of entropy guarantees, without God and His clear purpose, everything will evaporate into unusable energy. All existence will be as though it had never been and will bear the final seal of nothingness, as it fades into the lowest level of heat energy. All industry, education, art, and civilization will be as if it had never been. The eternal mark of meaninglessness will be infused across the vacuous plain of the former cosmos. All the hopes, dreams, and loves of the world will fizzle into the oblivion of raw energy as if they had never taken place. This is the ultimate hope of the atheistic materialist. A universe, without a purpose, meandering toward a terminal dark-out.

The Purposeless Purpose of Eastern Religions

Mankind is unique and has a God given purpose. Rocks will never learn Algebra; cucumbers will never strive to play Mozart. The human soul is always searching. Mankind knows there must be something more out there or up there. Something transcendent must exist, or we would never ask questions about purpose. Is this all there is? Many rich, powerful, and famous people live lives that do not satisfy their restless hearts. Many of them become so despondent that they commit suicide to try to relieve their pain. All their toys, all their wealth, and all their write-ups leave them without real purpose if they deny God.

The good news: God has a plan and a purpose. The eastern religions, such as Buddhism and Hinduism, do not have temporal or eternal good news. The ultimate goal of Buddhism is to escape into Nirvana and lose yourself. Your purpose is to become nothing. You become nothing, and you know nothing. Pondering and believing that can only bring despair, and weaken one's moral fortitude. Hinduism teaches man's goal is to break the karmaic cycle and become one small drop of water that falls into the great ocean of god. Hinduism's central doctrine of reincarnation cannot supply hope. Its goal is for everyone to dissolve into oneness. This world is an illusion, realize this, so you do not have to come back to the earth as another person or a cockroach. Experience eternal release, and just fall into the ocean of being, as you lose your personality and meaning. You lose your personhood, your family, and your soul. The ultimate purpose of eastern religions is, ultimately, that you have no purpose. Thinking on this can only envelop you with hopelessness and dolefulness. Scripture declares that God, the true and living God, has a marvelous purpose for all His beloved. Our ultimate purpose is to be in Christ, as the person He created. Our eternal goal is to honor, worship, and delight in God our Savior forever and ever. The universe may end in a cosmic heat death, but the one who created it, has built a place for all His people, a heavenly home that will never perish or burn out. An eternal home with God is a grand purpose, and a great destination of complete satisfaction.

A Real Atheist?

The Bible makes it clear that there are no real agnostics or atheists. All men know that God exists, and they are attempting to suppress this truth in unrighteousness. Philosophically there cannot be atheists. For one to propose that God does not exits, anywhere at any time, one would have to know all things, and be omnipresent, eternal, and infinite. That would make you God. So, the only person in the universe who could possibly not believe in God, everywhere, and always, would be God. One would have to be God to be a true atheist and that is theoretically, logically, and rationally absurd.

A Dialogue with an Agnostic

Mike: Are you a Christian?

Agnostic: No, I do not know whether God exists and neither do you!

Mike: How do you know that?

Agnostic: Uh, well, I don't care.

Mike: Do you use logic and reason in your life?

Agnostic: Yes, everybody does.

Mike: Where does logic come from?

Agnostic: The brain.

Mike: How do you know that?

Agnostic: I don't know.

Mike: Only God can supply the necessary preconditions for logic. Deny God and you have to deny logic, which would be absurd.

Agnostic: Why does God have to exist for logic to be real?

Mike: Christianity is the only worldview that supplies human reason a base for proper function. No non-Christian system of thought can furnish a foundation for the law of non-contradiction, so those systems of thought can only offer a self-contradictory worldview. All non-Christian thought results in futility because of the internal contradictions that they supply. Thus the contrary of Christianity is impossible because every anti-Christian worldview falls into a moronic ditch. They are all internally self-contradictory. They lead to conclusions that contradict their own terms. Christianity alone supplies the preconditions to make reality intelligible. The biblical truth is: without God nothing can make sense. The true and living God is the precondition for the intelligibility of reality and the understanding of all human experiences.

Agnostic: I'm not sure I know what you are trying to say.

Mike: Unless you believe in the triune God and His revealed word, you cannot consistently and logically believe in anything else. God is the precondition for all argument, proof, evidence, and reason. It is impossible for God not to exist for He is the precondition for all intelligent thought. The nonphysical, universal, and unchanging God alone provides the necessary preconditions for the use of nonphysical, universal, invariant laws of logic. To argue at all, you must presuppose that God lives because you are using logic. All non-believing thought cannot supply the necessary preexisting foundations for the laws of logic; this results in futility because of the internal contradictions that they supply. Therefore the contrary of Christianity is impossible because all contrary worldviews fall into absurdity because they are self-contradictory. They lead to conclusions that contradict their own assertions.

Agnostic: This sounds interesting but I like my life and there may be other worldviews just as true.

Mike: Only the true God can supply all the absolutely necessary preconditions for all human experience. Christianity is the only worldview that supplies human reason a foundation. Non-Christian systems of thought cannot furnish a foundation for the law of non-contradiction, thus those systems of thought can only offer a self-contradictory worldview. God is the precondition for all argument, proof, evidence and reason. It is impossible for God not to exist. He is the precondition for all intelligent communication because all human communication requires the use of the laws of logic. The omnipresent, transcendent, nonphysical, and unchanging God alone provides the necessary underlying conditions for the use of nonphysical, universal, and unchanging laws of logic. To argue at all, you must assume that God lives. Non-believing thought cannot supply the necessary preconditions underpinning the laws of logic. This results in futility because of the internal contradictions that they supply. Without God nothing can make sense. The true and living God is the precondition for the intelligibility of reality and the understanding of all human experiences.

Agnostic: I don't buy it.

Mike: Whether you affirm God or not, He still lives. And He demands perfection in keeping His moral law and you have broken His law. You need a Savior. Christ died on the cross and rose again. I call you to turn and trust in Christ.

Agnostic: I do not want to. I got to go.

A Meeting with a Buddhist

Mike: Do you believe in Christ?

Student: (a Buddhist man born in Japan): Well, no, I'm a Buddhist.

Mike: Have you heard that Christ came to the earth from heaven, He died on a cross for our sins, and rose again on the third day?

Student: Why, sure.

Mike: Are you attracted to that?

Student: You know, sometimes some people in Japan avoid a certain number because of Christ.

Mike: I didn't know that. The Bible instructs us that all men have made mistakes and have sinned. We have all failed and have broken God's law. We have worshipped other gods, we have put things above God, we have used His name in vain, we have at times lied, stolen, and have had sexual relations outside marriage. We have not kept all God's commandments. We are not perfect. Heaven is perfect. Only Christ's death on the cross can remove our mistakes, and sins so we can go to a perfect heaven when we die.

Student: OK.

Mike: If one believes Buddha or Muhammad and tries to follow their teachings, these actions cannot remove their sins. Christ died on the cross for the remission of our sins. Do you understand what Jesus did?

Student: Well… I don't know.

Mike: Every person on this planet has sinned. Heaven is perfect, without Christ, how would an imperfect person enter heaven?

Student: Well…

Mike: Everybody on the planet has sinned. What answer do you have? I'm not perfect, you are not perfect, how do you get to heaven?

Student: I don't believe that believing in Christ is important. Even the Buddha is not perfect, you know.

Mike: But Christ was and He rose again from the dead.

Student: I don't know; I don't know, that Christ was perfect.

Mike: Have you ever heard of the predictions and prophecies of Christ?

Student: I know.

Mike: Christ had over three hundred predictions of His birth, life, mission, and death. These prophecies were written down before He came to the earth to identify His person and purpose. These were written down before He was born. The Bible gave us over three hundred prophecies: the location of His birth, how He was to be born, the exact time He would enter Jerusalem, how He would die, and that He would rise again from the dead. These predictions, and hundreds of others, all came true in the life of Jesus. This identifies Jesus as the Son of God.

No other founder of a religion had numerous predictions written down in advance of their birth and appearance.

Student: Well…

Mike: The main truth you need to know is that the God of the Bible is the precondition for the intelligibility of this world. One cannot make sense out of anything in reality, without Christianity.

Student: Uh.

Mike: If I had a neighbor knock on my door late one night, and he told me that a Pepsi can spoke with him. He tells me that the Pepsi can told him to write down what it was saying. My friend says, "Mike, this is the answer to finding God. This can spoke with me and had me write out this book. If I follow the can, I will find peace, wellness, and paradise when I die." If he said this, I would ask him, "How do you know this is true?" He says, "Look, I have this book. I transcribed it. Just believe and then follow it, and you will have peace and eternal life." I ask him, "How can I know that it was God who spoke to you from the Pepsi can?" He again shows me the book and testifies. I tell him that is not good enough. There are hundreds of alleged holy books that claim to be from God. Except for the Bible, none of them stand out, and none of them offer me valid reasons to believe they are from God. Their proponents assert empty claims. Christ is different. He doesn't make vain assertions. He is the truth. Christianity is the ultimate basis for reason, logic, morality, and the ability for us to make assertions. Every founder from every religion, except Christ, is just like my friend with the Pepsi can.

Student: Yes.

Mike: Are you interested in becoming a Christian?

Student: Uh, no.

Mike: Would you like to visit our church?

Student: Yes.

Mike: Here is an invitation. It has a map and directions to the church. I'm glad I'll see you soon.

The Christian Has Certainty

> These things I have written to you who believe in the name of the Son of God, that you may know that you have eternal life, and that you may continue to believe in the name of the Son of God (1 John 5:13).

Christianity is absolutely certain. I can have certainty. Swinburne used Baye's Theorem to calculate the probability of the resurrection of Jesus Christ was a "whopping 97%" as reported by the *New York Times*. Swinburne is a very intelligent man, but God is not a "probable" theory. God is not even 97% certain to exist. God certainly exists, and I can have complete certainty of His sovereign being. Job announces that he "knows my Redeemer lives" (Job 19:25). Paul declares, "I know in whom I have believed" (2 Timothy 1:12). It is impossible for the Christian worldview to be false. I am saved by grace alone, and I have certainty through the Holy Spirit and His true word. It is impossible for God not to exist. Calvin said that scripture was so "clear and certain it cannot be overthrown either by men or angels."

Everyone has to hold to some universal and certain claims. The agnostic may deny certainty, but certain and universal claims are unavoidable. The agnostic might attempt to claim that no one can know anything for certain. Yet that is a claim to know that for certain. The agnostic's worldview makes nonsense of human experience, and falls into Quine's mire of the "baffling tangle of relations." Affirming the lack of certain knowledge makes nonsense of human experience. If the Christian worldview is not true, then knowledge is impossible.

If knowledge is impossible, one could not know that knowledge is impossible because that is knowledge. Christianity is unavoidable since one must rely on the Christian worldview to try to deny it. Only the Christian worldview supplies the preconditions necessary for logic, science, moral standards, and mathematics.

The intelligibility of human experience requires the God of the Bible. Christianity is the only worldview that provides human reason an unchanging foundation for knowledge. All non-Christian systems of thought fail to furnish a foundation for the law of non-contradiction. Thus they cannot provide the footing for knowledge. They can only offer an antithetical and incongruous worldview. Unless one believes in God's revealed word, you cannot account for anything in the universe. God is the underlying and infinite ground for all knowledge, proof, evidence, and logic. It is impossible for God not to exist. He is the precondition for all knowledge because all human knowledge requires the use of the laws of logic. The omniscient, nonphysical, and unchanging God alone provides the necessary preconditions for the use of nonphysical, universal, and unchanging laws of logic. To argue at all, you must presuppose that the true God lives because you must use logic. Non-believing thought cannot supply the necessary preconditions for the laws of logic, thus they fall into futility because of the internal contradictions that entangle them. Therefore the contrary of Christianity is impossible since all non-Christian worldviews fall into absurdity. They are self-refuting. They lead to conclusions that contradict their own foundational assumptions. Without the triune God, there cannot be knowledge, and nothing can make sense.

Plato (realms of being distinct from becoming), Kant (the realms of phenomena distinct from noumena), and Einstein (the realms of the material distinct from the abstract) knew that there is a gulf that separates the material world of concrete hard objects and the abstract world of idea's, logic, and mathematics. They tried to understand the distinction of the concrete world of physical objects from the immaterial world of nonphysical idea's, concepts, and forms. This gulf, between the real physical world of hard objects and the abstract realm of idea's, demonstrates the impossibility of materialistic atheism. Atheism collapses under its own non-concrete concept since it declares that only concrete objects exist. There is no possible way for concrete material objects to transform into nonmaterial idea's. What is absolutely required is a nonphysical intelligence to be the transcendent author of the realm of concepts. If the notion that human beings consisted only of hard bio-mass were true, it would be impossible to form that particular non-concrete notion.

If you went to the Horseshoe Casino in downtown Las Vegas, and you put a new quarter in the quarter poker machine and the machine rejects your quarter. You look at your coin, and it's the real deal. The U.S. Mint has stamped it and it is a good quarter. The poker machine identifies your new legal quarter as a slug. You should reject the machine as defective because of the impossibility of the contrary. You go to another poker machine, and according to it, your new quarter is exactly legal tender of a quarter. Therefore this new poker machine is correct and the first one was wrong. It is impossible and unthinkable for the first poker machine to be correct. You have validated the second machine using the argument of the impossibility of the contrary. You have proven the first machine was incorrect and broken. The U.S. Mint transcends the poker machines, hence you know which poker machine works from the impossibility of the contrary. God has "minted" His word and His way in the world. And it is impossible for Him not to exist. If you claim that God does not exist, you have to use His minted world, including logic and your senses, to attempt to prove He does not exist. This is impossible, thus God must exist.

CHAPTER FIVE

EVOLUTION: FROM A FROG TO A PRINCE

Men who believe in any personal or living agency in nature superior to our own, are in possession of the one essential element of all religion. [1]

The creation tale in Genesis is very impressive, even in modern terms (Atheist Isaac Asimov).

Solomon… although he excelled in the glory of treasure… of navigation, of service and attendance, of fame and renown… yet he maketh no claim to any of those glories, but only the glory of the inquisition of truth; for so he says expressly, "The glory of God is to conceal a thing, but the glory of the king is to find it out" (Bacon: *The Adventures of Learning*).

Natural selection is absurdly inadequate to explain the existence of conscious, reflecting, equation solving and poetry writing minds. [2]

---

[1]. The Duke of Argyle, *Reign of Law* (NY: Boies, 1884), p. 269.

[2]. Philip Johnson, *Reasoning in the Balance* (Downers Grove, IL: Intervarsity Press, 1995), p. 89.

The scientific method has no power to resolve disputes about value or teleology. Moreover, when it is trying to describe events in the remote past, such as the origin of life, or complex matters like human behavior, science has to rely on philosophical presuppositions. [3]

It is difficult even to attach a precise meaning to the term "scientific truth." Scientific research can reduce superstition by encouraging people to think and survey things in the terms of cause and effect. Certain it is, akin to a religious feeling, of the rationality or intelligibility of the world lies behind all scientific work of a higher order. [4]

Lo, heaven and earth exist: they cry out that they have been created… self-evident is the voice with which these things speak. You therefore O Lord, you are beautiful, made these things. [5]

If a Big Bang started the universe, who pulled the trigger? (Source unknown).

The universe is centered on neither the earth nor the sun. It is centered on God (Alfred Noyes).

If you eliminate the idea of divine purpose, you have no other logical alternative than to believe that the universe we know has developed by accident. On this principle, all our thinking which traces events back to the intentions or purposes is invalidated. Ever since science began we have been wrong to ask "Why this?" And "Why that?" If "Why?" Seeks to uncover an intention, a purpose; for there is ultimately no intention, no purpose. [6]

---

[3]. Ibid., p. 200.

[4]. Albert Einstein, *Essays in Science* (NY: Haddon, 1934), p. 11.

[5]. Saint Augustine, *Confessions* (Garden City, New York: Doubleday, 1960), p. 280.

[6]. Harry Blaimires, *On Christian Truth* (Ann Arbor, MI: Servant Books, 1983), p. 29.

> We cannot use electric lights and radio's and… at the same time believe in the spirit and wonder world of the New Testament (Bultman's inspirational dictum).

> The sky and the earth; see all that is in them and realize God made them out of nothing (2 Maccabees 7:28).

> But Saul increased all the more in strength, and confounded the Jews who dwelt in Damascus, proving that this Jesus is the Christ (Acts 9:22).

Evolution is just a theory. It is an ideology, and according to Darwinian Michael Ruse, it is a religion. It has never been and never will be a proven "fact." Macro-evolution is a hoax, a philosophical swindle, and a wicked fallacy. This chimera has hoodwinked, cheated, and duped more people than any vain philosophy in history. Evolution is false. The universe could not have started by an unguided big bang. If you watch a grenade explode, you will notice that the pieces do not move or revolve in mathematical alignments or orbits. The pieces go in different, non-ordered directions. An explosion results in chaos, not order. One needs an unguided big bang to start the process of evolution. Evolution is the champion delusion, hoax, and fallacy. This swindle of the ages has conquered many fields of science, but it is not long for this world or any other. It is a theory that self-destructs under just surface level examination. The technological advances in all fields of science have become the evolutionist's foe, not his comrade. Blind chance acting on matter cannot explain the machine like complexity and efficiency of one cell. It cannot explain how the cell is programmed, and where the information that is in the DNA code came from.

A Code Requires a Code-giver

All living organisms have a DNA code. It is a code. A code requires information. Information requires a mind, and all living cells have information encoded in them. If I walked down the beach and in the sand I read: "I love George, now and forever," I would know an intelligent source wrote that prose. Intelligence was needed to put the information on the sand, just as the DNA code requires an intelligence to encode it into every living cell. So it is blind faith that asserts that the information in a cell comes from blind chance. Chance producing life and information is one of the articles of faith within the evolutionary theory. Theists see design in nature, we say there is at least one designer; we see information, we know an intelligence put it there; we see machines running efficiently, and we say there was an intelligence that built that machine. This is what most would call: common sense. Most dictionaries define "stupid" as failing to utilize common sense. One, who asserts materialism or evolution in the face of all these "facts," is not being intelligent. But the facts are not the thrust of our apologetics. The true and living God does live. It is impossible for anything else to be true without Him. We are not to trade a factual blow with a factual blow in our verbal exchange with the evolutionist. We should take the knife out of his hand, disarm him, and show him that the sword we hold, the Bible, is the precondition for the intelligibility of our world.

> The conception of his (God's) counsel as controlling all things in the universe is the only presupposition which can account for the uniformity of nature which the scientist needs. But the best and only possible proof for God is that his existence is required for the uniformity of nature and for the coherence of all things in the world.[7]

Evolution of the species is a metaphysical claim dissimulated by those who believe they are composed of just an assembly of atoms. How could a mere assembly of physical atoms produce a metaphysical theory? This theory is religious, and it takes stone-blind faith to believe in it. Physical-only evolutionists are fundamentalists.

A Modern Fairy Tale

Darwinians believe in a fairy tale. This little fairy tale began once upon a time, billions of years ago. One small primal germ fitted and engineered itself together. It liked what it saw in the mirror and "decided" to reproduce itself. From the primordial soup and this seminal spore all living organisms evolved. These archaic bacteria decided that they would like to move up the "ladder," and grab life for all its gusto, and evolve into a mushroom. Then after a million years, the "it" found out that being a mushroom is not all that it is cracked up to be, being a spore is highly overrated. So it gathers

---

[7]. Cornelius Van Til, *The Defense of Faith* (Philadelphia: Presbyterian & Reformed, 1955), p. 103.

all its resolve, and musters up all its determination, and with its own innate force, after millions and millions of years, it evolves into a tadpole. The tadpole gets bored, and marshals up enough resolve to morph into a fish. The fish decides, after a great period of time, because it gets sea sick, to develop into a reptile, so it can experience how sand feels between its toes. The fairy tale goes on to weave its tale, and the reptile evolves into a bird. Then the feathery creature develops a phobia of flying, so it grunts and groans, and after centuries and centuries, it develops into a mammal. The mammal evolves into an ape, and the ape decides it likes poetry, music, and football, so it decides to become a man. In this tall tale, instead of a princess kissing a frog and the frog becomes a prince, with evolution: a frog evolves into prince without even a kiss. It takes sightless faith to believe in such mythology. I know that in the beginning: God created the heavens and the earth. Without this as our assumed starting point, nothing makes sense, and we fall for delusions as silly as pixy-tales.

It is beyond difficult to believe that the universe produces everything from star dust to Da Vinchi, germs to Beethoven, tad poles to Shakespeare, and the primordial soup to Michael Jordan slam dunks. It is not just straining on credulity to believe that we are only turbocharged apes; it is impossible for this to be true. The problem with evolution is not just Spencer's "unknowable mystery." It is impossible to account for morality, reason, and mathematics when confined to the materialistic evolutionary worldview. Huxley ranted that we all came from a "murky pale of protoplasm." Not only is he stuck in the mire of mere assertion, his statement, as all others based on materialism, is self-stultifying and self-defeating. It is destroyed by "its own credentials." If we are the result of a physical-only process of matter and motion, the person asserting evolution cannot justify the nonphysical logic he uses in forming his argument. If he is correct and there is nothing beyond the material realm, then his theory is the byproduct of a physical process alone and cannot be trusted. The material evolutionist cannot account for his use of reason. Thus employing reason to propagate the theory of evolution is self-refuting.

Bacteria are the Fittest

I have never heard the scientific grounds for a bacterium to evolve into a "higher" form. The bacteria are the fittest creatures on the planet, only rivaled by cockroaches. These two types of organisms do not need to evolve. They survive quite nicely. Nothing is more tenacious, more resilient, more stout, and produces more functioning and self-procuring offspring than bacteria. Why would they need to evolve? Why would cockroaches need to evolve? They could survive a nuclear bomb. The organisms that evolutionists claim as the "higher" creatures, die off easier and quicker, and produce far less offspring. The higher up the ladder, the more likely the organism is extinct or is put on the endangered species' list. Look how fragile the whales and the great apes are as species. Large body mass creatures are much less fit than the tenacious organisms like bacteria and cockroaches. The evolutionists do not have to deal with just a missing link; the whole chain is gone. Only God and His revelation can give us a foundation for science. The theory of survival of the fittest does not comport with the reality of ultra-resilient cockroaches because they do not need to evolve into higher forms. They do just fine without knowing Mickey Mouse or Plato. Bacteria would not become more stout and produce more survivable offspring if they could read poetry or applaud Tiger Woods. Bacteria do not have determination or conviction. Even if they did, how could that resolve give them the innate force to evolve? They would need purpose and the means to fulfill that purpose, a teleological reason. This can only come when there is intelligence and purpose. A matter-only universe cannot produce teleology, hence evolution is a myth; it is fable for profligate adults. It not only does not gel with the facts; it is impossible for it to be true.

Odds, Probability, and Certainty

Hoyle, the Cambridge Astronomer, once said that the odds of life arising by chance have about the same probability of "a tornado blowing through a junk yard and forming a Boeing 747." That is devastating to those who submit to the blind faith of evolution. Yet it is much worse than that. There are no odds for the existence of God. There are no probabilities. It is impossible for the God of the Bible not to exist. Without God, one cannot discuss or argue about the theory of evolution. S.E.T.I., the Search for Extraterrestrial Intelligence, scans the heavens for codes, information, language, and patterns. They base their work on the theory that finding a radio signal with a code would prove there are intelligent beings out there in the vast reaches of the universe. The premise is: a code presupposes a code-giver. A code-giver has intelligence. Within the Christian worldview, this makes sense. The baffling thing is to watch the scientists, who study the DNA code, fail to make the same deduction. They would if an alien sent a simple code over the air waves. A code-giver presupposes an intelligence, yet this is often ignored by many scientists. This type of fuzzy reasoning is the problem with the theory of evolution.

Unbelieving men suppress the truth in unrighteousness. The Christian is not to battle in the trenches with our facts against the Darwinian materialist's facts. We must demonstrate that without the true God, as the pre-requirement of all our thought, we cannot make sense of anything in the abstract or in the biological. My uncle is not a monkey, and my grand dad is not a polliwog. I am not a product of monkeydom; I am created in the image of God. Mozart, Milton, and moms are not the product of unguided animated star dust. Evolutionists want their father to be a muskrat and their mother to be an opossum. They delight in the fairy tale that their great aunt was a tadpole or snapping turtle. But if man evolved from an animal, then all humans are animals, and this gives them license to behave like animals. The funny thing is the doctrine of evolution presupposes God since this false notion employs logic. Science presupposes God. Induction presupposes God. So all their crazy theories require God. All true and false postulations need God and His revelation as the precondition of their intelligibility.

Most arguments against the theory of evolution claim to be probable. They do not speak of certainty. The Bible speaks of God as the Creator with absolute certainty. There is not a cosmic odds-giver crunching the probability of the existence of God Almighty. We are told that one cell is made up of 100,000 molecules; that 10,000 finely tuned, interrelated chemical reactions occur concurrently. That a cell contains, in its nucleus, a digitally coded database larger than thirty volumes of an encyclopedia. The apologists then explain that the odds of this happening by chance are overwhelming. They say the evidence is beyond a reasonable doubt, so it's probably true. The truth of the matter is God's existence is not a probability. The odds-giver should not give a thousand to one odds that this world was created by a Creator. There is absolute certainty that God lives, and that He created all things in the heavens and the earth, period. We must have God, as the pre-essential of creation, or nothing in the cosmos can make sense.

> The wicked in his proud countenance does not seek God; God is in none of his thoughts. His ways are always prospering; Your judgments are far above, out of his sight; as for all his enemies, he sneers at them. He has said in his heart, "I shall not be moved; I shall never be in adversity" (Psalms 10:4-6).

A Put Up Job!

Hoyle dispels evolution by setting forth the following: "The laws of nuclear physics have been deliberately designed with regard to the consequences they produce inside stars. If this is so, apparently random quirks have become part of a deep-laid scheme." He called creation a "put up job." The Lord's fingerprints are imprinted on every part of the universe, from the tiniest atom to the largest galaxy. I enjoy examining the proof of God's design and engineering. But within my worldview, everything is evidence of God having created time, space, and matter. There is nothing in the world that is not evidence for a Creator, when I affirm biblical presuppositions. The believer is not to defend the faith with probabilities.

It is impossible for God not to be the Creator. We have a perfect certainty that God hurled and fashioned this universe together for His glory. We must stand on God's word and say to the world: God lives, and He is not silent. There is no doubt that He lives, due to the fact that doubt presupposes the triune God. All doubts depend on logic, reason, and morality. All those elements presuppose God.

> In the beginning God created the heavens and the earth (Genesis 1:1).

I rejoice when I discover that if the earth were 10% larger or 10% smaller, life would be impossible; that the earth is tilted at just the correct angle; it has the exact gas mixture in its atmosphere; our planet has a moon at the perfect distance and size; and the earth is at the right distance from the sun for life to be. No other known planet is organized with this precision to ensure that life can survive. This evidence will convince all believers. These are very happy facts. But they are not uninterpreted or brute facts. A skeptic could dismiss and explain them away. The facts do not explain themselves. But the cool skeptic does not care. He holds to a different worldview, and believes in different presuppositions. The battle is not over facts. It is over worldviews and foundational assumptions that interpret facts.

The fossil record has not produced birds with one-half or one-quarter wings. And what use would a halfway-evolved wing be in the struggle for survival. The nonfunctioning appendage would get in the way and inhibit survival, not enhance it. We do not find fish with one-half or one-third fins because these would not assist in the survival of the species. The extra weight and frozen body part would hinder it and natural selection would not select it. Body parts, not fully formed (incomplete lungs, warm blooded hearts, partial eyes, and ad infinitum) would be a hindrance to any organism trying to survive. And when did the fish or the birds get together and decide to grow wings and fins? "Hey, Hal I'm bored, lets do something different tonight and grow some quarter wings, so our future ancestors will grow full wings, and be able to fly in a few million years." That sounds ridiculous and it is. It involves teleology or striving for a goal. That is the reason it sounds so preposterous. Unanimated matter and animals, void of reason, cannot decide to embrace teleology. Yet the skeptic will still invent fanciful theories explaining how animals evolved wings and fins. Our job is not to trade "evidence," and dodge the evolutionist's bullets. We should take his gun away. We do this by using the word of God to obliterate his worldview and his materialistic presuppositions. We demonstrate to them that without God, you cannot account for facts of any kind.

> The heavens declare the glory of God; and the firmament shows His handiwork (Psalms 19:1).

Information Presupposes Intelligence

I was taught in public school that all my cells contain DNA. DNA is in every cell of every living thing. I was fascinated to discover that DNA works in a partnership with Messenger RNA. DNA is a code, and it sends off a message. Any time I see messages or information in my world, I assume that an intelligent being placed it there. If I go to Maui, and I take a long stroll through the jungle, and I observe writing on a tree trunk that says: "Joe loves Lori now and forever." I know that the wind, acting upon some stick, did not write that by chance. Why? Because there is information in the writing on the tree. The precondition for information is intelligence. DNA has a readable code. Thus intelligent design is a precondition for living things. Many psuedo-scientists are pointing microphones into grave yards and "haunted houses" hoping to hear from intelligent beings in another dimension. What are they looking for? They are searching for language and a code. But an otherworldly intelligent being has already contacted mankind. God has written a code and a message in all our cells, declaring that He lives. Most important of all, He has revealed His person and His way in the Bible. It takes a person gifted in self-deception to conclude that the information, in every cell on the planet, came by chance.

Nowhere else do we find information, codes, or messages coming from chance. When you read the plethora of articles on cloning or gene therapy, notice how often they use words like: book, map, code, tissue engineering, design, patterns, message, blueprint, reading, deciphering, and many other words which presuppose intelligence. This is devastating to the atheist. An intelligent God designed us, and He implanted the DNA blueprint in all living creatures.

Every cell, in every living thing, has a digitally coded database that is more voluminous in information content than a large stack of biology books. The intelligible information, stored in one microscopic DNA molecule, would fill a stack of books that from the earth would reach the moon. This information is encoded in the DNA and RNA by numerous enzymes. These active proteins are capable of reading, deciphering, and communicating that information to and fro. All these different parts and mechanisms must be set up independently and simultaneously, or the individual part would not be of any use. All these varied mechanisms must be independently and precisely set up, wired, and installed at the same time. The odds, of all these different intelligent machine-like processes, evolving by chance, simultaneously, with precision and complete compatibility, are unthinkable.

Poems, written advertisements, and DNA all have "specified complexity." They have a high information content. High information content demands an intelligence behind it. All living cells have DNA and a set of chemical instructions written with amino acids and proteins. If you stumbled upon a bunch of rocks on a mountain side and they were placed in a formation that spelled-out: "I love USC!" After reading this, you would know, rain water beating on the rocks, mixed with air bombed bird doo-doo that dropped on the dirt, could not write this message. You would recognize that some intelligence formed this sentence: maybe a hiker or maybe a Trojan fan. Either way, you would know it took intelligence to write this message. And DNA must have a rational being as its author. It has complex and specific information that requires a thinking being. These written codes could not come from chance plus time, acting on matter. Maybe an alien, or a pantheon of gods, or Hume's big vegetable, wrote these biological missives in all cells. The information theory, outside the Christian worldview, cannot prove the biblical God. But within the Christian worldview it is a powerful "proof."

Macro-Evolution is Impossible

Evolution is impossible. Macro-evolution is not just implausible; the theory is impossible. Biologically sturdy ants would not evolve into the top-ten list of endangered species, like a great ape. The stout rat would not evolve into a fragile wolf or giraffe. A strong and resilient bacteria would not evolve into a weak and easily extinct Dodo bird. The so called lower species are usually the ones that are the strongest and most fit to survive. If reproducing, the strongest and greatest number of offspring, is the means of specie preservation, then the ant and the rat are a couple of the "highest" species. The following "facts" make evolution impossible: Live amino acids are in a different form than nonliving amino acids and they do not switch over into nonliving amino acids in non-biological systems. Living molecules could not form without an oxygen rich atmosphere, yet oxygen eats-up the pre-protein chained amino acids. Without the element oxygen, a living organism could not live: there would be an absence of a life demanding ozone layer. Furthermore, a pre-biotic cell would be destroyed, in an oxygen environment before it could evolve into a living cell, by the oxygen itself. Thus oxygen is mandatory for life, yet it kills off the pre-life before it can live.

Many modern scientists have discovered that every cell in every living organism has many interrelated, interconnected, and inter-depended parts. These bio-pieces could not evolve simultaneously to produce already functioning mini-machines in living cells. Behe uses the mousetrap to illustrate this problem of "irreducibly complex" biological systems. For the mouse trap to work it needs many parts in the system functioning at the same time. The catch, the spring, the holding bar, the hammer, and the platform all have to be a functioning part of the mousetrap simultaneously. The living cell has many different systems that have dozens of parts. The biological system cannot work without all the parts functioning concurrently. This removes any chance that a biological organ had numerous, slight, successive modifications that gradually produced change as required by the theory of evolution. The odds that all these bio-machine parts, within the organ, evolved into a perfect fit, simultaneously, are mere fancy. Darwinian evolution is impossible, and the very theory of macro-evolution presupposes God. Logic is a precondition for any theory, including a fallacious theory, like Darwinism.

A Few Questions for the Evolutionist

The following is a list of a few simple questions that I have found can stump an evolutionist. These questions cannot "prove" that God exists. But pressing three or more on the evolutionist will help humble them, in the hope that they will turn to Christ.

- Where in the fossil record are the transitional forms between invertebrates organisms and vertebrates organisms?

- How did the human eye, capable of performing ten billion calculations per second, evolve by chance?

- How do lifeless chemicals come alive?

- What is the evolutionary advantage of an organism having a half-wing on its way to a full wing? Would not the extra weight, of the less than fully formed wing, and the potential clumsiness of the useless appendage, lower the chance of survival and not enhance it?

- Does a worm, with a mutation that causes a leg to evolve, increase its survivability? Would not the new leg reduce its chance for survival?

- How did warm-blooded birds evolve from cold-blooded reptiles?

- Does the doctrine of the survival of the fittest assert that the organisms that produce the greatest number of surviving offspring are the most fit? If so, why would a cockroach or bacteria ever ascend, and eventually evolve into large body-mass organisms that are extremely susceptible to extinction, and produce much fewer offspring? Do the simple organisms of bugs and bacteria need to evolve?

- Can information, such as the DNA code, come from non-intelligence? Is there anywhere, where we observe non-intelligence producing information?

• Can chance plus time plus agitation produce information? (try putting a pen and paper in your clothes dryer, and turn it on high heat).

• How can chance plus energy plus time produce the "bristling high-tech machinery" of the living cell? These tiny living machines are fitted with "sensors, gates, pumps, and identification markers." Can all this automated biological machinery, equipped with "power plants, automated workshops, and recycling units," all be produced by mindless chance?

• How can we believe the theories that scientists are postulating today, when these will be challenged by five new theories tomorrow? Every month, a new fossil find overturns last year's theory. There are too many gaps and guesses for the Darwinian theories to be true. Charles Hodge, over a century ago, warned us: "What concerns the origins of things cannot be known except by a supernatural revelation. All else is speculation and conjecture… and… is in the region of speculation, and is merged into philosophy, and is subject to its hallucinations."

• Is it because science cannot supply the conditions for morality that it is prone to fakes, forgeries, and frauds? Many of these frauds have been exposed in medical and scientific studies. The investigators discovered that the dishonest scientists were seeking grant money which motivated them to lie about their medical research. This dishonest research on testing medical treatments is very harmful. Add to that the January 2000 story of the Archaeoraptor: It was touted, by the *National Geographic* magazine, as a bird. Later it was found to be a fake! Why is there such a long history of scientific hoaxes and fraud?

• Deny God, and affirm evolutionary materialism, and you undermine morality. Nature offers scores and scores of "inhumane" conduct. Are humans to follow the animals that kidnap and force females to have sex with them? Should we act like praying mantises and black widows

> that devour their males? One finds a plethora of beastly killings, forced intercourse, and voids of egalitarianism in nature. Monogamy, self-sacrifice, and enduring love is missing in most of the animal kingdom. Without God, there is no reason mankind should not practice the same brutality.

The Brain Thing

The materialist atheist asserts that the mind is the physical brain. There are not any nonphysical actions taking place in the human brain. But if the human mind consisted only of hard chemicals and neurons bouncing around in the skull, human thoughts would be no more true or valued than an afternoon tamale food-belch. Both are just chemical reactions. This means that there is no rational reason to count my thoughts more important than a burp; they are just meaningless and empty chemical reactions. This of course is self-voiding. If my thoughts and words are meaningless, then they are not true. Hence my thoughts cannot be meaningless. My thoughts are not just concrete chemical reactions.

A mind, distinct from the brain, destroys the theory of evolution. Evolution materialists do not believe mankind has a spirit. His soul is only "a little wind and smoke." Research on the brain can lead to the conclusion that the mind is independent of the brain. Some legitimate science has uncovered reasons to believe that life survives the physical death. Some scholars have said that they would "bet yes" that the afterlife is a fact. When one submits to God's revelation, there is no betting. It is impossible for God and the afterlife that He reveals not to exist. To ask the question about a possible afterlife presupposes that God lives, and His word is true. When the atheist backs up in a conversation and says, "Hold on, I'm searching for a word," point out the inconsistency. I like to ask them: "Who is searching?" Those who claim that only the physical world exists, and that their mind is just a block of flesh, cannot answer that question. Frequently, they will quickly see their dilemma. Thomas Huxley, in one of his moments of weakness, asked, "How is it that anything so remarkable as the state of consciousness comes about as a result of irritating nervous tissue, is it just as unaccountable as the appearance of the Djinn, when Aladdin rubbed his lamp?"

Research has demonstrated that there is a distinction between the mind and the brain. One study had brain surgeons open up the skull of brain surgery patients to expose their gray matter. The researchers then electrically stimulated the area of the brain which lifts the right arm. They stimulated it, and the arm lifted without the patient's permission. Then the scientists instructed their patients to resist the lifting of the arm when they stimulated the same spot in the brain. They stimulated that area, and all the patients could resist the lifting of their arm. This proved that the mind can control the brain. Another study, conducted by U.C.L.A., had doctors give depressed patients two sets of pills. One was an antidepressant medicine and the other was a placebo pill. Both groups said they experienced relief of symptoms: 52% of those who received the medication and 38% of those who received the sugar pill. The interesting thing was the discovery that the brain waves, of the placebo-taking patients, acutely changed after taking the fake pill. Their brain chemistry and brain waves were altered without any medication, merely from their own "minds." The mind controls the gray matter and can change it; the mind is distinct from the brain. The researchers reported that they were "stunned" because there were actual "hardware" changes in the brain, by the power of suggestion. The power of suggestion comes from the mind working the brain. The mind can change and "alter" how the brain works. This is clear evidence that the mind moved the brain and is distinct from the brain tissue. This is proof. Evidence is good, but remember that evidence can be interpreted in ungodly ways.

Rocks and Dogs Appreciating Rembrandt?

Without presupposing the God of the Bible, one cannot account for any theory, even the theory of evolution. One cannot supply the necessary preconditions for the use of reason without God. Remember, the materialist proclaims that only material objects exist, so he cannot account for the nonphysical logic that he puts into service in forging his theory. He uses logic, but he cannot account for it. The nonbeliever has to steal from the Christian worldview to make any pronouncement, about any object, or any concept in the world. One cannot even account for science, without the Christian worldview. Pastor T. Dewitt Talmage wittingly said, "Science and scripture are the bass and soprano of the same tune." He likened the skeptic Robert Ingersoll's attack on the Bible as to "a grasshopper on a railway line when the express comes thundering along." He also quipped that "science is a boy and revelation is a man." He was demonstrating that revelation is more mature and reliable than science. This is true. I would go beyond that, and say that without the man, a father, the boy cannot even exist. One cannot have science without God. The God of the Bible is the precondition for science. Science uses induction, empirical testing, logic, and morality. One cannot account for any of those dynamics without God and His revelation.

The atheistic worldview proposes that mankind, with all his skyscrapers, opera's, supersonic jets, art, and literature, is merely a more complex block of whirling subatomic particles than rocks, carrots, and squirrels. An atheist can use science, but he can never account for it without God. The God and His revelation are the foundation for science. The Christian is not to be a concordist. One who attempts to find agreement or concord between revelation and science. The truth of God is the precondition for true science. Science needs God and His revelation. God does not need science.

The False God of Chance

Blind chance acting on matter cannot explain anything, including itself. If you spill your beer by accident, you don't ask the beer how it got there. The beer is an accident, and it cannot explain itself. The Bud isn't wiser. One needs a person to explain the beer spill. If our world is an accident, just some cosmic sneeze, then we cannot explain ourselves, including the statement that we cannot explain ourselves. This is one of those self-refuting statements that destroy atheism. Statements that if they were true, they are false (see chapter six for more on self-refuting statements). Thus the proposition, we are an accident that cannot explain itself, is a false statement. It is self-demolishing. As you read through this book, you will notice in the dialogues and in the commentary, everything that a person articulates that is not based on the Christian worldview is false. There is nothing that is true that an atheist can assert that contradicts Christianity; those assertions will always be erroneous. Understanding this will build your faith and give you confidence in witnessing to skeptics. The God of the Bible has all the answers, and without God, you will not have an answer to any question. Jesus announced that He was "the truth." He is the truth, and the Holy Spirit is the Spirit of truth. To make any consistent and true statement, one must base it on the God of truth. Anything written or spoken that attempts to contradict God's revelation, will be self-defeating and fallacious. We know we are not just a random accident profused from an ancient impersonal big-bang. An explosion does not have order. The universe has order. This demonstrates that we are not an accident. We call living things: organisms. An organism presupposes that it has organization and structure to it. Who organized the organisms? We cannot be the product of self-organizing stardust. That theory uses logic and logic presupposes God. Without God one cannot account for the logic needed in creating that hypothesis.

> Contend earnestly for the faith which was once for all delivered to the saints (Jude 1:3).

The mathematician, J.W. Sullivan, described evolution as "an article of faith." When I believed in evolution (and I did "believe"), I was troubled by the fact that in the fossil record, one-half giraffe's necks were never found. I shook my head in bewilderment, when I mused on the fact, only a fully developed eye would help an organism survive. A third of an eye, and a three-quarters of an eye would hinder the fitness and the survivability of an organism. The DNA code also bothered me. If one saw a neon sign flashing: "Loosest Slots on Jupiter," one would assume intelligence designed the sign and put the information on it. The information would not have gotten there by chance. Could the non-intelligent process of chance really create the universe by some cosmic explosion? Could life come from non-life? Could intelligence come from non-intelligence? Could slime evolve to ponder the divine? Could a frog evolve into a prince? Rocks and cats do not appreciate Rembrandt, why do I? These questions that bounced around in my non-Christian head, made sleeping at night very difficult. I usually had to have loud music blaring, so I would not ponder these refutations of my faith in evolution.

The Self-Refuting Nature of Naturalism

> By the word of the LORD the heavens were made, and all the host of them by the breath of His mouth. For He spoke, and it was done; He commanded, and it stood fast (Psalms 33:6 & 9).

Refuting evolution is easy. The evolutionists live and testify on blind faith. They tell us that living things "give the appearance of having been designed for a purpose." It is easy to refute such drivel with compelling evidential arguments. But we are not to exchange evidence with the evolutionist and believe that the one who is the best lawyer, wins the argument. We should answer the evolutionist's objections to Christianity the same way we answer all objections. We must uproot all their foundations and demonstrate that only Christianity can give a foundation for science and knowledge. Evolution is a faith-based system. It cannot account for or justify the use of induction, logic, and morality.

Evolutionists have a pre-commitment to "metaphysical naturalism." This is a religious and philosophical system that asserts that the universe and everything in it, are made up solely of matter and motion. Naturalistic skeptics have a nonphysical presupposition that assumes only the physical reality exists. That is why the staunch evolutionist Dawkins begins his book *The Blind Watchmaker* with the confession: "Biology is the study of complicated things that give the appearance of having been designed for a purpose." He then attempts in the remainder of the book to refute this admission, and he does this without even blushing. This inconsistent materialism is behind the theories of Dawkins and all the evolutionists who attempt to marshal empirical facts to support their non-empirical theory. This hypothesis insists living organisms only "appear to be designed." That demonstrates the bias of the evolutionist's foundational pre-commitments and that materialism is the presupposition behind their theories.

The biggest problem for the evolutionary theory: It is a theory. A theory is not a material object by definition. It is abstract and nonphysical. The material-only evolutionist posits the idea, only the physical exists, while he is asserting an idea that is not physical. An idea, a theory, and a hypothesis are not physical objects. They are nonmaterial. The evolutionist uses a nonmaterial theory to assert that it is only possible for the material cosmos to exist. One can discern, with just a superficial examination of the materialist's claims, that their theory is self-nullifying: it commits philosophical suicide. We should place this reality before them and drive them to the truth that their theories are absurd. We must defend the truth in Christ to the extent that all men bow to His Lordship or remain silent. The mouths of the anti-theists will be stopped up as you expose their self-contradicting and self-terminating propositions. The goal is for their knee to bow and their tongue to confess that Jesus Christ is Lord. If not, let their tongues hang silent.

Hume famously demanded that "Any volume… let us ask, does it contain any abstract reasoning concerning quantity or number? No. Does it contain any experimental reasoning concerning matter of fact and existence? No. Commit it to the flames; for it can contain nothing but sophistry and illusion." Hume makes a self-refuting blunder here. His own statement must be thrown to the flames because it lacks any "reasoning concerning quantity and number," as well as "any experimental reasoning concerning a matter of fact or existence."

A Complete Theory

> If we should discover a complete theory... we shall... be able to take part in the question of why it is that we and the Universe exist. If we find the answer to that it will be the ultimate triumph of human reason - for then we would know the mind of God. [8]

Sagan looked up at the stars, set against the dark backdrop of the night, and declared that only the cosmos exists. He assumed omniscience in this boast. A fanciful boast that could never be verified. As Sagan the pagan matured, he seemed to sober up to the reality that the universe and living organisms exhibit order, complexity, and design. So he plunged with his eyes wide shut farther into aphotic folly, proposing that the design might have come from alien life forms seeding our globe. He reduces the human race to an ET science project as he reveals his bias against theism. Sagan's speculations require blind faith to believe. There is no empirical evidence for extraterrestrials. Unlike God, they are not the precondition for the intelligibility of the cosmos.

> The unbeliever's presuppositions (worldview) would consistently lead to foolishness and the destruction of knowledge. [9]

No school of science has ever frightened theists as much as geology. Many geologists proclaim that the strata of the earth contradict the Bible. But the layered strata of the aftereffects of the Mount St. Helen's eruption resulted in no disagreement between geological "facts" and the Bible. Many scientists may expose alleged biblical contradictions, but they are only contradictions if one begins with faulty presuppositions. Steve Austin, of the Institute of Creation Research, has demonstrated that layered strata could be formed in an instant by volcanic activity, like the Mount St. Helen's eruption in the 1980's. Either way, the "facts" do not speak for

---

[8]. Roy Peacock, *A Brief History of Eternity* (Wheaton,Il: Crossway Books, 1990), p. 145.

[9]. Bahnsen, Greg, *Answering Objections, Biblical Worldview* (VII; Feb., 1991), Covenant Media Foundation, p. 1.

themselves. All facts must be interpreted through the eyes of philosophical presuppositions.

My presupposition: God has spoken. With this presupposition, I can justify reality and my investigation of reality. When I base my worldview on God and His word, I can justify science, induction, the evaluation of evidence, and my use of reason. The nonbeliever cannot justify one item in all reality. He cannot provide the necessary preconditions for the investigation of reality. Thus the nonbeliever cannot account for geology and science. When you are witnessing to a nonbeliever ask him: How do you know that induction is true? How do you know, when you test something and you get the same result a thousand times, you will get the same result the next time? You don't know under your worldview. I put my hand in the fire, and I will get burned. Why can I depend on that the next time? The Christian can justify that because God's revelation has told us that induction is true and we can count on it. The nonbeliever cannot justify induction, he uses it, and takes it for granted, yet he cannot account for it. It just, is.

The non-Christian has to live by blindfolded faith. The Christian worldview is the precondition for science. We do not need to try to get scientific approval for the Bible. Science needs approval from God's word. Charles Spurgeon, in his book *The Greatest Fight in the World Rightly Maintained*, wrote: "If scientists agree to our believing part of the Bible… Their assent is of no more consequence to our faith than… the consent of the mole to the eagle's sight." We don't need the affirmation of scientists; they need the affirmation of God's revelation. Without scripture, the scientists cannot provide the rational preconditions needed for science.

Many have a pre-commitment to materialism. Yet they cannot justify that commitment. Justifying anything transcends materialism because justifications are not material objects. If materialism is valid, we could get as much truth from the purring motor of a Chevy, a machine, than from the machine of human cognition. However, we do not observe journalists waiting to interview race-car motors after a race. They always seem to interview the driver, who has a brain. A mind is more than just a material machine. There is a "ghost in the machine." The human spirit that helps make up a soul.

A Talk with an Average Joe

I have discussed the "myth" of Darwinian evolution with a number of people from all walks of life. I have never had one muster any logical arguments that could withstand some prying questions. Here is one such conversation with Joe the evolutionist:

> Mike: Hey, I noticed your car has a Darwin fish on it. Do you believe in evolution?
>
> Joe: Of course. Are you one of those fundamentalists that are stuck in the tenth century?
>
> Mike: That's quite a question. Actually, I like to discuss the theory of evolution with people that hold that position, and pray that they repent and trust in Christ. Have you studied the science of DNA?
>
> Joe: Yes I have. It provides great evidence for the evolutionary process. Human DNA is almost 98% identical to ape DNA. This is strong evidence.
>
> Mike: Does DNA have a code and information content in it?
>
> Joe: Yes. That's one of its main functions.
>
> Mike: Have you ever seen information come from anything but an intelligent being?
>
> Joe: Well, uh, no.
>
> Mike: Information requires intelligence. If I heard someone tapping on the other side of wall, in a language such as the Morse code, and it spelled out: "Help me I have been kidnapped by a circus clown with bad breath." I would assume that there is an intelligent being behind the wall in need of help. The reason I would know that there must be a person behind the tapping is it came in the form of a code. It was not just the random tapping of

> a bird or a machine. The code requires intelligence. And biologists call it the DNA code. Code! Can you explain, without an intelligent being writing the DNA code in the cells, where the code came from?
>
> Joe: Well, I have never thought about it that way.
>
> Mike: I never did either until I started learning to think in a critical manner. I would encourage you to turn from your ways and trust in Jesus Christ. You and I have sinned. We have broken God's law by lying, stealing, hating, missing church, lusting and many other sins. Jesus died to remove all the sins of His people. Here is a tract with an invitation to our church. Come by and check it out.
>
> Joe: Thanks.

Remember when you use the general outlines of these conversations in your witnessing, you must stay focused on your point, graciously bear the weight of it on them over and over. Many evolutionists will attempt to divert the subject throughout your conversations. Do not let them change the subject, but stick to your point.

In The Beginning

> In the beginning God created the heavens and the earth (Genesis 1:1).

The opening verse of the Bible declares that God created the heavens and the earth. God created the universe out of nothing. Most non-Christian scientists, for many decades, did not believe that the universe had a beginning. Today, most scientists believe that the universe had a starting point. This is one of the many reasons we are not to submit God's word to modern science. All science must be submitted to God's word. No other ancient philosophy or religion asserts that the whole universe was created out of nothing, at one point in time. The Hindu's believe Brahma created the water from an eternal universe. He then moved over the water and out of his eye went the sun. Out of his lips went the fire, and out of his ear went the air. Then Brahma got tired and laid down his tired self for over four million years. After that little power-nap, this Rip Van Winkle god, destroyed the world, and then out of the chaotic material, created the world again. He did this again and again. He continues to sleep, wake up, destroy the universe, and then make it again. Creation and demolition, then four million years of sleep. Brahma and all the false gods may sleep, but the true and living God neither slumbers nor sleeps. He alone created the whole universe out of nothing at one moment in time. Only the true God supplies the basis to study, analyze, and make theories on the origin of the universe. Only the living God allows us to account for the logic, induction, and ethics required to make scientific discoveries.

The earth is always changing. One cannot vest his hope, his thought, or his philosophy of life on the earthly. One cannot base his ethics, reason, and nobility on a system of thought which is built on the physical universe that is in a constant state of flux. A changing cosmos cannot produce unchanging things like the laws of logic. Again, those entities transcend the physical universe. Your thought, submitted to God's revealed word, is the only means to have a worldview that can make sense of the universe. Kepler said it best in describing the creation as a "sacred sermon, a veritable hymn to God the Creator."

No God: No Meaning

Existentialists, like the atheist Sartre, claim that life has no meaning. The assertion of the absence of meaning presupposes meaning. There has to be a standard of meaning to assert that there is no meaning in life. If one feels isolated in a sea of meaninglessness, one has to be isolated from something. The schools of philosophy that promulgate the meaninglessness of all things, presuppose meaning, which presupposes the living God. To make a claim that something is not, presupposes something that is. Isolation and meaninglessness presuppose the God of scripture. One cannot escape God through vain philosophy of any stripe. If life is meaninglessness, then that would include the theory that life is meaningless, which would be self-nullifying. Life has meaning. And the claim, life does not have meaning, presupposes God. The non-believing existentialist wants to rest in his self-imposed ignorance. Lewis said, "Heaven understands hell and hell does not understand heaven." Non-Christians do not want to be stimulated out of their self-deception. We, as Christians, have the joyful duty of being a philosophical alarm clock.

Every existential cynic and iconoclast relies on logic, language, and ethics to propagate their views. The precondition for logic, language, and ethics is God Almighty. The existential escape itself is no escape. There is no escape from reason, morality, language, or God.

The Inescapable Truth

All non-Christian thought, including Darwinism, in principal, ultimately destroys the possibility of logic, science, moral codes, and all aspects of human experience. Christianity provides the preconditions for human experience, and it is inescapable. It is the only worldview that does not make nonsense of the cosmos and human experience. If Christianity is not true, then knowledge is impossible. Christianity is certain and unavoidable. It, alone, rejects man's autonomy. Human beings are not omniscient or omnipotent, thus humanity cannot account for the universals in the laws of logic and mathematics, without God. The Christian worldview declares that God has spoken and humanity is not autonomous. With Christianity out of the picture, one affirms autonomy, which leads to self-contradiction: disqualified on its own terms. Christianity declares a worldview that supplies a means to understand human experience. It announces that the sovereign God has revealed knowledge of Himself and the cosmos. All non-Christian worldviews including naturalism are autonomous and cannot provide the preconditions for the intelligibility of the world because they are non-universal and self-stultifying. All species of thought contrary to Christian theism are arbitrary, self-contradictory, and impossible. Autonomous thought is impossible because it is contradicted on its own assumptions, hence it grabs a shovel and digs its own grave. The triune God has spoken in Jesus, and the Bible. He is the precondition for the intelligibility of all human experience. Without God one must fall into self-contradictions.

Without the triune God, all reasoning fails, thus there cannot be science. There isn't a non-Christian view of the creation that can make sense out of reasoning, science, and morality. An atheist scientist cannot account for his use of nonphysical logic in his scientific reasoning. Logic is not physical. It is transcendent, universal, and abstract. Only the Christian world and life view can supply the necessary preconditions for the nonmaterial, unchanging, and universal laws of logic. The laws of logic cannot be found in a beaker or a test-tube. You cannot purchase a set of laws of logic on sale at Target. They are not concrete and physical. Only the transcendent, immutable, universal, and nonphysical God can provide the necessary preconditions for transcendent, immutable, universal, and nonphysical laws of logic. This demonstrates that it is impossible for the atheistic scientist to be correct in declaring nothing exists except the physical world. For even that declaration is nonphysical, hence it is false. It is impossible for God not to exist.

> They are like children sitting in the marketplace and calling to one another, saying: "We played the flute for you, and you did not dance; we mourned to you, and you did not weep." But wisdom is justified by all her children (Luke 7:31-35).

CHAPTER SIX

WHAT'S TRUE FOR YOU ISN'T TRUE FOR ME; THAT'S TRUE

> Presuppositional apologetics is... a helpful tool... With it we attempt to discover what a person believes and why they believe it. We can then draw their belief system to its logical conclusions, showing the fallacy of such a system. This is often enlightening to a nonbeliever because many have never thoroughly thought through what they believe. We can contrast their belief system with one based on Biblical truth. [1]

> I am beginning to feel that without contradiction and paradox I cannot get anywhere near that truth which will set me free. [2]

> *Se non e vero, e ben trovato* (Italian canard that means: Whether it is literally true or not, it's still true).

---

[1]. Danny Lehmann, *Bringing Them Back Alive* (Springdale, Penn.: Whitaker House, 1987), p. 46.

[2]. Madeleine L'Engle, *The Genesis Trilogy* (Colorado Springs, CO: Waterbrook Press, 1997), p. 108.

If there is no tomorrow, there is no today (Source unknown).

Heartless? Inhumane? Maybe We've Just Redefined Inhumanity Here (An *Associated Press* newspaper headline describing the despicable and nefarious action of the nurse who hit a man with her car and left him in her windshield moaning and pleading for help for over a day and ignored his cries as he died by bleeding to death in her garage).

O Dear Lord, you are equal to everyone. For you there is no distinction between your sons, friends or enemies. [3]

The law of non-contradiction is the foundation upon which all rationality is established. [4]

Freedom is slavery. Two plus two make five. [5]

Beware lest anyone cheat you through philosophy and empty deceit, according to the tradition of men, according to the basic principles of the world, and not according to Christ (Colossians 2:8).

For the weapons of our warfare are not carnal but mighty in God for pulling down strongholds, casting down arguments and every high thing that exalts itself against the knowledge of God, bringing every thought into captivity to the obedience of Christ (2 Corinthians 10:4-5).

Self-Refuting Statements

The obedient believer is one who counts the Word of God as the surest truth he knows, as his presupposition... The unbeliever is one who rejects that presupposition...

---

[3]. Swami Prabhupada, *Krishna* (NY: Bhaktivedanta, 1970), p. 123.

[4]. R.C. Sproul, John Gerstner, & Arthur Lindsey, *Classical Apologetics* (Grand Rapids, MI: Zondervan 1984), p. 72.

[5]. George Orwell, *1984* (New York, NY: Signet Classic 1949), p. 228.

> The commitment of his heart is to oppose God, and so he seeks to escape his responsibility to obey any scriptural law, including the norms of knowledge. But he cannot succeed. Indeed, he cannot even attack the law without assuming its truth, and thus his thinking is muddled. [6]

> "Your own wickedness will correct you, and your backslidings will rebuke you. Know therefore and see that it is an evil and bitter thing that you have forsaken the LORD your God, and the fear of Me is not in you," says the Lord GOD of hosts (Jeremiah 2:19).

The definition of a self-refuting statement: A universal statement that is not based on God's word. It self-destructs on its own proposition because it is a statement that invalidates itself. It is self-contradictory. If the statement is true, then it is false. A self-refuting statement is self-defeating and self-invalidating. It nullifies itself. It cannot be true, forasmuch as it is true, then it is false.

The Self-Deceived Assert Self-Refuting Statements

A self-refuting statement fails to satisfy its own premise. It is necessarily false. Nietzsche demonstrates this when he wrote this self-refuting statement: "There are many eyes. Thus there are many truths. Hence there is no truth." My question to him would be: "Is that true?" If it is, it is false, if it is not true, it is false. Thus it cannot be true. People want to be self-deceived and will assert contradictory statements to avoid the truth found in Christ. Skepticism and every non-Christian assertion will always self-destruct. What they attempt to justify confutes itself. If you will be rational, you must be a Christian to account for the preconditions of the intelligibility of reason. We do not have to go around refuting every infidel's errant proposition. It will refute itself and is destroyed by its own credentials. If their proposition contradicts the Bible, it commits philosophical suicide. There are internal inconsistencies in all non-Christian systems of philosophy and thought. They are riddled with self-contradictions. And they are self-defeating and self-voiding. The Christian

---

[6]. John Frame, *The Doctrine of The Knowledge of God* (Phillipsburg, NJ: P & R, 1987), p. 63.

faith has total certainty, and we must demonstrate that the unbeliever has total uncertainty. Any notion that is contrary to biblical thought is false.

The following list of self-refuting propositions is given to demonstrate the gaping defects that non-Christian thought is intrinsically bound. Self-nullifying statements fail to satisfy their own premise. They are necessarily false. The self-refuting statement is written first and is followed by the stultifying question or appropriate response.

• You can't know anything for sure.
Are you sure of that?

• You shouldn't judge.
Is that your judgment?

• You shouldn't push your views on others.
Are you pushing that view on me?

• There is no certainty.
Are you certain of that?

• All things are relative.
Then that statement is relative, so it is not true, thus all things are not relative. If a statement is relative then it is not binding, so all things cannot be relative.

• You can't know anything.
Do you know that?

• No one can know anything about God.
Do you know that about God? To assert that God is unknowable, is to say a lot about God.

• Everyone's opinion is equally valid.
Well, my opinion is that your opinion is wrong, so your view is false, thus not everyone's opinion is equally valid.

• What is true for you is not true for me.
Well, what is true for me is that you are wrong.

• I feel that I'm right!
I feel that I'm right, and I say you are wrong.

• Logic is just sophistry and isn't always true.
That's self-refuting because the claimant used logic to attempt to disprove logic. To declare that the law of non-contradiction isn't true, is to prove that law is true. It has to be true for the assertion to be made.

• There are no laws of logic.
The attempt to refute the laws of logic requires the employment of the laws of logic. Logic is an invariant and universal truth. The laws of logic are nonmaterial, invariant, transcendent, universal, and necessary. They require God because He is nonmaterial, immutable, transcendent, and necessary.

• The only true knowledge of reality is discovered through the positive sciences.
That statement is not true because it is not found in the positive sciences.

• We can't be married to any idea.
Are you married to that idea?

• Philosophy can add nothing to science.
Is that your philosophy for your science?

• Philosophy about science is not a meaningful enterprise.
Does that philosophical assertion of science have any meaning?

• How to Believe in Nothing and Set Yourself Free
(a title of a book).
Is that what you believe?

• Language is not useful for a definition.
Is that your definition in which you employ language?

• I can't believe in anything that I can't see or feel.
Can you see or feel the point of that statement?

• There are no wrong needs.
I need that to be wrong.

• All knowledge begins with experience.
Did you experience that?

• God is indescribable.
Is that your description of God?

• All speculations of the reality of absolutes are an illusion.
Is that statement an absolute? If it is, it is an illusion, thus it is false.

• Everything is just an illusion.
Then that statement is an illusion, so it is false, thus all things are not illusions. If people really believed this, they wouldn't look both ways when crossing the street, but they do, proving they can't consistently hold this view. They must depend on the Christian worldview.

• "Pundits all make over $50,000.00, so they can't understand anything" (Chris Matthews, wealthy pundit).
Chris, do you understand that?

• "All knowledge is confined to the realm of experience" (Immanuel Kant).
Have you experienced all knowledge?

• The whole notion of truth must be scrapped and replaced by the ongoing process of refutation.
Then that statement is not true.

• Every assertion is false.
Then that assertion is false.

• I believe only in science and the scientific method.
Is that statement scientifically testable?

• No truth is immutable.
Then that statement is mutable, so it is not true.

• True knowledge is only the knowledge which we experience.
Did you experience that statement?

• Truth can never be rationally attained but remains an elusive myth and an erroneous pre-commitment.
Then that is an elusive myth and is not true.

• True knowledge is only that knowledge that can be empirically verified.
Can you empirically verify that statement?

• Reality is not fixed, hard, and foundational.
Is that statement fixed, hard, and foundational?

• "That intelligence, when froze in dogmatic social philosophy generates a vicious cycle of blind oscillation" (John Dewey).
Is that statement frozen in dogmatic philosophy? If yes, its blind oscillation, therefore it is false.

• All reality is limited to the mind of the observer.
Then that statement is limited to the mind and not a universal truth, so it's false.

• Truth is not a boxy, dogmatic thing with hard corners attached by dogmatists.
Are you dogmatic about that?

• Truth does not consist of words, propositions or assertions that can be communicated by language.
Are those words or assertions communicated by language?

• Truth depends on your experience.
Did you experience that proposition? No. then it is false on its own terms.

• Here, we have no rules.
Is that your rule?

• Lies, lies, everywhere you turn are lies.
Is that a lie?

• We and our existences are non-existences.
Does that statement exist?

• We can only discover truth by testing and experimentation.
Are you able to test that assertion?

• Apart from mathematics, we can know nothing for sure.
Is that proposition a mathematical equation? No. Then you are providing in what you say, the very basis to reject what you say.

• I enjoy the sound of silence.
Silence is the absence of sound.

• Commit to the flames any propositions or assertions that do not contain mathematics or facts obtained from observable experiments.
Did you test that statement with experiments or does that statement contain mathematics? No. Then commit it to the flames on the basis of its own statement.

• The only genuine knowledge is obtained by the positive sciences.
Is that proposition verified by the positive sciences? No. Then it self-destructs. It saws off the limb it was sitting on.

• We can know nothing about reality.
Do you know that about reality?

•"The line of demarcation between knowledge and mere opinion is determined by one criterion: falsebility by empirical evidence, by observed phenomena" (Popper).
Did you observe that? If not, then that is just mere opinion.

• Knowledge is what our peers let us get away with saying.
Your peers have decided they will not let you get away with that statement, so it's false.

• Alexander Campbell said the following absurdity in describing the anti-creed position of the Church of Christ movement: "Our religious association is free from all mixture of human opinions and inventions of men."
Is that your human opinion?

• The only thing that is predictable is unpredictability.
Do you think that prediction is unpredictable?

• Only things that are blue are true.
Is that statement blue?

• I doubt everything.
If you tried to doubt everything, you would be clipping off the rope you're holding onto, because the notion of doubting, itself, presupposes certainty.

• Nothing can be ultimately justified.
Is that statement ultimately justified?

• There are no good reasons for holding to the belief in objective knowledge.
Is that objective knowledge?

• We cannot achieve certainty because it is based on postulates.
Are you certain about that postulate?

• Nobody's right.
Are you right about that?

- Every attempt to fashion an absolute philosophy of truth and right is a delusion.
Is that true and right?

- All I believe in are the laws of logic.
Is that statement one of the laws of logic?

- Everyone's opinion is equally valid.
Is that assertion more equal than others? My opinion is that assertion is false.

- All knowledge comes from observation.
Have you observed all knowledge? The assertion does not make possible its own ground of proof.

- The whole world is an illusion.
If that assertion was true, then it is also an illusion, so it is false. The whole world is not an illusion.

- Nothing is good or evil.
Then that statement is not good, thus it is false.

- All English sentences consist of four words.
This sentence comments on all English sentences, including itself. It fails to meet its own demands, hence it is false.

- Seen on display in a store: "I Love You Only" Valentine cards: Now available in multipacks.

- My philosophy is that if it isn't difficult, it isn't worth doing.
That is easy to say, so according to your philosophy you should not have uttered it. If you must utter it, speak it while you are crawling backwards up a mountain.

Turning the self-refuting statement on itself demonstrates that it is absurd. Suppose you walked into a public restroom and on the wall of the stall someone had written; "The proposition written on the other side is false." You step out and read what is written on that side and it says:

"The proposition on the other side of the wall is true." The self-refuting assertion, on its own grounds, demonstrates that it is false and is reduced to absurdity. If it is true, it is false. It is like trying to ride two horses going in the opposite direction at the same time. The views within the statement have assertions that lead to their own destruction. Christianity is the only system of thought that is self-consistent. All non-Christian systems are self-contradictory, inconsistent, incoherent, and self-nullifying. Beyond that, Christianity is the precondition for the intelligibility of our world and all that is in it. The attempt to refute Christianity actually concedes the inevitability of the Christian faith because Christianity has to be fully true to attempt its denial. The employment of logic and morality, in striving to refute Christianity, is an implicit acknowledgment of the absolute certainty of God. The Christian has absolute intellectual certainty. Any comment, premise, theory, or assertion that contradicts a universal truth in the Bible is self-refuting and self-impaling.

> Therefore let all the house of Israel know for certain that God has made this Jesus whom you crucified, both Lord and Christ (Acts 2:36).
>
> But Saul increased all the more in strength, and confounded the Jews who dwelt in Damascus, proving that this Jesus is the Christ (Acts 9:22).

One of the main tenets of modernity is relativism. The self-refuting philosophy that asserts "all things are relative." Another spin off: "What is true for you isn't true for me." And: "You can't know anything for sure." These are statements that cannot be true because they invalidate themselves. If they were true, they are false (see the list above). Allan Bloom, in his insightful book *The Closing of the American Mind*, bemoans the fact that "there is one thing a professor can be absolutely certain of: almost every student entering the university believes, or says he believes, that truth is relative." [7] I have to agree with Mr. Bloom. I have found (having spent much time exchanging ideas on university campuses across America) the only thinking tool most students have developed is the art of avoiding the tough questions. They declare that all things are relative out of one side of their mouth. Then they defend environmentalism as if it is always true, out of the other side of their mouth. They know that relativism

---

[7]. Allan Bloom, *The Closing of the American Mind* (NY: Simon and Schuster, 1987), p. 25.

is not true! Obviously, relativism is a self-voiding notion. They just do not want to be tough minded and think life's important issues through. The responsibility of the believer is to show them the folly of anything that opposes the truth of Christ, including relativism.

Everyone Has An Opinion

> Pronounce them guilty, O God! Let them fall by their own counsels; Cast them out in the multitude of their transgressions, For they have rebelled against You (Psalms 5:10).

If your friends, loved ones, or witnessing contacts throw the slogan around: All things are relative; ask them whether mistreating slaves is wrong, or murdering homosexuals is wrong, or dumping nuclear waste in the ocean is wrong? Almost every relativist will agree that those things are wrong. At this point, they are not relativists. The Christian can objectively decry the mistreatment of humans and the environment since we know that God told us not to abuse people and nature. Those who deny absolute truth and values cannot live within the boundaries of that philosophy. No one can consistently live out a life based on relativism. They will stand for something. Just ask them what they think is important in our society. They will name: racism, human rights, the right to vote, or something that is of great value to them. Once they assert that something should be done or not done, they have borrowed from the Christian worldview. No other worldview can give an unchanging, perpetual, universal, and absolute standard for ethics and morality. All systems of ethics and science will ultimately be relativistic except for Christianity. The Christian ethical law is based on the eternal, unchanging, and absolute nature of God. All other systems are based on opinion, the opinion of the masses or the men of letters. Either way, it is their opinion and opinions change. There are some absolutes, some things that are immutably true, some things that are not subject to an opinion.

Absolutes are established on God's nature and His law. If someone tries to assert that there are no absolutes, he must use an absolute statement. This, as we have now learned, is self-impaling. If it is true, it is false. The only absolutes that are not self-refuting are those from God. So anytime a relativist asserts that something is true universally and immutably, they are wrong because their own worldview cannot provide unchanging, universal, and absolute truth. That is devastating. And the truth found in Christ devastates and demolishes all vain imaginations.

> Casting down arguments and every high thing that exalts itself against the knowledge of God, bringing every thought into captivity to the obedience of Christ (2 Corinthians 10:4,5).

Dr. Robert Morey dismisses atheism with a very powerful illustration. Morey instructs the atheist to put a dot on a piece of paper. He tells the atheist that the dot represents himself. He then tells him to draw a circle around the dot. Morey goes on to explain, "Inside the circle is all you know. Everything that you have ever learned." He asks the atheist, "How much knowledge would you say you know?" Morey then tells him to "put one percent in the circle." He explains that this is a much larger amount than the atheist really knows. "But lets say this is what you know. Now how much knowledge is outside the circle?" The atheist responds, "Ninety-nine percent." Morey then places an X outside the circle. He then puts the atheist on the spot and poses the problem: "This X represents God. Is it possible that God exists in that ninety-nine percent of the knowledge that you admit you do not have?" The atheist has to answer, "Yes" or run. He is now a professed agnostic and no longer can claim to be an atheist. The point of the illustration: It is impossible for a true atheist to exist. This exercise totally debunks the idea of atheism. Philosophically, atheism is impossible because it is possible for God to exist in a sphere beyond our limited personal contact. Only a being who is omnipresent would know that there is no God, everywhere. Only God can be omnipresent, thus this would require the being to be God.

Answering an Attack

Ingersoll promulgated the following Bible attack list. The refutation is written under his false statement:

> 1. The Bible is cruel.
> Response: By what standard do you measure cruelty? Deny God's word and you deny the possibility for morality including a standard that can claim that something is cruel.

2. The Bible is impure.
Response: By what standard do you measure purity? Deny God's word and you deny the possibility for moral purity including claiming something is impure. Purity presupposes God. God and His word are the precondition for purity.

3. The Bible is contradictory.
Answer: This statement assumes the laws of logic. Logic presupposes God. Deny God and you deny logic, which is self-refuting.

4. The Bible is unscientific.
Answer: Science assumes induction. Induction presupposes God. Deny God and you must deny induction, which is the foundation for science.

God is True

> Jesus said to him, "I am the way, the truth, and the life" (John 14:6).

> In the matter of just and unjust, fair and foul, good and evil, which are the subjects of our present consultation, ought we follow the opinion of many and to fear them; or the opinion of the many who has understanding? (Plato quoting Socrates).

> Let God be true and every man a liar (Rom. 3:4).

To have a consistent and functional worldview, one must have absolute standards and laws. If one asserts laws that do not come from God's revealed word, these assertions will be self-contradictory and self-defeating. When the non-Christian claims that there are no absolutes, he is asserting an absolute standard and a law. A standard that is self-stultifying. The statement: There are no absolutes, is an absolute statement. This statement is a contradiction and is self-refuting. For it to be true, it would have to be false. Therefore it can only be false. There must be absolutes in logic and in morality, or we can assert nothing and account for nothing. That is impossible.

Unchanging standards do not reside in matter. They cannot be empirically quantified, examined, or put into a flask. They cannot be conventions or subjective theories made up by mutable man. The absolutes of ethics transcend time, space, and matter; they cannot be tested in a lab. But all labs assume absolutes and use them in all their science. They cannot solely be the result of neuron firings in the brain because that would make them mutable and by definition they would not be laws. The material-only atheist cannot explain where laws come from or justify them. If one claims there are no absolutes, one is employing absolutes to make this claim. Again, this means the claim is self-negating.

Discussion on Truth

It has been spun: "Reality is that which doesn't go away when you stop thinking about it." There is a real reality. The contrary is impossible. When a person claims that there is no reality, he is a real person talking to another real person, which presupposes reality. Yet many deceived people attempt to deny the undeniable. The following is a conversation I had with a young man who professed not to believe in absolute truth:

> Mike: Hello, here is a tract that will tell you about God.
>
> Jim: Well, I have my own religion. I believe that everyone has their own truth, and you shouldn't push your religion on others.
>
> Mike: How do you know that's true?
>
> Jim: I believe it's true.
>
> Mike: How do you know that?
>
> Jim: I just know it for me. There is no truth out there anyway.
>
> Mike: Is that true?
>
> Jim: Well, I told you that I do not want you pushing your religion down my throat.

Mike: As of this moment, I haven't told you anything about Jesus Christ. I haven't told you that you have broken God's law by not keeping the Ten Commandments and that you and I, without Jesus, are doomed to hell for lying, stealing, cheating, avoiding Church, using ungodly anger, coveting, and many other sins. I did not exhort you to repent and trust in Christ. I did not recount the glories of His death and resurrection. Now I have, and I haven't "pushed" it down your throat.

Jim: I don't believe a word of what you said. I told you there is nothing that is true.

Mike: Again, I ask you, is that true?

Jim: Ah…

Mike: And how do you know that there is no truth?

Jim: I just do.

Mike: On your worldview, one could not forbid the torture of minorities, and the plundering of third-world countries by the superpower nations. If there is no truth, you cannot declare that anything is right or wrong. And you will have to give up science, medicine, school, governments, and everything else that is assumed to be "true."

Jim: No, I believe that the West is wrong when it subjugates third-world countries and rapes their natural resources.

Mike: Why is that wrong? By what standard do you assert that anything is wrong?

Jim: Well, it just is.

Mike: It just is? You cannot account for your claim. You must live strictly on blind irrational faith. Let me ask you another question: Where does mathematics come from?

Jim: I don't know.

Mike: Where do the laws of logic come from?

Jim: I don't know.

Mike: Where does your personality come from?

Jim: I don't know and I do not care!

Mike: It is very apparent that you do not have any answers. You should humble yourself and learn from God's word.

Jim: I don't believe in that.

Mike: That's strange because the Bible can supply all the answers to the questions you cannot answer. Yet you want to avoid the Bible.

Jim: I have my opinion and you have yours.

Mike: Not really. My opinion is based on God's word. His word is the precondition for logic, science, mathematics, morality, and personhood. God's pure word alone provides the necessary preconditions for all the questions and answers in life. You, in contrast, have no answers for anything. It's not a matter of opinions; it's a matter of truth. You do not have the truth. God's word is the truth.

Jim: Well, I'll just do my best.

Mike: You need to turn from your ways, flee to Jesus and away from hell. Christ will save your soul and transform your life. Christianity will also supply the only worldview that can give you a foundation for declaring evil actions as evil and truth as true. Without Christ, you have proven you cannot make sense out of this world. You are living in an inconsistent and messed-up worldview, and you need to come to Christ.

Jim: No thank you.

Mike: You are now left in a life philosophy that can supply no answers, no truth, and no morals. I have demonstrated that your view of life is self-refuting and absurd, and it will lead you to hell. Is this what you want?

Jim: I'm happy where I am.

Mike: Well, read that tract when you have a chance. I will pray for you.

Is There a Right and Wrong?

Many of the unredeemed are relativists who believe that no one is right or wrong, and that morality is based on individual taste. This is a huge problem in America and the West. The following is a fictitious conversation compiled by commingling many real conversations I have had in the market place:

Christian: The Bible instructs humanity that homosexual acts are evil.

Relativist: I believe that there is no right or wrong. And you should not push your morals on me.

Christian: Do you think that I am wrong in doing that?

Relativist: Yes!

Christian: Well, you just insisted that there is no right or wrong, yet you scolded me, and told me that I was wrong in my moral view about homosexuality.

Relativist: I just think that you shouldn't force your morality on me.

Christian: Are you forcing that moral view on me?

Relativist: OK. You shouldn't push your moral views on others.

Christian: Why not?

Relativist: Because it is wrong.

Christian: Again, I remind you that you said that there is no right or wrong.

Relativist: I only insist that you don't push your morality on others.

Christian: Are you still pushing that morality on me? And are you saying that we should let large industrial corporations burn down the rain forests?

Relativist: No way; that would be evil!

Christian: Would you want to push that morality on those big corporations that want to burn down the rain forests and damage the environment? If you claim that there is no right or wrong, you are also saying that the abuse of women, the murder of children, and the enslavement of minorities is acceptable. But you need to know that discussing morals is not a game. If we reject God's word, we are left with sinful men making personal moral decisions based on selfish gain. There must be moral absolutes to distinguish virtue from vice, right from wrong, and good from evil. If there is no objective moral standard, all manner of evil will flourish.

God is an Exact God

The triune God of glory is an exact God. Precision, truth, and judgment presuppose an exact God. Only the God of the Bible is exact and true. God's geometry is exact, there is a square, square; a triangular, triangle; a circular, circle. Geometry presupposes a transcendent God because nowhere in our physical universe can one find a perfect square, triangle, or circle. They exist in the perfect state in theory. They exist only in theory. Yet mathematics has proven, in theory, that there are perfect squares, circles, and triangles. Why do we have an abstract principle that does not exist in the physical world? An atheist cannot give an answer to this problem. Ask the skeptic: "Why are there not perfect geometric entities in our world when they exist in theory?" The only objective basis one can find for perfect circles, squares, and triangles, is a perfect God who transcends our non-perfect world. Mathematical theorems assert that there are infinite numbers. Yet there is nothing infinite in our physical world. Infinite numbers do not exist in our physical reality. Only an infinite God can justify the truth of infinite numbers.

God is also the precondition for time. Everyone knows that time exists in past, present, and future. We believe that time passes. This may appear to be self-evident. But time can only be justified by presupposing God. It is 11:55 and 57 seconds. Before the secondhand hits 58 seconds, the second can go infinitely forward, and this can seemingly never end. 57.1 seconds, then 57.2, 57.3, and on and on. I can break that time down by asking: Did it ever become 11:55 and 57.1 seconds? 57.12 seconds? Yes. 57.123…, and on and on, in an infinite progression. Hence without the triune God, as the source and foundation for the one and many, I cannot even account for time. Without the infinite God, who is the foundation for infinite numbers, the non-Christian cannot solve this paradox. This is not a problem for the Trinitarian whereas he believes in an infinite and eternal God. Non-Christians use infinite numbers, yet these numbers have no end, hence they do not comport with their worldview. One must presuppose the triune God. The unbeliever cannot even account for time. Each second, God is an exact God, and time presupposes this God.

The Mire of Mere Assertion

People can declare anything they want. The mere declaration does not make it true. If you borrowed ten thousand dollars from a relativist and when it was time to pay them back, you told them that the ten thousand dollars was just twenty dollars to you. All things are relative! Ten thousand dollars may be true to you, but it is not true for me. Twenty dollars is. This approach will bring out the inconsistencies of the relativist, as well as a red and livid face. As the steam is blowing out of his ears, ask him whether you can drop a fifty-pound rock on his foot since the rock, to you, is light as a feather? He will not go for that anymore than he will allow you to not pay him all the money you owe him. He may state that all things are relative, and what is true for me, is not true for you, but he cannot live out his worldview. The Christian can. We know that God has commanded us not to steal. And that He has made our world so what is ultimately true, is true for everyone. One plus one is always two, no matter who you are or where you are. Mathematics and all absolutes are justified from God.

People can assert anything. The mere assertion itself does not make it true. The assertion must be justified and valid to be true. Without the Bible, one cannot justify anything. God's word alone supplies truth and the means to discern truth.

Below I have recorded a conversation with a gentleman who was stuck in the "mire of mere assertion":

> Mike: How's it going? Do you have a moment to talk about God?
>
> George: The cosmos is God
>
> Mike: How do you know that? That statement is arbitrary.
>
> George: Well, the Christian God is false.
>
> Mike: How do you know that?
>
> George: The Bible has been corrupted through the ages.
>
> Mike: How do you know that?
>
> George: We know UFO's have come and the backwards people of the Bible thought that the aliens were God.
>
> Mike: How do you know that? That statement is arbitrary.
>
> George: Well, the pyramids tell us that aliens came and seeded the earth.
>
> Mike: Again, how do you know that?
>
> George: I hate getting into religious quarrels. All religions are basically the same anyway.
>
> Mike: How do you know that? That statement is also arbitrary.

George: You keep saying that!

Mike: Yes. Anytime a person asserts something that is not based on the truth of the Bible, that assertion is unjustifiable. They will be stuck in the mire of mere assertion. One's assertion doesn't make anything true. If anyone says something contrary to scripture, all I have to ask them: "How do you know that?" They will have no way to account for their opinions, when those opinions conflict with God's word. And your assertions are just the opinion of a man, and they are arbitrary and cannot be rationally justified.

George: Well, that's just your opinion.

Mike: No, my worldview is based on the Holy Bible. The Bible provides justification for my beliefs. It is impossible for the Bible not to be true. Without God's word you cannot account for logic, reason, morality, induction, love, and mathematics. God is the precondition for the intelligibility of this world. All assertions must be based on God's word and the principles that come from it.

George: The Bible is not the only truth.

Mike: How do you know that?

George: I'll see you later.

Mike: Think about what I said, without God you cannot account for anything in this world. Jesus is the truth. I'll pray someday you will turn and trust in Him.

I have had many conversations like the one listed above. This is a good way to demonstrate to the unbeliever that his opinion is meaningless and absurd if it conflicts with scripture. If you are ever at a loss for an answer to a skeptic, just keep gently asking the person: "How do you know that?" This question will demonstrate that the unbeliever has no justifiable answers. His claims are arbitrary.

Autonomous Reason

Mankind has demonstrated throughout history its propensity to attempt to rely on autonomous reason. We desire to rule ourselves, without God's revelation, by depending on reason alone. Yes, we should think and behave "rationally." We are logically obligated to be rational. As soon as you attempt to deny reason, you must use reason to assert that denial. A man cannot deny his rational nature without refuting himself. He must resort to employing reason, even in the vain attempt to resist rationality. One, no matter how much philosophical ingenuity he employs in denying reason, must always use reason to do so. And the only foundation for reason is God and His revelation. Deny God and one has no immutable source of reason and logic. This is no empty claim. Without God there is no reason to trust our reason, which, again, is self-refuting. We can trust human reason when it is built on the foundation of God and His revelation.

An Alien Experiment?

The trouble with the worldview of non-belief is it cannot account for any idea or object in the universe. The nonbeliever cannot prove that he is not just a super hi-tech computer chip in an alien Pentium computer. An entity that does not really exist, only thinks he does. A matrix machine that believes it is a human. If you ask an unbeliever: How does he know that he is not an alien computer chip? He cannot give you proof, unless he presupposes the truth of scripture. The Bible reveals who we are, and what God's plan is for mankind. And it is impossible for the Bible not to be true. All my questions and speculations, and even science fiction writing, presuppose that God lives, and He has revealed himself to men.

Many atheists attempt to label religious faith as a crutch. They charge that theists are afraid of death, and God is just a projection of our own needs to comfort that fear. Again, any statement regarding anything, for it to be rational, God must live. With the skeptic, always tout the truth that God is the precondition for any investigation or rational discourse. The claim that Jesus is a crutch, in one sense is true, but I would go even further. Jesus is not just my crutch; He is my wheelchair. Without His grace and strength, I could not live a full and healthy life. When a nonbeliever pushes the psycho-babble assertion that the only reason we believe is because of fear or psychological weakness, we can turn this argument around on him. That type of statement is a double-edged sword. I tell the unbeliever that they reject God because of fear. They know hell exists, and they are afraid of its reality, so they convince themselves that God doesn't exist. They do this for the comfort of their minds. God's nonexistence is a projection of their minds because of fear, so they actively suppress the truth of God in their mind. Darwin said that Christianity was a "damnable doctrine" because he despised the thought of hell.

> Serpents, brood of vipers! How can you escape the condemnation of hell? (Matthew 23:33).

The foundation for absolutes is only found in scripture. The Bible is true. Christianity alone can account for logic and reason. No other worldview can supply the preconditions needed for discerning truth. The Bible must be true if anything is true. Numerous self-deceivers, infidels, profligates, and wreckers have assaulted scripture. Paine, a real cultural pain, rolled up his sleeves and exerted much labor against scripture (as if he received high commissions for his critiques). Yet, when he was confronted and asked whether he owned a Bible, he admitted that he did not have one in his house or study. Many have tried to destroy the Holy Bible: Hume, Voltaire, and Russell have all tried their hand at it. All their critical essays and books are in reality faith builders for the Christian. Their writings fortify our faith forasmuch as all their criticisms presuppose God and scripture. Thus their attacks against the Bible need the Bible to furnish an ultimate foundation that allows them to issue their arguments. The God of Holy Writ is the necessary precondition to be able to argue intelligibly. He is the precondition of all criticisms and intellectual attacks. Calvin said of scripture, "The beauties of scholars and philosophers will almost entirely disappear; so that it is easy to perceive something divine in sacred scripture, which far surpasses the highest attainments and ornaments of human industry." That is true. But it is beyond that. All philosophy, even errant philosophy, presupposes God and His revelation. Without God, one cannot justify the use of reason, logic, and ethics that the godly and ungodly philosophers marshal in their postulations and theories.

One needs God to attempt to refute God. Chesterton said, "To disbelieve in God would be like waking up in the morning, looking in the mirror and seeing nothing." To see and to understand anything, one must stand on the Christian worldview. God must be, or we cannot make sense of any fundamental phenomenon. No wonder the infidel philosopher John Stuart Mill acknowledged on his death bed that this philosophy never gave him any "peace, comfort, or consolation." He admitted that his life that opposed

Christianity was a failure. An unbeliever, when asked to account for logic or morality, can only say: "They just are," or: "They are solely the result of molecules and motion; the physical world alone gave us these nonphysical dynamics." These statements cannot be true because that would mean they are not universally or unalterably true; logic and morality would have no transcendent foundation, which undermines everything they assert. All their propositions would be unintelligible, self-refuting, and untrue. Christianity is true, and any attempt to refute it will always lead to rational self-destruction. The non-Christian cannot contend against God in view of the fact that he has fighting instruments that come only from the Christian arsenal. He has to unsheathe God's logic, morality, and induction to battle God. He needs God to propose anything that opposes God. Deny God and all is unintelligible. It is impossible for the Christian faith not to be true.

It is Impossible for God Not to Exist

It is impossible for God not to exist. He is the precondition for the intelligibility of all reality. It is not just that our DNA code presupposes thought, and thought, a thinker. It is not just that the universe appears to be designed, and a design presupposes a designer; and a plan, a planner. I believe and affirm all this. But I am a Christian, and everything I see in the world is proof for God's existence. The skeptic does not hold the same presuppositions as I do. Hume demonstrated the fallacy of arguing for God's existence using proofs. It is brain straining to believe, as atheists do, that something came from nothing, order came from chaos, harmony came from discord, and life came from non-life. I do not have enough faith to believe in such nonsense. I do not believe that our solar system is an accident any more than a wristwatch is one. But this is not convincing to a skeptic who holds atheistic presuppositions. God exists, and it is impossible for Him not to exist. Even the discussion of His existence presupposes that God lives. Without God, one cannot account for the logic used in any conversation regarding the existence of God.

The Bible does not lead us to believe there is enough evidence that gives one a good rational reason for confidence there is a God. God is not a probability: He is alive. And He is the precondition for all rational thought. He is not a mere probability. He must live, or everything is meaningless and absurd, which would mean that statement is absurd, so it is fallacious. God lives, and He doesn't need any proof. Everything is proof. There is no doubt in my mind that God is there, and He is not silent. Even if I fall into doubt, my doubt uses logic, so even my doubt presupposes God. It's like the story of the little girl; who was being grilled for believing in the Bible and the story of Jonah. She said to the scoffer, "I believe every word in the Bible. I know Jonah survived in the belly of a whale, and I will ask him how he survived when I get to heaven and see him there." The skeptic then asked her, "What if Jonah isn't there?" She replied, "Then you ask him." Simple faith is not just simple; it's also powerful. God gives us faith and without Him and His word, nothing in the world is intelligible.

Evil Presupposes God's Law

> God has been conceived as the foundation of the metaphysical situation with its ultimate activity. If this conception be adhered to, there can be no alternative except to discern in Him the origin of evil as well as good. [8]

The argument: If God were all good and all powerful, He would defeat evil; evil exists, thus God does not exist. This is a fallacious argument. Inasmuch as this argument presupposes God. The argument itself depends on God's existence. Even an argument against God's existence, depends upon the Lord to propose it. The argument from evil that attempts to disprove God's existence utilizes logic, morality, and a distinction between good and evil. God is the precondition for logic and morality. He is the basis for making a distinction between good and evil. Without God, everything just is. There can be no objective moral truths. There can be no truths. When a man asserts good and evil, he presupposes that God lives.

Many atheists frame the argument of evil like this:

> 1. If God is all good and all powerful He would defeat evil.
> 2. Evil is not defeated.
> 3. Therefore God does not exist.

The transcendental argument demonstrates that this argument presupposes God. But the syllogism itself is not even valid. A Christian

[8]. Alfred North Whitehead, *Science and the Modern World* (NY: Free Press, 1925), p. 179

should never accept the syllogism as it is written above. The way we should pose the formula:

1. If God is all good and all powerful He can defeat evil.
2. Evil is not yet defeated.
3. Therefore God will defeat evil in the future.

The Bible testifies that one day, God will rinse the world of evil. Evil will be defeated. When one makes an argument, one has God as the ultimate ground for the logic that is employed in the argument, including an argument from evil. The Christian is to examine the argument, and only accept it if it is consistent with the teaching of scripture. The atheist has no way of knowing, in the future, God will not defeat evil. The believer has God's word on it. The atheist is left holding an empty bag, a bag that God made. The grounds, from which an atheist attacks God, are based on God's revelation. The atheist has to borrow from the Christian worldview to attempt to disprove God. Only in the context of the Christian worldview is good and evil intelligible. The existence of God is well beyond just a reasonable proof. God is the foundation for knowing anything at all. Deny God, and a man cannot make sense out of anything, including good and evil.

Give Answers with Meekness and Respect

We must never respond to questions about evil in a nonchalant, callous or detached way. We must have compassion for those who struggle with this paradox. Many of those, who focus on this question, have lost loved ones through criminal actions, disease, or natural disasters. A post September eleventh Barna survey found:

• Those who believe in an all-powerful, all knowing God dropped from 72% pre-attack to 68% afterward.

• Confidence in absolute moral truths dropped from 38% to 22%.

People are emotional. Both lost people and saved people live on emotions. We are instructed by scripture to be ready to give a defense of our hope with meekness, gentleness, and respect.

Truth can transform, and it is beautiful. Love rejoices in the truth, but truth is more than this. Truth is fully true, and it is not false. There are real and true things that are objectively true; regardless whether we like them or not. We should stand for the truth, but with the understanding that our witness is not just an academic debate. There are real, hard hitting, and unpleasant issues we must tackle with love and humility. We must care. I pray over and over that I would care for people. I ask God to give me compassion. Jesus' ministry was known for its compassionate thrust. Truth should always be enjoined with love and humility. Often, people will have stern intellectual problems with Christianity, yet, when you answer them with love and truth, they will melt and almost brake down in tears. Jesus wants His followers to touch minds and hearts. The Holy Spirit is the Comforter. He comes when we minister to the lost, and He touches them in the depth of their souls. The individual's problem with evil is usually a spiritual and emotional problem more than an intellectual one.

There Must Be Certainty

If the Christian worldview is not true, then knowledge is impossible. The only way to avert skepticism is to have an unchanging, infinite, infallible, and exhaustive authority. The God of the Bible alone has these attributes. The statement that "knowledge is impossible" is a claim of knowledge, hence it is false. God is the precondition for intellectual certainty. And there must be certainty. The statement that asserts that there is no certainty is self-refuting because it claims certainty. There must be a certain, immutable, and infallible authority. That authority is God Almighty. Other starting points are self-contradictory.

Only Christianity supplies the foundation that is necessary for logic, science, moral standards, and mathematics. Non-Christian systems of thought cannot furnish a foundation for the law of non-contradiction. Thus those systems of thought can only offer a self-nullifying worldview. The true God is the primordial requirement for all knowledge, proof, evidence, and logic. It is impossible for God not to exist. He is the precondition for the intelligibility of reality. He is the universal and necessary rational given. The non-corporeal, transcendent, timeless and immutable God supplies the necessary preconditions for the use of non-corporeal, transcendent, timeless, universal, and immutable logic. To argue at all, you must presuppose that God lives. Non-believing thought cannot supply the necessary preconditions for the laws of logic. Hence it results in futility because of the internal contradictions that it supplies. Therefore the contrary of Christianity is impossible. All other worldviews fall into absurdity inasmuch as they are self-contradictory. They lead to conclusions that contradict their own primal assumptions. Without God, nothing can make sense. The true and living God is the pre-essential for knowledge, and for the understanding of all human experience. Christianity is the inescapable truth. It alone provides the preconditions for the universal and unchanging laws of logic. Universal and certain claims are unavoidable, and Christianity alone provides the preconditions for universal and certain claims, thus Christianity must be true.

CHAPTER SEVEN

THE TRINITY: THE SOLUTION NOT THE PROBLEM

> Science has gone a very long way towards proving the essential unity of all phenomena. [1]

> The Absolute may explain everything; it cannot explain anything in particular. [2]

> We really believe that the deity is tri-personal - not mono-personal, but tri-personal. The doctrine teaches that there are three persons in the one Godhead, and not one. [3]

> If it is necessary in our thinking about God to move to a position beyond naturalism and supra-naturalism, this is no less important in our thinking about Christ. Otherwise, we shall be shut up… to a sterile choice between the two. [4]

---

1. Julian Huxley, *Religion without Revelation* (NY, NY: Mentor Books, 1957), p. 45.
2. Walter Kaufmann, *Critique of Religion and Philosophy* (Garden City, NY: Anchor Books, 1961), p. 127.
3. John Gerstner, *Theology in Dialogue* (Morgan, PA: Soli Deo Gloria, 1996), p. 42.
4. John A.T. Robinson, *Honest to God* (Philadelphia, PA: Westminster Press, 1963), p. 64.

For, in the name of God, the Father and the Lord of the universe, and of our Savior Jesus Christ, and of the Holy Spirit, they receive the washing with water (Justin Martyr's First Apology, LXI).

Thus the connection of the Father in the Son, and the Son in the Paraclete, produces three coherent Persons, who are yet distinct One from Another. These Three are one essence, not one Person, as it is said, "I and my Father are One," in respect to unity of substance, not singularity of number (Tertullian on the Trinity).

We believe in one God, the Father Almighty, maker of all things… And in one Lord Jesus Christ, the Son of God, begotten of the Father; that is, of the essence of the Father, God of God, Light of Light, very God of very God… being of one substance with the Father… And in the Holy Spirit (The Nicene Creed).

The Trinity also means that God's creation can be both one and many. Secular philosophy veers between the two extremes of monism (the world is really one & plurality is an illusion) and pluralism (the world is radically disunited and unity is an illusion). Secular philosophy moves from one extreme to the other because it does not have the resources to define a position between the two extremes, and because it seeks an absolute extreme or another-as if there must be an absolute oneness (with no plurality) or else a universe of unique, unconnected elements, creating an absolute pluralism and destroying universal oneness… But the Christian knows there is no absolute unity (devoid of plurality) or absolute plurality (devoid of unity)… The Christian knows that God is the only absolute, and that the absolute is both one and many. Thus we are freed from the task of trying to find utter unity or utter disunity… When we search for ultimate criteria or standards, we look… to the living God. [5]

[5]. John M. Frame, *Apologetics to the Glory of God* (Phillipsburg, NJ: P & R, 1994), p. 40-50.

The Scriptural Support

There are numerous scriptures that reveal to man that God is three persons in one God. This is important since there are many cults and false religions that appeal to the Bible in their attempt to deny the Trinity. The following scriptures are some of the key passages on the doctrine of the Trinity. I will offer a very incomplete list. I recommend that you read some apologetic books on the Trinity and some books on the cults. Ron Rhodes has written a couple of fine books on the cults that discuss the Trinity at length. Dr. Robert Morey's book on the Trinity is the best I have ever read on that doctrine.

Some of the tri-unity scripture verses:

Genesis 1:26, 3:22, 11:6; Psalms 45:6-7;
Isaiah 6:8, 48:11-17; Hosea 1:7;
Zechariah 10:12, 12:10;
Matthew 28:19; 2 Corinthians 13:14.

Bible verses that reveal that God is one:

Deuteronomy 6:4; Isaiah 43:10, 44:6, 45:5-6, 48:3-16.

The scriptures that reveal that the Father is God:

Matt. 6:8; John 4:23, 17:3; 1 John 2:23.

The verses of Holy Writ that teach that Jesus is God:

John 1:1, 8:58, 10:30; Hebrews 1; Isaiah 9:6, 7:14; Colossians 1:15; Acts 20:28.

And without controversy great is the mystery of godliness: God was manifest in the flesh, justified in the Spirit, seen of angels, preached unto the Gentiles, believed on in the world, received up into glory (1 Timothy 3:16).

> And Thomas answered and said unto him, "My Lord and my God" (John 20:28).
>
> Behold, he comes with clouds; and every eye shall see him, and they also which pierced him: and all kindreds of the earth shall wail because of him. Even so, Amen. I am Alpha and Omega, the beginning and the ending, says the Lord, who is, and who was, and who is to come, the Almighty (Revelation 1:7-8).
>
> The Bible verses that instruct us that the Holy Spirit is God:
>
> Acts 10:19-20, 13:2, 21:11; 1 Corinthians 12:11; Galatians 4:6; John 15:26, 16:7; Micah 2:7; Isaiah 61:1, 63:10-11; Psalms 55:11, 139:7.
>
> Then the Spirit said unto Philip, "Go near, and join thyself to this chariot" (Acts 8:29).

Most of the cults teach that Jesus is heter-ousia: a different substance or essence from the Father. But the Bible declares that Jesus is one with the Father (John 10:30). The Trinity is reasonable. However, I do not fully understand God's nature due to the fact that there will always remain some mystery about the being of God. Mysteries are not contradictions. The one true God is the Father, Son, and Holy Spirit.

The Attacks on the Mystery of God

Many non-Christian religions and philosophies attack the Trinity as a contradiction. They declare that the doctrine of the Trinity breaks the law of non-contradiction. Hume, Russell, Kant, Muhammad, and Jefferson were critical of the Christian God. Kant declared that the Trinity "provides nothing… even if one claims to understand it." Jefferson scoffed, "When we have done away with the incomprehensible jargon of the Trinitarian arithmetic… we shall then be… worthy disciples." The reason for the mocking and irritation is the unbeliever's mind is darkened and they apply the wrong arithmetic. Everyone knows that one plus one plus one, equals three. Not one. But what does one multiplied by one and multiplied by one, equals? One. The Trinity is a mystery. It is not what someone of old quipped: "a riddle wrapped up in a puzzle and buried in an enigma."

God is three persons in one being. God in His Almightiness is a mystery. We do not know how the doctrine of the tri-unity of God works. We just know that the Trinity is true and without the Trinity, as the one true God, we cannot make sense out of anything. Reject the Trinity and you cannot account for personhood, love, equality, mathematics, justice, morality, and logic. The Trinitarian nature of God is the precondition for understanding reality and truth. Many Christians recoil at defending the Trinity because they think it is a contradiction and a problem. It is not. It is the solution. The Father is God, the Son is God, and the Holy Spirit is God. And there is only one God, three persons in one being. This concept does not break any of the laws of logic. If the doctrine taught that there are three persons in one person, or three beings in one being that would be a contradiction. The Bible teaches that there are three persons in one being. This doctrine is a mystery, not a contradiction. The Trinity violates no known law of logic. And remember, the mathematics of the triune God is not one plus one plus one, equals one. It is one times one times one, equals one.

> We worship one God in Trinity, and Trinity in Unity; neither confounding the Persons: nor dividing the Substance. For there is one Person of the Father: another of the Son: and another of the Holy Spirit. But the godhead of the Father, and the Son, and the Holy Spirit, is all one: the Glory equal, the Majesty co-eternal (Excerpt from the Athanasian Creed).

The modern Jewish religion, Islam, and the Jehovah Witnesses proclaim that God is an absolute one, a monad, a unitarian deity. The famous Rabbi Rashi, in his commentary on the third day of creation, taught that before God created the universe: "He was *yachid ba' olam*: all alone." Only the Christian God, the true God, did not create out of necessity, but out of liberty. He is self-existent, He has aseity and needs nothing. God does not need the creation to have someone to care about and love. Within God Himself, He is love and "love happens." God is a noun and a verb. He is a triune being who is actively involved within Himself and His creation. He is stupendous, magnificent, and resplendent in His infinite triune glory. A god who has "needs" is not perfect and infinite. That god cannot possibly exist. It is not just reasonable to believe in the deity of Christ and the triune nature of God, the contrary is impossible. God is Trinity. The Trinity is a mystery among us, and above us, and beyond us. He dwells within all Christians by faith, and this mystery is the key to understanding our world. The sundry religious theories about God demonstrate the ineptness of man's unaided reason. Without God's revelation in His word, all man-made religions create a god who is a divine monad, or the plural pantheon of gods in polytheism. Mankind needs revelation to discover the only true and living God.

God is a self-complete and self-contained unity. There is but one God. God is an absolute personality. There are three persons in the Godhead, the Father, the Son, and the Holy Spirit. Within the being of God, diversity is no more fundamental than unity. God is a tri-unity. The persons of the one God are mutually eternal and exhaustive of one another. The Holy Spirit and the Son are ontologically equal with God the Father. This is the solution to the problem of the "one and the many." We baptize in the name (singular) of the Father, the Son, and the Holy Spirit (plurality). The unity of the particulars is grounded in the being of God. There is a unity and a diversity in God and there is a unity and diversity in the cosmos. The cosmos is called the universe. It is a unity and a diversity. A unity and a diversity make up the physical reality. The cosmos has unity that is on par with the diversity because in the nature of the triune God there are no particulars not in equal relationship with the universals. There is nothing universal that is not equally ultimate in the particulars. God said, "Let us (plural) make man in our (plural) image (singular) and our (plural) likeness (singular)." No aspect of the universe is more ultimate than the other. The unity in the universe is equal with the diversity in the universe. They are equal because the triune God created and sustains them. All non-Christian worldviews sacrifice the unity for the diversity or the diversity for the unity. Only God in three persons can provide the solution to the problem of "the one and the many." Thus other systems of thought are false.

God in Trinity as the only Starting Point

> There are three persons in the Godhead: the Father, the Son, and the Holy Spirit and these three are one God; the same in substance, equal in power and glory (Westminster Shorter Catechism).

> And this is eternal life, that they may know You, the only true God, and Jesus Christ whom You have sent (John 17:3).

The God of the Bible in Trinity is the starting point for epistemology, apologetics, and philosophy. The triune God is reflected and revealed everywhere in the material and nonmaterial worlds. The Trinity "confronts" humanity and all creation everywhere at all times. You cannot look into a microscope or a telescope or a mathematical table and fail to be confronted by the God alone who is the Father, the Son, and the Holy Spirit. The triune God is the foundation and the solution to the problem of the one and the many. God is the solution and not the problem. Within the being of the triune God: unity and diversity, the one and the many are equally ultimate and infinite.

We see God in His triune nature revealed from Genesis to the book of Revelation. We must declare the truth of the Father, Son, and Holy Spirit, one God in three persons, the blessed Trinity. He is not the god of the philosophers or the pagan religions. God is the Alpha and Omega, the First and the Last. We must affirm, trust, and love the true and living God. The triune God is the solution that makes sense out of everything in the world. This is one reason the believer is to study theology. Theology is the study of God. Many Christians confess that they dislike theology and try to avoid it. John Muether wrote in the journal *Modern Reformation*, "For many people theology is like underwear - you need it, so you are glad you have it on, but you sure hope it doesn't show." [6] But the foundation for all reality, and understanding that reality, is the triune nature of God. The explanation of all entities, phenomenon, things, laws, and concrete objects begins with God. Beginning with any starting point or presupposition other than the Trinity is self-defeating.

The God revealed in scripture is the standard for truth, philosophy, and science. This is not a debatable predication. We must begin, move, and finish with God, or we cannot justify anything we do. The Trinity is the solution to all questions, and the source of all true knowledge. All thought presupposes the true God. This does not mean that we cannot do anything without employing theological rhetoric as Gregory of Nyssa lamented in his time, "If you ask for change, someone philosophizes you on the begotten and the unbegotten. If you ask is the bath ready, someone answers the Son was created from nothing." Presupposing the Trinity, as the solution to all questions and the standard for truth, doesn't mean that we must construct a theological postulation just to perform simple mundane tasks. Yet every simple task, and every piece of routine communication presupposes the triune God because we use logic and morality in all

[6]. John Muether, *So Great a Salvation* (Phil., PA: Modern Reformation, Vol. 10, Nu. 3. May/June 2001), p. 8.

those endeavors. God is the precondition for all logic and morality. If we presuppose anything other than God as our starting point, we end up with absurdity and contradictory affirmations. God, the Father, the Son, and the Holy Spirit, is inescapable if we want to make sense out of our world. If you reject the triune God, you end up asserting your philosophical demise. Deny God and you commit logical suicide.

God's Nature Reflected in Nature

> He is before all things, and in him all things hold together (Colossians 1:17).

We have a tri-unity in the universe composed of time, space, and matter. Each aspect is comprised of its own tri-unity. In the universe these are three distinct dynamics. All three of these are also divided by three. Space is comprised of height, width, and depth - a tri-unity. All is space, yet a distinct aspect of space. Matter is comprised of solid, liquid, and gas which make up a tri-unity of matter. Time is past, present, and future. Each "time" is fully time. We can see God's nature reflected in His creation. The Trinity is not a problem, but the solution. The Lord is the starting point and the finishing point. The Lord is the Alpha and Omega, the Beginning and the End.

Not only is the tri-unity of God not a contradiction and not a problem, but it is the solution to the intelligibility of our world. Without the Father, the Son, and the Holy Spirit as one God, we cannot account for love, motion, communication, relationships, mathematics, and every atom in the universe. God's triune glory is reflected in His creation. A lonely monad god cannot be the solution for the problem of the one and the many, and this false god is not reflected in the creation. Gregory Nazianzus mused in sweet transport, "I cannot think of the One without immediately being surrounded by the radiance of the Three; nor can I discern the Three without once being carried back to the One."

The Precondition for Mathematics: One God in Three Persons

> Your throne is established from of old; You are from everlasting (Psalms 93:2).

Mathematics has demonstrated that infinite numbers exist in theory. Only presupposing an infinite triune God can justify infinite numbers. One can count: 1, 2, 3, 4,... and go on infinitely. One can count backwards: -1, -2, -3, -4,... and go on infinitely in that direction. Yet our universe in finite. God is the precondition for infinite numbers. Without an infinite God, one cannot account for infinite numbers. The Triune God is the precondition for making sense out of our world. The true God has to be tri-unity. A god who is a solitary person would be in unitary aloneness before he created the angels or mankind. This would mean that love, justice, communication, relationship, and mercy cannot be a necessary attribute of this god. Only the one tri-personal God of scripture can have these traits as part of His being and nature.

> Great is our Lord, and mighty in power; His understanding is infinite (Psalms 147:5).

The study of mathematics presupposes the Father, and the Son, and the Holy Spirit: One God. He is "infinite, eternal, unchangeable, in His being, wisdom, power, and holiness." In the material world, we do not see the infinite. However, mathematical theory irrefutably demonstrates that infinite numbers exist in the realm of the abstract. Draw a line that is a foot in length. You can divide it in two. Then you could divide those two lines in two. You could repeat this abstract division, dividing the lines in two, and you would never have to stop. Mathematically, you could divide any size line forever and ever, infinitely. Ask the unbeliever if an infinite number of marbles could exist in the universe? If he answers in the affirmative, then follow up with this question: If someone played a game of marbles and shot one of the infinite number of marbles out of the universe: What is infinity minus one? If that is not enough to get your head spinning, ask yourself: "How many squares can fit into a five-foot square?" The answer is an infinite number of squares. These types of puzzles that employ infinities do not make sense in our finite physical universe. However, mathematics has proved that there are infinities. The materialist, who claims that only the physical, material world exists, cannot account for the infinite entities, in a finite material-only world. A world that they assert exists. Infinite lines and infinite entities do not exist in a concrete, material-only world.

> How precious also are Your thoughts to me, O God! How great is the sum of them! If I should count them, they would be more in number than the sand; When I awake, I am still with You (Psalms 139:17,18).

Christ sustains and holds all things together. This is the reason that mathematical truth applies to the physical sciences and physics. Christ lays the foundation, so that rational mankind can trust and utilize mathematics and physics. The diverse parts (diversity of particular things - the many) and specific applications of mathematics agree (unity - the one) with one another because of the tri-unity of God. Without God, one could not study mathematics because it is a theological study of the unity and the diversity in our world. The eternal and infinite God is the absolute precondition that makes mathematics possible.

The use of mathematics and of logic requires morality. Disclaim God and His moral law and there is no obligation to affirm that two plus two equal four, and that "A" cannot be "A" and "non-A" at the same time, in the same way. "Must" I affirm mathematical or logical truth? If so, I must provide objective unchanging moral grounds for the obligation. And that requires an unchanging God. For two plus three not to be four, anywhere at any time, requires a universal truth. Which presupposes an all-knowing God (who supplies the moral law). God's law commands all men to tell the truth and forbids lying. This is the reason we "ought" to affirm two plus three equal five.

God as a Crutch?

Many skeptics frequently hurl the charge that God is just a projection of your own imagination. They argue that Christians have a lack or a wanting in their lives; some type of psychological co-dependence syndrome that needs to be filled with belief in a benevolent God. God is just a crutch, and Christians have psychologically projected God to fulfill their needs. The problem with that explanation: The biblical God is not the type of God we would make up. People create a god in their own image. The Muslims create a blood thirsty god for a blood thirsty culture. Newagers create a god like themselves: A sinner that lacks the attributes of righteousness, justice, and holiness. The average secular American creates a god who is a mellow combination of Santa Klaus, Bewitched, the Force, and Shirley McClain. The holy and awesome God, who makes men tremble, is not the type one would invent.

The God of scripture is not a God that we would make up if we were left to ourselves. Christian theology declares a revelation from a source that transcends mankind. Christians must proclaim that God is the Father, and the Son, and the Holy Spirit: one God, unique, and indivisible; alone in majesty, clothed in splendor, might, and holiness. The triune God reveals so much of His nature that is awesome and frightening; that is righteous and unbending. There is so much of the sovereign God that is mysterious and overwhelming. Even some Christians attempt to apologize for God's attributes, and many professed believers are unwilling to follow Him. They want to make Him more "seeker friendly." They attempt to do a little tinkering with His character, so that God comes across more acceptable to them. We must resist this compromise with all that we are and proclaim from the housetops: I believe in God, the Father Almighty, Maker of the heavens and the earth, I believe in His dear Son, and I believe in the Holy Spirit. This is our God, and He is almighty in His mightiness.

God Is Love

> Love suffers long and is kind; love does not envy; love does not parade itself, is not puffed up; does not behave rudely, does not seek its own, is not provoked, thinks no evil; does not rejoice in iniquity, but rejoices in the truth; bears all things, believes all things, hopes all things, endures all things. Love never fails… For now we see in a mirror, dimly, but then face to face. Now I know in part, but then I shall know just as I also am known. And now abide faith, hope, love, these three; but the greatest of these is love (1 Corinthians 13:4-13).

A very tough question for the unbeliever: What is love? Is it a pat on the head, a hug and a kiss of a loved one? If yes, one can ask the question: when your loved one is too busy to hug or kiss you, does he now not love you? All men know; real love transcends the material world. Yet many claim that love is just the chemical firing of neurons in the brain. If so, why do we love and miss our loved ones when they die? Love not only points clearly to God, but without God, one cannot account for love. The Bible defines love much differently than the secular world. Love does not seek its own, it rejoices in the truth, and it never fails. God is love. Love springs from the triune Lord. God's inter-personal, reciprocal, and communal love for one another. We are created in the image of God, thus we have love, give love, and seek love.

The Truth of the Trinity Confronts a Former Christian Present Muslim

A Muslim man over heard a discussion on Islam that I was having with a friend. He interrupted and engaged us in the following conversation:

> Muslim: If you guys are concerned about Muhammad's holy wars, you need to know that the Christians engaged in the Crusades and other horrors.
>
> Mike: I would agree that many men who claimed to be Christians committed wicked acts in war and other atrocities. The difference between Islam and Christianity is that the founder of Islam commanded his followers to wage war, and he led many bloody wars himself, while the founder of Christianity commanded his people to be loving and just. Jesus never led a military war, and He commanded His followers to love their enemies. If a Muslim goes to war in the name of Islam and kills people because they will not convert; he is being consistent with his religion. If the Christian murders people who refuse to convert in the name of God, he is doing the exact opposite of what he is commanded to do.
>
> Muslim: Well, you believe in three Gods.
>
> Mike: No. We believe in the Trinity. Can you define the Trinity?
>
> Muslim: It is three Gods that are one God. It doesn't make sense.
>
> Mike: No. That is not the proper definition of the God of the Bible. He is three persons in one God. He is not three gods in one God or three persons in one person. The Trinity is the doctrine that declares three persons in one God. This does not break the logical law of non-contradiction.
>
> Muslim: Tell me what is one plus one plus one?

Mike: Well, the better question that I have for you: What is one times one times one?

Muslim: One.

Mike: Exactly. Not only is the Trinity logical, it is impossible for God not to be the Father, the Son, and the Holy Spirit, one God. Let me ask you a question: if God is just a monad, a single person God, where did love come from? Who did Allah love before he created the angels or men? Love needs an object. Allah and all monad deities cannot have love as a basic part of their nature. Only the triune God of scripture is true and living.

Muslim: Well, I can't answer your question right now.

Mike: Let me ask you another question, where did the notion of equality come from? We believe all men are created equal. We know there are perfectly equal triangles and perfectly equal lines in geometric theory. Moreover, we never see in our physical universe two lines or two triangles that are perfectly equal. Where did the notion of equality come from if we cannot see it in our material world? Within the tri-unity of God: The Father, the Son, and the Holy Spirit were and are co-equal. That is the unchanging basis that man has for equality among humankind. Humanity is created in the image and likeness of the triune God, thus we have an objective standard for equality. With Allah, can you justify unchanging equality?

Muslim: I have never thought of that.

Mike: One last thing, all men have sinned. You and I have broken God's law. God is perfect, and heaven is perfect. How can a sinner get into a perfect paradise? Only Jesus Christ has the solution in His atoning work on the cross. He died to rinse away the sins of His people, and true Christians have justification before heaven's court. That means my sins are taken away and Christ's perfect law

> keeping righteousness is imputed to me; it is credited to my spiritual account. If you died tonight would you go to heaven?
>
> Muslim: No. I try my best. Can we get together? I would like you to come over my house and talk to me and my wife?
>
> Mike: Yes, let me get your e-mail and your phone number.

The Triune God Must Exist

A solitary god would depend on men and angels to fulfill some inner-lacking. This unitarian god would lack love, communication, and equality in his essential nature and being. Without the attributes of love and fellowship, he cannot even be a personal being. If this solitary god needed to create angels, jinn, or men to give and receive love that would imply that this god depends on his creation. This is not God at all. Love, fellowship, equality, and personhood are essential to God's being. Only the biblical God has these attributes as essential to His being. God is God, and He does not depend on His creation for anything. Without people and cherubim, God would still love and have fellowship, and not lack anything. Francis Schaeffer rightly summed up the solution that the Trinity provides:

> The Nicene Creed - three persons, one God... Whether you realize it or not that catapulted the Nicene Creed right into our century and its discussion: three Persons in existence, loving each other, and in communication with each other, before all else was. If this was not so, we would have had a God who needed the universe as much as the universe needed God. But God did not need to create; God does not need the universe as the universe needs Him. Why? God is a full and true Trinity. The Persons of the Trinity communicated with each other before the creation of the world. This is not only an answer to the acute philosophic need of unity in diversity, but of personal unity and diversity. The unity and diversity cannot exist before God or behind God because whatever is farthest back is God... The unity and diversity are in God Himself - three persons, yet one God... this is not the best answer;

> it is the only answer. Nobody else, no philosophy, has ever given an answer for unity and diversity... Every philosophy has this problem, and no philosophy has an answer. Christianity does have an answer in the Trinity. The only answer to what exists is that He, the starting-place, is there. [7]

If the triune God does not exist, then knowledge is impossible. This is self-contradictory, and it is impossible because it is a knowledge claim. Only the Christian worldview supplies the foundation necessary for love, logic, science, moral standards, and mathematics. Non-Christian gods and systems of thought cannot furnish a foundation for the law of non-contradiction, therefore those systems of thought can only offer a self-contradictory worldview. God in Trinity is the precondition for all knowledge, science, and logic. It is impossible for God not to exist for He is the precondition for the intelligibility of the universe. The nonphysical, transcendent, timeless, and immutable God supplies the necessary preconditions for the use of the nonphysical, transcendent, universal, timeless, and immutable laws of logic. To argue at all, you must presuppose that the triune God lives. Non-Christian thought cannot supply the necessary preconditions for the laws of logic, thus it is false. The contrary of the Trinity is impossible because all non-Christian worldviews fall into absurdity because they cannot explain the universe and are self-contradictory. They lead to conclusions that contradict their own primary assumptions. Without the one God: the Father, the Son, and the Holy Spirit, nothing can make sense. The true and living God is the precondition for knowledge, and the understanding of all human experiences, including the problem of the one and the many. One God in three persons is the inescapable truth. He alone provides the preconditions for the universal and unchanging laws of logic. Universal and certain claims are inescapable. The Christian God alone provides the preconditions for universal and certain claims, hence Christianity must be true.

> The grace of the Lord Jesus Christ, and the love of God, and the communion of the Holy Spirit be with you all. Amen (2 Corinthians 13:14).

---

[7]. Francis Schaeffer, *Trilogy: He is There And He Is Not Silent* (Westchester, IL: Crossway, 1990), p. 288-289.

CHAPTER EIGHT

WITNESSING FOR THE NON-EVANGELIST

Nobody wants to be known, even when he realizes that this heal-hand salvation depends upon such knowledge. [1]

I just want the best for my son. I think I've told him what's right, but if he don't want to hear it, that's fine. He'll ultimately have to deal with a higher being. When he does, I hope he goes in there with a lot more positives on his record than negatives (Floyd Mayweather Sr. speaking about his son, boxing champ Floyd Mayweather Jr., who fired him as his trainer).

It is Christianity… to do right in everything. If we do this, and remember the life and lessons of our Lord Jesus Christ, and try to act upon them, we may confidently hope that God will forgive us our sins (Author unknown).

I will go to heaven when I die because I am basically a good person (average non-Christian's opinion on their eternal destiny).

---

[1]. Paul Tillich, *The Shaking of the Foundation* (NY: Scribner's Sons, 1948), p. 43.

The terror of the law, for it is only when we stand... naked and trembling before the Lawgiver and Judge, that we recognize our great need and cry out for a Mediator. The law given at Sinai was a ministry of condemnation (2 Corinthians 3:7-9), in which the very beasts were punished if they trespassed. [2]

Perhaps the greatest error of the Church in the 20th century has been to forsake the use of the Law in its capacity to act as a schoolmaster to bring sinners to Christ. [3]

Every sin, both in original and actual, being a transgression of the righteous law of God, and contrary thereunto, does, in its own nature, bring guilt upon the sinner, whereby he is bound over to the wrath of God, and the curse of the law, and so made subject to death, with all miseries spiritual, temporal, and eternal (Westminster Confession of Faith, VI. 6).

Do what thou wilt shall be the whole of the law (Aleister Crowly, the late self-proclaimed Beast and 666). [4]

Not choosing itself is a choice. [5]

Repentance... must be a great earnestness about it and a deep hurt if the old man is to be put off. When lightning strikes a tree or a man, it does two things at once; it rends the tree and swiftly slays the man. But it also turns the face of the dead man... toward heaven. [6]

---

[2]. Jim Nance, *The Mountain* (Moscow, Idaho: Credenda Agenda, Vol. 11/ Number 3), p. 14.

[3]. Ray Comfort, *The Ten Commandments* (Bellflower, CA: Living Waters, 1993), p. 180.

[4]. Aleister Crowly, *Magic in Theory and Practice* (NY: Castle), p. 193.

[5]. Hans Kung, *Does God Exist?* (Garden City, NY: Double Day, 1980), p. 61.

[6]. Roland Bainton, *Here I Stand* (Nashville, TN: Abingdon, 1950), p. 67.

> Repentance is necessary: "Except ye repent, ye shall all likewise perish" (Luke 13:5). There is no rowing to paradise except upon the stream of repenting tears. Repentance is required... It is not so much to endear us to Christ as to endear Christ to us. Till sin be bitter; Christ will not be sweet. [7]

> Since the law is holy, just and good that which breaks the law must be unholy, unjust, and evil... Since sin is a transgression of God's good law, the sinfulness of sin appears by the commandment. [8]

> Carnal hearts, until grace fully subdues them, are very loath to know their wretched condition. They love to not hear of anything that reveals to them the misery they are in. [9]

> Only knowing the goal of perfection where one should dwell, can one have definite purpose in life. [10]

> The first message of the cross is not God loves you, but God's law has been broken. Viewing the cross without the law is like trying to assemble a jigsaw puzzle in thin air... the spirit of the cross is eternal love, but the base of the cross is eternal justice. [11]

> Without the true knowledge of the Law, the corruption of nature lies hid... Men are ready to soothe up themselves... being ignorant of the Law of God... they bless themselves

---

[7]. Thomas Watson, *The Doctrine of Repentance* (Carlisle, PA: Banner of Truth. 1668), p. 63.

[8]. Ralph Venning, *The Sinfulness of Sin* (Carlisle, PA: Banner of Truth 1997 Edition), p. 145.

[9]. Jeremiah Burroughs, *The Saint's Treasury* (Ligonier, PA: Soli Deo Gloria 1991), p. 118.

[10]. Confucius, translated by Lin Yutang, *The Wisdom of Confucius* (NY: Random House, 1938), p. 139.

[11]. Ernest C. Reisinger, *The Law and the Gospel* (Phillipsburg, NJ: P & R Pub. Co. 1997), p. 158.

and think they are well… the Law of God… shows men their sins, and it makes men see and feel themselves as dead men. [12]

Flip or fry; turn or burn; change your stroke or go down in smoke (outdated fundamentalist slogans).

It's a small world, but I wouldn't want to have to paint it? [13]

Therefore you shall be perfect, just as your Father in heaven is perfect (Matthew 5:48).

Sinners do not bear the call of Christ because they do not think they are sinners. So men are unsaved not because of their sins, but because of their "righteousness." All is well, if only we can realize, all is not well. [14]

Evangelism… means summoning men to receive Christ Jesus as all that He is - Lord, as well as Savior - and therefore to serve Him as their King in the fellowship of His Church… work for Him on earth. In other words, evangelism is the issuing of a call to turn, as well as trust; it is the delivering, not merely of a divine invitation to receive a Savior, but a divine command to repent of sin. And there is no evangelism where this specific application is not made. [15]

---

[12]. Edward Elton, *Treatises, "Triumph of a True Christian"* (London, 1648), p. 86 & 89.

[13]. Steven Wright, *Quoted from Credenda Agenda Volume 11/ Number 4* (Moscow, ID. 1999), p. 17.

[14]. John Gerstner, *The Early Writings: Volume 1* (Morgan, PA: Soli Deo Gloria 1997), p. 215.

[15]. J. I. Packer, *Evangelism and the Sovereignty of God* (Downers Grove, IL: Inter Varsity Press, 1961), p. 39-40.

> Knowing, therefore, the terror of the Lord, we persuade men (2 Corinthians 5:11).
>
> Your people shall be volunteers in the day of Your power; In the beauties of holiness, from the womb of the morning, you have the dew of your youth (Psalms 110:3).
>
> Hear the word of the LORD, you who tremble at His word (Isaiah 66:5).
>
> But we know that the law is good if one uses it lawfully (I Timothy 1:8).
>
> The law of the LORD is perfect, converting the soul (Psalms 19:7).
>
> By the law is the knowledge of sin (Romans 3:20).
>
> For I am not ashamed of the gospel of Christ, for it is the power of God unto salvation to everyone who believes (Romans 1:16).
>
> Moreover, brethren, I declare to you the gospel… by which also you are saved… that Christ died for our sins according to the Scriptures, and that He was buried, and that He rose again the third day (1 Corinthians 15:1-4).

Our Glorious Duty

The duty of the witnessing Christian is to be faithful to scripture. This demands that we set the law of God on the sinner, before we offer the grace of God through the gospel. Reisinger amplifies this use of God's law:

> Every creature under heaven should be concerned about his or her duty to the Almighty Creator and judge of all the earth. Therefore the question: What duty does the Creator require of His creatures? Is always relevant. The biblical answer is that God requires personal, perfect, perpetual obedience to His revealed will… that… is summarized in the Ten Commandments… The Commandments demand

> both external and internal obedience. Addressing the will and the heart, as well as outward actions… Not only murder, but hate. Not only adultery, but lust. Not only stealing, but coveting. [16]

The truth of man's rebellion against God's holy law is to be brought before the eyes of the unbeliever to both convince and convict him of his sins. Using clear, specific and particular commandments, in asserting the sinner's pollution before a holy God, is the first stage of faithful witnessing. This is the instrument we should use to humble him, and provoke a sense of misery and wretchedness that will drive him to Jesus for cleansing, forgiveness, and redemption. Iain Murray quotes Nathan Bangs, who reported that the preachers during the Great Awakening "disturbed the false peace of the lukewarm, awakened the conscience of the sleeping sinner, and gave him no rest until he surrendered to Christ." [17] Do you remember Elijah? During Elijah's ministry, he was labeled a troublemaker by the king. It always seems that when Christians follow God, and seek to obey His commandments, they are called troublemakers. Our goal should not be to have people like us at the cost of truth. Our duty is to speak the truth, even if this results in people disliking us. Yes, our witness must be filled with grace and compassion, but these virtues should never dislodge our call to stand for the truth and righteousness.

Faithful witnessing consists of the believer placarding the terror of the law on the lost, and then offering the grace of the gospel to those that tremble at God's word. Christians are not to preach a controllable god, a god who is only there to meet the unbeliever's needs. Such a god becomes a divine bellhop who must jump at our call. Much of the Christian world seems to be embarrassed by the true God, and they try to change Him into a more user-friendly deity. An almighty sovereign God, full of awe and righteousness, is not what the world wants. And He is not what many churches "share." The Bible reveals that "the fear of the Lord is the beginning of wisdom" (Proverbs 9:10). We should press God's law on the sinner with compassion and patience. We are not to dazzle them with proud grandiloquence or blast them with an uncaring scolding. We must warn them. We should sincerely care for the state of their souls through the graceful preaching of the law and the gospel.

---

[16]. Ibid., Reisinger, p. 69-71.

[17]. Iain H. Murray, *Revival and Revivalism* (Carlisle, PA: Banner of Truth, 1994), p. 70.

God's Word

M'Cheyne offered this inspiring quote: "If the mercies and if the judgments do not convert you, God has no other arrows in His quiver." The terror and thunder of Sinai will invoke fear and holy fright in the sinner. Then if God changes the sinner's heart through the gospel, the convert will flee God's judgments and hurl himself upon Christ and His eternal mercy. We are not to shrink back in declaring God's holiness and His law to the lost. We must declare the holiness of God until the unbeliever shakes in terror and flees to Christ or flees from us. If we do not see knees knocking and hearts broken, we haven't preached the holiness of the true and living God. This will not make friends, but by God's grace, it will make true disciples, and simultaneously, it will reduce the number of pretenders.

God's word and His sovereign grace convert and reform sinners. A South Sea islander, who was a reformed cannibal and a convert to Christ, proudly displayed his Bible to a G.I. during World War II. The soldier mockingly said, "We have outgrown that sort of thing in America." The native smiled back and said, "It's a good thing we haven't. If it weren't for this book, you would have been a meal by now." The Bible is a book of transformation. It is the instrument that the Holy Spirit uses to save souls and reform sinners. Our job is not to astound and electrify people with human wisdom, but to preach God's holy word to the lost.

> I say to you that likewise, there will be more joy in heaven over one sinner who repents than over ninety-nine just persons who need no repentance (Luke 15:7).

When one shares the love of God without preaching God's holiness and His law, it weakens the sinners sense of sin. Then the lost sinner is not interested in the grand truth of the cross and justification. The law and the gospel, these are the means God uses to save lost sinners through His Spirit. Drama's, light shows, uplifting music may stir emotions and bring people to large and opulent church buildings, but they alone will not save a hell bound sinner. The lost need to hear the bad news of the wrath of God, the judgment of righteousness, and the offer of God's great grace in the person and work of Jesus Christ. Our job is not to be cute or funny, but to love the lost with the truth. The unpleasant reality, the lost person's position before a righteous God, is the reason that they must cast themselves upon the mercy of God in Christ. Entertainment in the right setting for the right reason can be very edifying and stimulating. But we must follow Paul and preach Christ: "to know nothing but Christ and Him crucified." We are to placard Christ, the righteous King, whom all men have offended in every point of His holy law, and that same Christ the Savior dying for our transgressions, of that very same law.

The Tool of our Witness

The witnessing that is consistent with the Bible preaches the law and the gospel. The law was given at Sinai, amid the fearful thunderings and lightnings, beclouded and dark; trumpets were blasted and the words written by the very finger of God were transmitted to God's people. That law opens our eyes to see our sin and our need of a Savior. The law is given to instruct us on how to live for God, and the law is to be used to restrain evil in civil society. It is imperative that the Christian urges God's commandments on the unbeliever. The irreligionist needs to understand that he must have a loving Savior. He must have authentic atonement, forgiveness, and redemption. God's holy law is the tool we use to make him aware of his need. This requires that you learn the Ten Commandments. Studies have shown that most American Christians do not know them. So learn them first for your own sake, teach them to your family, and then press them on the unsaved.

> The Law also shows us our great need—-our need of cleansing, cleansing with the water and the blood. It displays to us our filthiness, and this naturally leads us to feel we must be washed from it if we are ever to draw near to God. So the Law drives us to accept Christ as the only person who can cleanse us, makes us fit to stand within the veil of the presence of the Most High. The Law is the surgeon's knife that cuts out the proud flesh... The Law kills, the Gospel makes us alive; the Law strips, and then Jesus Christ comes in and robes the soul in beauty and glory... All the commandments... direct us to Christ, if we will but heed their evident intent (Spurgeon). [18]

---

[18]. Ibid., Comfort, *The Ten Commandments*, p. 187.

The Wicked Despise The Law

The law of God is to be used to terrorize and threaten the unbeliever. The law, as Moody posed, "chases us to Calvary." The law is shared, and the sinner then sees his depravity. When we use specific sins, like lying or stealing, then the sinfulness of sin is understood by the lost soul. At that point, you will get different reactions. Hopefully, by God's grace, the person repents and asks you: "What must I do to be saved?" You then have the privilege of sharing the comfort and mercy of the gospel (1 Corinthians 15:1-4). The other reaction can be very difficult. The unbeliever, hearing that they have broken specific commandments of God, can immediately get angry. Nietzsche considered the words of Jesus a "damning approach to life." Of the Sermon on the Mount he said: "If a society was driven by such an ethic, in effect it is controlled by losers." He went on to say: "Christianity is the one great curse, the one innermost perversion." This brings to mind all the odious rancor of Ted Turner, who called Christians losers. Nietzsche proved to the world, once again, you reap what you sow. He died insane, after years of muttering and rambling that he was Jesus Christ.

We must not hold back, the truth of the sinner's lost and miserable condition, just to avoid persecution. We should never be combative in our witness. We must try to avoid provoking a hostile response from the unbeliever. We are called to invoke the truth of God's law with kindness and love, not forsaking our duty because of fear. I have been called every name in the book, and some that are not in the book. But I delight in following my Lord in my witness. I also have had hundreds of people tell me they appreciated the way I presented the truth to them. Many were atheists and allotheists. A lot of them came to the Lord in humble repentance. If you are derelict in your duty of sharing the law with the unbeliever, you may reduce your chances of persecution, but you may also miss numerous opportunities to see the lost, found.

The Long Stare of a Holy God

Sartre claimed that he became an atheist because a man stared at him in public. He felt uncomfortable and dehumanized by becoming an object of the long stare of a stranger. He then reasoned: God is omnipresent, hence God must have His eyes perpetually on Sartre. But he did not like God gazing upon him. Thus he denied God because of his quirky shyness. God is everywhere present and looks upon everyone always. He sees all the iniquity of mankind, and we should remind people of that fact. All their law breaking is observed and recorded. Sinners hate this fact. Yes, if you preach the law and the gospel, frequently you will receive the full cocked fury of sinners in the form of insults, spitting, cursing, and screaming, just as the Lord Jesus received. The Bible tells us that the lost are suppressing the truth in unrighteousness. They do not want you upsetting their active denial. Do not worry, Jesus told us that we are blessed when we are persecuted. We do not look for and cultivate persecution, but we know that the scoffer will get what he deserves if he does not turn and trust Christ.

The bombastic atheist O'Hair and her two grandchildren were murdered in a horrible fashion. She was forced to watch her grandchildren get tortured to death by a fellow atheist who had stolen their organization's monetary assets. O'Hair was the cantankerous lady who lifted up and shook her deviant fist and yelled at God, "I don't believe in you; I reject you." If she didn't believe in God, who was she yelling at? She knew God was there. And now that she is deceased, she surely knows. Yet sadly, because of her worldview, she couldn't morally argue against her attacker for torturing her and her loved ones. An atheistic worldview cannot assert an objective and unchanging morality. Murder should be looked on as a good thing in the atheist worldview. If their creed is survival of the fittest then those who murder are more fit than their victims. Therefore the atheist cannot say that murder is wrong. If anything, they should delight in the killing of weaker members of an evolving species. The species is progressing through natural selection, by the hands of murderers. This will provide a more stout gene pool for the ascent of the species. Christians can justify their outrage at murder, and proclaim in a consistent manner that all murder is morally wrong. We do this through God's holy law. No other worldview can assert that murder is universally, unalterably, and objectively evil, and remain consistent. Christianity is the precondition for morality and ethics, including the forbidding of murder.

Jesus: a Stone of Stumbling

The more I witness, the more I am still surprised at how angry people can get when you share the law and the gospel with them. People who claim to be Christians, and others who claim to be atheists can get steamed really quick when you mention the name of Jesus. It is interesting that if you are at a dinner party, and you share words about Buddha, Krishna, or Muhammad, no one gets upset and many people eagerly listen. But if you professed faith in Jesus, at just the mention of His name, the crowd gets animated with anger. If you continue to speak of Christ, the inflamed host will ask you to leave. In our world, one can babble on and on with New Age prattle, and recount the vain glories of eastern mysticism, and such a person is received as a man or woman of wisdom and culture. The only ideology that must be put in the closet is Christianity. People, who are actively suppressing the truth, do not want to be confronted with Jesus and His law. The conversation recorded below is an example of how quickly an unbeliever can get rankled and combative over God's word.

Burgers, Fries, and Rage at In-N-Out

At the fast food restaurant In-N-Out Burger, we handed a woman and her friends gospel tracts and we were drawn into a conversation:

> Lady customer: Please do not push your religion on us. We just lost a friend who died.
>
> Mike: We are not trying to push our religion on you. We just want you to know we care and that Jesus is the only solution to our heartache and our sins.
>
> Lady: I don't want to hear about sins!
>
> Mike: Well, we all have broken God's law, I have and you have. Jesus takes away the sins of those who put their trust in Him.
>
> Lady: Quit preaching to me.
>
> Mike: I'm not preaching to you. I'm trying to be kind, soft spoken, and patient. If you want to see preaching, come to our church on Sunday.
>
> (She obstinately and heatedly started preaching at us in front of the whole restaurant.)
>
> Lady: All you guys are a bunch of hypocrites. You are phonies, and you push your religion on people! I don't need you to tell me I'm a sinner. I don't need anyone preaching to me!

> Mike: Miss, it looks like you're preaching at us. We are sorry that you are angry. We just care about you guys.
>
> Lady: You don't give a rip about us. You just want to push your religion on us and preach to us.
>
> (She then cusses at us and hollers as she leaves.)

The Nations Rage

> This negligence in a matter where they themselves, their eternity, their all is at stake, fills me more with irritation than pity; it astounds me and appalls me; it seems quite monstrous to me. [19]

I pray and attempt to be kind, temperate, and gracious when I go out as a witness for Christ. But, the fact of the matter is, anybody who shares the law and the gospel, will at times face persecution. Most often, one is attacked through verbal outbursts. In another situation, I saw how furious people can get when you gently urge God's law on them. Even when you communicate with respect and kindness. A group of my friends and I were at Arby's and we heard a young gal curse God's name. We gently called her attention to that fact and exhorted her to repent. She and her boyfriend threw out some colorful language on their way out the door. Then in less than a minute, she came back in and asked: "What did you say?" We told her that she blasphemed; she then apologized to us. We respectfully told her that she didn't sin against us, but God. She then scowled and screeched some very ugly curse words at us, and she personally cursed our children eating next to us. We knew the Bible instructs us that for covenant people, the curses of sinners are actually blessings, so we weren't concerned about our children or ourselves. We were deeply grieved at her pubic display of wickedness and blasphemy. We prayed for her. Often, the reaction of the unbeliever can be very contentious. These types of hostile conversations may promote fear in some Christians, but they should not. God's word informs us that "perfect love casts out all fear." The insults of the profligate and miscreant Americans are nothing compared to the persecution that has been carried out through the sword of Sudan's Muslims against the Christians. Those regions have had real persecution. A persecution that

---

[19]. Thomis Morris, *Making Sense of It All* (Grand Rapids, MI: Eerdman, 1992), p. 23.

leads to death, slavery, and brutality. We American believers should be able to endure some cursing and threats for our Lord. We face next to nothing compared to the believers in Muslim or communist countries. Let us be thankful, and use the opportunities that the Lord has given us in our country to preach the truth.

> But he said to him, "If they do not hear Moses and the prophets, neither will they be persuaded though one rise from the dead" (Luke 16:31).

Missing Vocabulary

> The wrath of God is like great waters that are damned for the present: they increase more and more and rise higher and higher till an outlet is given… Nothing but the mere pleasure of God… holds the water back (Jonathan Edwards).

Many people, Christian and non-Christian, recoil at the sound of the words "hell" and "repent." There are whole movements within the Church that have (as part of their mission and purpose) the goal of not offending the nonbeliever by avoiding using words such as "hell fire," and "repent," and "sinner." Much of modern American Christianity is getting mushier and mushier in order not to offend "seekers." Many believers will say it is better to motivate people with love and not with fear. Love is a very strong way to motivate, but fear is also necessary. If my four-year old leans over a balcony or lunges toward a hot stove, I will not softly tell him how much I love him to protect him from bodily injury. I must warn him. That warning may take some loud and strong words to prevent an injury. Strong warnings are important tools of protection and security. We need not pit love against fear.

Jesus loved people more than anyone in history, and He spoke on hell more than any person in the Bible. He motivated people by using love and speaking the truth in love. When the whole truth was proclaimed by Christ, fear was often the result. Frequently, the world gets very livid when you press the truths of these words on them. Unless, of course, God is softening their heart and saving their soul. We are not to shrink back in declaring the whole counsel of God, even if it is unpleasant and hurts people's feelings. I have heard Christians proclaim that God doesn't use scare tactics to bring people to Christ. Instead of buying into that wishful thinking, you should respond to the unbeliever's indifference by pleading in the manner of the Puritan Joseph Alleine. He breathlessly announced:

> Men and brethren, heaven and earth call upon you: yea, hell itself preaches the doctrine of repentance to you. The ministers of the churches labor for you. The angels of heaven wait for you, for your repenting and turning unto God. O sinner, why should devils laugh at your destruction, and deride your misery, and sport themselves with your folly? This will be your case, except your turn. And were it not better you should be a joy to angels than a laughing stock and sport for devils. Verily, if you would come in, the heavenly hosts would take up their anthems and sing… The true penitent's tears are indeed the wines that maketh glad both God and man. [20]

I have had many unbelievers complain about my use of the words "hell" and "repent." Frequently they are repulsed at such words. They do not have much of a problem with the mush of the ultra-tolerant, decaffeinated, warm, and fuzzy modern religion. But they are very much discomforted by the believer who warns them about the wrath to come. They tell me that it is distasteful to use fear as a way to motivate people to become Christians. The salty atheist Bertrand Russell declared: "Religion is based, I think, primarily and mainly upon fear."[21] Since this declaration is from an atheist; it can be turned back upon him. I would respond to this accusation by asserting that the atheist is afraid of hell, and due to his fear; he tries to deny the unpleasant reality of hell. He builds his worldview primarily upon fear, the fear of a real hell. He acts like a philosophical ostrich, sticking his head in the sand, hoping that the truth of hell, will just go away by his denying its reality. My faith is built on love and a respectful fear of a Holy God. The hell denier lives in fear, the fear of hell. He is passionate when the subject is brought up because he knows it is true. Thus he suppresses the truth in unrighteousness, as he hopes hell will just go away. He lives and moves in fear of hell. Hell is real and so is heaven. Everyone will spend eternity in one of those two destinations. Henry Buckle wrote: "If immortality be untrue, it matters little whether

---

[20]. Joseph Alleine, *A Sure Guide to Heaven* (Carlisle, PA: Banner of Truth, 1671, reprinted 1989), p. 130.

[21]. Bertrand Russell, *Why I Am Not A Christian* (NY: Simon and Schuster, 1964), p. 22.

anything else be true or not." That is how important eternity is. If there is eternal life, then that truth is one of the most important issues people must deal with. This should motivate the unbeliever to come to Christ and compel the believer to share his faith.

> If we say that we have no sin, we deceive ourselves, and the truth is not in us (1 John 1:8).

A Bold Public Witness

Christians should be the boldest, most passionate, and most charitable people on the planet. We have the promise of the Spirit, and He has us. We have the gospel: the power of God unto salvation. We serve the Lord of Hosts, and He is the maker of heaven and the earth. We should be patient, gentle, and zealous followers of Jesus. Every situation with the public is an opportunity to exalt the name of Jesus through preaching His word, and living a pious life.

I have been blessed to see a Jehovah Witness cult member repent and come to Christ in front of the Mormon temple in Salt Lake City; I have seen a young man lead seven teens to Christ in the parking lot of a grocery store; I have seen deeply troubled men and women, who were crushed and broken, made whole on the Las Vegas Strip, in parks, at universities, and in the market place. I would not have had those blessings if our teams did not go out on the limb and preach Jesus. Out on the limb is where most of the fruit abides. I understand that bold and loving witnessing gives most modern Christians a hissy-fit. But you can't make hell go away simply by ignoring it. We should obey our Lord and not men. Yes, one of the best ways to inculcate the nonbeliever away from Christianity is with uncaring, pugnacious, flame throwing evangelism. Zeal is usually not loud, and it is never to be belligerent. Real Holy Spirit birthed zeal is militant in its mercy and its love for the truth. What we need is the phrase that Pascal had kept sewn in his clothes; his testimony which climaxed in the words: "Fire. God of Abraham… not of the philosophers… God of Jesus Christ." We need the fire of God to burn a love for the lost into our hearts. So pray for boldness, read God's word for inspiration, keep gospel tracts on your person, study the apologetics in this book, engage in role play witnessing drills, and step out in faith. You can be a witness and have the privilege of watching a sinner turn from his wickedness and come to salvation. What an honor and blessing, God has set before us!

Christianity: The only Place where Justice and Grace Meet

The law of God requires justice. Man's law requires justice. The Christian is to demonstrate to the nonbeliever that they have broken God's holy law. We must enjoin holy incriminations on their harden conscience. We should spiritually charge them for breaking God's law. All unbelievers are cosmic criminals, just as we were before we came to Christ. The law is to be used to send them to Christ. And after regeneration, we send them back to the law to obey all God's commandments out of gratitude. Before we instruct them on how the penalty has been paid by Jesus, they must understand that their good works cannot pay the penalty for past sins, only Christ can. Nor can the believer's good works erase past transgressions. If I receive a speeding ticket, and I go to court and the judge asks, "What do you plead?" I say, "Guilty, but I promise I will never speed again. Judge, please forgive my ticket on account of my future obedience." The judge would say, "It is good that you will not speed again. That is your lawful duty. But you still have to pay the fine for your past mistake of speeding." The good news is Jesus Christ, as judge, came down, took off His robe and paid the fine Himself for all who trust in Him.

All thirty thousand religions, except one, believe that your future good works will help you get to heaven, nirvana, freedom from the karmaic cycle, or paradise. Yet our good deeds can never erase bad deeds. If I murder nine people; later I help feed ten thousand people at a shelter; I am still a murderer. If caught and tried, the good works will not rinse away my capital crimes. We all have sinned. The unbeliever tries to deny this truth. John Piper sets this before us with the following: "God warns with His wrath and woos with His kindness." Thus we are called to expose the unbeliever's cosmic crimes. We have the grand blessing to explain to them that the only solution for their sin and iniquity is the atonement of Christ. The atonement expiates the sins of the Christian and rinses his transgressions from his spiritual record. Then God graciously imputes Christ's righteousness to the believer's account. We enter heaven free from past sins, and clothed in the righteousness of Christ through faith alone and by grace alone.

> To you first, God, having raised up His Servant Jesus, sent Him to bless you, in turning away every one of you from your iniquities (Acts 3:26).

We use the law to compel the unbeliever to flee to Christ and avoid the wrath to come. The gospel is the instrument that God uses by His grace to save the elect's soul. Paul announces: "The gospel is the power of God unto salvation." The law exposes the nonbeliever's sin and lostness. When he turns and believes the gospel: the life, death, burial, and resurrection of Christ, his sins are forgiven by God's good grace. The law, without the gospel, cannot change anyone. You can put lipstick and a party dress on a pig, but you still have a pig. The pig, all gussied-up, has the same nature he had before the makeup. And a lost person, who outwardly appears to keep religious law, is still lost. He must have his nature changed by God's grace through faith in the gospel. When he turns and trusts in Christ, he is forgiven of all his sins. God's great grace credits him with the perfect righteousness of Jesus Christ. The believer is now in right standing with God, and at his death he will enter heaven's glory because of Christ alone.

Evangelism: Just Do It

There are so few who have what Spurgeon called a deep "tenderness." These are the ones who carry an anguish of soul for the fate of the ungodly. They break out of their complacency and seek by any means to save that which was lost. The love of Christ compels them (2 Corinthians 5:14). The Greek word used denotes that His love arrests them, preoccupies and presses them to reach out to the lost... They go to battle. [22]

Many preachers have quipped, "That compared to evangelism and witnessing, everything else that the Church does is like rearranging the furniture while the house is on fire." While we should never pit one of God's commandments against another, the importance of preaching the gospel to the lost cannot be overstated. Our desire and passion should be for the lost to come to Christ. Our perennial goal must be to glorify God in all things. If we attempt to win the hell bound sinner with unfaithful and unscriptural means, we fail to glorify God. If multitudes of radical Muslims have an unbending zeal to commit wicked acts in the name of a false god, then Christians should be willing to have more Holy Spirit zeal to preach Christ and Him crucified. My experience, in the western United States, is that most believers do not obey the Lord in sharing their faith in the local market place. Surveys of Christians have revealed that ninety-percent

---

[22]. Ray Comfort, *God has a Wonderful Plan for Your Life* (Bellflower, CA: Living Waters, 2000), p. 115.

of believers have never brought another person to Christ. [23] Many are afraid, some are too busy, some do not care, and a number of them would share their faith if they felt they were competent enough to witness to strangers. If you want to rid yourself of "witness-a-phobia," ask God to plant a deeper love for the lost in your heart. Jesus promises that the Holy Spirit will be in and with His followers in a special way when they are sharing their faith: "But you shall receive power when the Holy Spirit has come upon you; and you shall be witnesses to Me in Jerusalem, and in all Judea and Samaria, and to the end of the earth" (Acts 1:8). Notice the disciples start preaching in Jerusalem, their Jewish home town. They started in the place where they lived. The real solution to the fear of witnessing is to start where you are, and step out in faith. Plan the time, pray, and just do it!

Life is Like a Vapor

Christians, who do not have time to hit the streets or the shopping malls to preach the gospel, need to examine their priorities (planning one day a month to go witnessing is a good way to start a consistent life of evangelism). Schedule a time to go and prayerfully follow through. Do not allow yourself excuses. We are very talented and imaginative when it comes to finding "reasons" we cannot go witnessing. Be faithful, prayerful, and radically obedient. The Christians among us who do not care about the fate of the lost, need a wake up call. Every person you will ever see will die one day and face a Holy God. Homer put it this way in the *Iliad*, "Death in ten thousand shapes hangs ever over our heads, and no man can elude him." The one thing that all humans have in common: We will all die. The clerk at the corner store, your neighbor, your family, and your friends will all see death.

Our prayerful and hopeful goal should be for them to come into the presence of the righteous God with Jesus as their Savior. Ponder the realities of hell; remember hell and forever always seem to go together in the Bible. Your duty is to care for those who are on their way to hell. Yes, our God is sovereign, but He ordains the means as well as the ends. The instrument that God uses to save souls is believers preaching the gospel. We should be like the persecuted Baptist preachers of eighteenth century America. Who, upon their arrest for preaching without a state license, were described by a prosecuting attorney: "These men are great disturbers

---

[23]. C. Peter Wagner, *Church Growth; State of the Art* (Wheaton, IL: Tyndale, 1986), p. 53.

of the peace; they cannot meet a man upon the road but they must ram the text of scripture down his throat." [24] We do this out of a passionate love for our wonderful Savior, and a compassion for those who do not know Jesus. Pray for compassion; scratch out a time in your date book, and go share what you have been given in Christ.

> Knowing, therefore, the terror of the Lord, we persuade men; but we are well known to God, and I also trust are well known in your consciences (2 Corinthians 5:11).

We have to ask God for a heart full of compassion. When we urge the holiness and the dread of God's commandments on the lost, there is a real danger of looking as if we are the narrow, isolated, self-righteous types. We have to care as much as we warn. We must witness with as much patience as truth. As we witness to the lost, it can be easy to get caught up in pride because of the blessings we have received through being in covenant with God. The nonbeliever is without hope, and without the covenant promises of God. They have nothing, and all Christians have everything. Let us be humbled by this reality and become gracious prosecutors who freely offer pardon, expiation, justification, and the healing balm of the gospel. We should always remember, before Christ called us, we were in the same dreadful place of condemnation.

Our main goal is to be faithful to God's word and glorify Him in all we say and do. We should strive to communicate in a warm manner, a winsome manner, and with a lack of pretense. We should put away all the fluff, dazzle, and phoniness; lift up Christ and Him alone. He is the Savior, and He is full of grace and truth. Blowing smoke, being a phony, does not honor God's word. Having a burning passion, a fiery zeal does not equate with being a misanthrope or a hypocrite. We must follow Jesus and Paul and share the truth in love. Our petition to God is for us to burn for Christ, as John Bunyan pleaded at the threat of imprisonment, "How can I close my mouth when God has called me to preach." Spurgeon declared, "Have you no wish for others to be saved? Then you are not saved yourself." Tough words that make our ultra-tolerant culture cringe. True words that make our carefree seeker friendly churches recoil. A faithful Christian is to have the desire to see the lost come to Christ. Let thoughts of your own salvation inspire you to step out and share your faith.

---

[24]. Ibid., Murray, p. 67.

Comfort describes a time when he "approached a young man who was using a string of profanities… I asked him to try the I.Q. test (a test on a tract that exposes the sinner's law breaking). He said, 'he had told a few white lies, lifted things here and there, and of course, lusted.' When I gently said that God saw him as a lying, thieving adulterer at heart, he widened his eyes and he used the name of Jesus in blasphemy, to which I replied, 'And a blasphemer!' He looked horrified and exclaimed, 'G-d.' I said, 'Twice over!' he then put his hand on his mouth and muttered, 'You make me feel like going to confession… I am so embarrassed!' Conscience did its duty. He didn't need a priest; he needed a Savior." [25] The law is a supernatural tool to break down the unbeliever's pride. God, by His grace, breaks up the fallow ground of the most hardened heart through the power of His holy word. Our job is not just to be nice, but we should care enough for the lost person standing in front of us that we tell them of the difficult and unpleasant truth of their law breaking. They need Jesus and the best way to demonstrate that truth is through the law of God.

Go and Tell

> And when He got into the boat, he who had been demon-possessed begged Him that he might be with Him. However, Jesus did not permit him, but said to him, "Go home to your friends, and tell them what great things the Lord has done for you, and how He has had compassion on you." And he departed and began to proclaim in Decapolis all that Jesus had done for him; and all marveled (Mark 5:18-20).

In this passage, Jesus commands a freshly freed former possessed man to go and tell others of the great things God has done. One of the first witnesses for Christ was not a seminary graduate. He was not an expert in apologetics. He was not a close disciple nor was he an expert in theology. It was not John or Paul; Jesus found his first witness in a cemetery. He was a graveyard lunatic, an ancient Charlie Manson type. He cut himself with rocks. That was a mode of Satan worship in antiquity. This cemetery dweller must have been like Jeffrey Dahmer, David Berkowitz, and Tex Watson; all mass murderers who professed faith in Christ after being

[25]. Ibid., Comfort, *The Ten Commandments*, p. 174-175.

imprisoned for capital crimes. This graveyard crazy was a very unlikely witness until he met Jesus. If he can go and tell others about the glories of God in Christ, certainly we can. The statistics on death are very impressive. One out of one person dies. Two hundred and forty an hour, every day, and every year. Most of them die without Jesus. The woman at the well had a troubling past and was in a mess with her marriages. She came to Jesus and God saved her. Jesus then sent her to tell her hometown about Him. If she can go tell the lost about the Lord, we can go and be a witness. The mission of every believer is to pass on to others what we have received from Jesus. Witnessing is part of our earthly warfare.

During the Gulf War America had 119 casualties. A Baptist chaplain reported that twelve hundred men came to the Lord and professed Christ during the conflict. This might have been the first time in history when more people got saved than were killed on our side. I know, I seldom think of sharing my faith as an engagement of war. But it is war and we must behave as soldiers who are waging war. We must ask God to reawaken us to the reality of the holy battle for souls. God is sovereign and God wins. He has ordained the instruments to bring the lost to Jesus, and He does this by enlisting all Christians into His army.

Southern Utah University: From Sad to Glad

We had a witnessing team ministering at Southern Utah University. I saw a sad looking young lady sitting on a bench and went over to chat with her about the Lord:

Mike: How are you doing today?

Annie: Fine.

Mike: Do you have a moment to talk?

Annie: Not really, I'm studying.

Mike: What's your major?

Annie: Psychology.

Mike: Interesting. Do you believe in God?

Annie: Yes.

Mike: Do you know that heaven is a perfect place, God is holy and perfect and you and I are not?

Annie: Nobody is perfect.

Mike: Well, I know you are busy, but I just want you to know that Jesus died for the sins of His people. Today, right here, if you come to Him, repent and trust in Him, He will always be there for you.

Annie: I'm not sure.

Mike: You know that Jesus died on the cross, was buried, and rose again on the third day. He loves His people that much. Come to Him today, He cares for you when no one else will. People may leave you, but Jesus always stays close by. If you come to Him, He will never, ever leave you.

(She started weeping and sobbing.)

Mike: Jesus cares for you so much, He even sent me from another state to tell you what He did on the cross and that He cares. We all have broken His commandments, we have failed so often, yet those who turn and trust in Jesus, have all their guilt rinsed away.

(She started weeping on my shoulder.)

Mike: Can I pray for you?

Annie: Yes.

I prayed for her. And she confessed her need and desire to trust Christ for salvation. She professed faith in the person and work of Jesus and couldn't thank me enough. I got her name and phone number and told her I would pass it onto a local church. This conversation went extremely well. This was one of those mountain top moments. Sometimes the Lord comes in His sovereign grace and changes a heart right in front of you. It is a marvelous experience; a wonderful honor to be used by God to preach the gospel, and see a lost soul come to the Lord. Whenever someone comes to profess faith in Christ, I get their address and phone number and give this information to a church. The encounters that bear immediate fruit, are fairly rare. But if you go out witnessing consistently, you will have the privilege of watching God transform a soul right before your eyes. You are called to be a witness.

> And a servant of the Lord must not quarrel but be gentle to all, able to teach, patient, in humility correcting those who are in opposition, if God perhaps will grant them repentance, so that they may know the truth, and that they may come to their senses and escape the snare of the devil, having been taken captive by him to do his will (2 Timothy 2:24-26).

When you have a dialogue with an unbeliever, you are to imprecate the commandments on their heart, and offer the gospel to redeem them from the curse of the law, and to soothe their souls. When you do this, you must keep in mind that the sinner wants to suppress the truth; he does this by holding onto his false presuppositions. We must always be aware that the non-Christian holds to a different foundational lens than the Christian; as they look at reality. They are like Lord Nelson, when a communication signal was flashed before him that he wanted to disregard, he would put his telescope to his blind eye and say, "I really do not see the signal." This is how the unbeliever lives. He does not want to see the signal of God's revelation that he is a lost and doomed sinner. He wishes to suppress the truth of Christianity. He doesn't want to embrace Christianity's consistent presuppositions, so he tries to put the lens of God's revelation on his blind eye. He wants to evade the truth, suppress the truth, and disregard the truth. He whistles in the dark, hoping to avoid the unpleasant task of facing the reality of God's revelation in Christ Jesus. Our job is to placard the holiness of the law, and the merciful work of the cross. We must not just throw flowers and kind platitudes at them. The non-Christian must be cut to the heart like the three thousand converts on the Day of Pentecost. Let us boldly follow the example of the Apostles and the early Christians.

> That utterance may be given to me, that I may open my mouth boldly to make known the mystery of the gospel, for which I am an ambassador in chains; that in it I may speak boldly, as I ought to speak (Ephesians. 6:19,20).

Justification: Declared Righteous

> Clouds and darkness surround Him; Righteousness and justice are the foundation of His throne (Psalms 97:2).
>
> Mercy triumphs over judgment (James 2:13).
>
> Therefore, having been justified by faith, we have peace with God through our Lord Jesus Christ... For when we were still without strength, in due time Christ died for the ungodly. For scarcely for a righteous man will one die; yet perhaps for a good man someone would even dare to die. But God demonstrates His own love toward us, in that while we were still sinners, Christ died for us. Much more then, having now been justified by His blood; we shall be saved from wrath through Him (Romans 5:1-9).

Justification is a doctrinal term. This truth is found in the book of Romans (chapters three through eight, in First Corinthians) and in other portions of scripture. It is unique to Christianity. Justification: The believer is declared righteous, his sins removed, and Christ's righteousness imputed (credited) to the believer's account by grace alone through faith alone because of Christ alone. No other religious system has a means to erase our record of iniquity, and grant us a righteous record so we can enter a perfect heaven. Justification is a legal, forensic term that implies prior condemnation, and results in a pardon through a judge's judgment.

During the time when China held American service men and their aircraft, the government of China demanded a legal apology from the United States government. The Chinese told the world that the U.S. aircraft was an illegal spy plane that purposely downed a Chinese jet. They told the American government that they would not release our service men and women without an apology. China is the one that sent the aggressive pilot that clipped our plane, and the pilot died due to his own aggressive actions. Yet China, a nation that never apologizes, demanded and received an apology. During the negotiation for this legal "I'm sorry," the U.S. government discovered that the Chinese have three types of apologies. *Yi Hah* is a mild ambiguous apology that means "I wished it didn't happen." *Bao Qian* is a more serious form of I'm sorry, usually accompanied with a bow. *Dao Qian* is a forensic, legal and formal apology in which the speaker accepts full responsibility for his actions. *Dao Qian* is the strongest version of an apology. This is what China demanded from the American government, a legal and formal apology. In the same manner, the holy God of the universe, demands a formal, forensic righteousness. Not because He is capriciously harsh, but because He is completely righteous. God is not arbitrary; He is holy and perfect. One must be righteous to live with Him in heaven. Every man has broken God's holy law; the only solution for man's sin and depravity is a formal, legal justification through Christ by grace through faith.

> But to him who does not work but believes on Him who justifies the ungodly, his faith is accounted for righteousness (Romans 4:5).

Most Christians understand that because Christ died on the cross, their sins are forgiven and rinsed away. This is the negative aspect of justification. Something is subtracted, namely, our sins. The positive aspect of justification is usually overlooked by the average modern Christian. The positive element: God imputes or credits the believer with the righteousness of Christ. Jesus not only died for us; He lived for us. His perfect, holy, and righteous life record is given to those who trust in Him. We know that Jesus atoned for our sins and disobedience on the cross, but His work was not merely negative and passive. During His life of thirty-three years, Jesus lived in perfect accord with God's law, fulfilling all righteousness on our behalf. The saved believer stands before the Holy God, not just guilt and sin free, but they are actually declared righteous on account of Christ. All that Jesus did on the earth is imputed and credited to the believer's account. We are justified before God through the active and passive obedience of Jesus. We are saved by His life and His death. That is good news. Only Christianity can bestow justification. All the world's religions are based upon the religionist's good deeds and his personal merit. The problem is heaven is perfect, God is holy and nothing unholy and unrighteous will enter God's heaven. Biblical justification is the only solution to man's sin and Adam's disobedience.

The Eternal Blessing of Imputation

> And he believed in the LORD, and He accounted it to him for righteousness (Genesis 15:6).

> Therefore, having been justified by faith, we have peace with God through our Lord Jesus Christ (Romans 5:1).

> For they have healed the hurt of the daughter of My people slightly, saying, "Peace, peace!" When there is no peace (Jeremiah 8:11).

Justification forensically renders the believer righteous and gives him peace with heaven. Without justification, the unbeliever has no peace with God. This is one reason we must not flippantly declare that God loves everybody. We must never assert that there is peace, when there is no peace between the ungodly and God. Without justification by grace alone, there can be no real peace. Imputation is the biblical term for the positive element of justification. Through God's grace by faith: The believer is judicially constituted as righteous. He is declared righteous. Christ preached in Matthew 5:48, "Be ye perfect as your heavenly Father is perfect." The law demands perfect obedience. This is a perfection equal to the Father's perfection. Nobody except Christ has pulled that off, so we need a perfect righteousness that is not our own. We need to be justified by the works and righteousness of another. Justification is a forensic term which speaks of the Christian's legal position before God. The believer is declared righteous despite his unrighteous deeds.

The justified are given an alien righteousness. A righteousness that is not their own, but is imputed to the believer by faith alone. Not having a righteousness of our own insures that God gets all the glory. We should delight in the good news of our justification and get stirred-up to teach others this stupendous truth: Christ came to save sinners. When we witness, we must hoist the person and work of Christ. After pressing the law on the heart of the wicked, share the gospel and justification with them. Pray that God changes their hearts, and that they cast themselves upon the person of Jesus Christ.

> We cry down the law when it comes to our justification, but we set it up when it comes to our sanctification. The Law drives us to the Gospel that we are justified, then sends us to the Law again to show us our duty now that we are justified (Thomas Boston).

Pray, Pray, and Pray

> You therefore must endure hardship as a good soldier of Jesus Christ. No one engaged in warfare entangles himself with the affairs of this life, that he may please him who enlisted him as a soldier (2 Timothy 2:3,4).

Evangelism without prayer is salesmanship. Our life is to be one of prayer and witnessing. Augustine put it this way: "Pray as though everything depended on God, and work as though everything depended on you." Prayer is absolutely necessary to see the unsaved come to Jesus. God answers prayer, but He will not answer a prayer that is unasked. Begin by writing down a list of people who do not know Jesus that you can contact. Compile the names of all the unbelievers in your life: the super market cashier, the man at the Seven-Eleven store, your coworkers, your friends, and your family members. Most of us are not called to go out on the corner, waving a Bible and shouting at people to repent. Nonetheless, we are all called to tell others about the great things God has done in history and in our lives. We need to recalibrate our prayer sights on the lost people who live in our circle of influence. We should ask God to soften their hearts and draw the wayward to His dear Son. All members of the Church need to be shaken out from their self-centered daze of indifference. We cannot be apathetic regarding the plight of the unbeliever. We are not all gifted with the gift of evangelism, but we all have the mandate to pray for the lost, and preach the gospel to the sinner.

> He who continually goes forth weeping, bearing seed for sowing, shall doubtless come again with rejoicing, bringing his sheaves with him (Psalms 126:6).

In 1940, a butterfly collector was out in Utah trying to enlarge his collection of bugs. At dusk, he returned from his excursion, and he shared with his companion that he had heard a loud moaning and a cry for help. Someone was calling for assistance down the stream. His friend asked him whether he stopped and looked for the man who was in trouble. He said, "No, I had to get a particular butterfly." The next morning the corpse of a gold prospector was discovered in what later was named Dead Man's Gulch. Are we like the indolent butterfly collector? People are all around us, dying in their sins, and we are too busy or too dull to reach out to help. Is your life a spiritual Dead Man's Gulch or is it a life saving station? I want to care like Whitefield cared. He pleaded: "Weep out, if possible, every argument, and compel them to cry, 'Behold, how He loves us.'" A long time ago, I decided I didn't want the sum of my life to be just a bunch of stuff in storage and zero's in a money market account. I discovered I wanted my life to count for eternity. I asked God for a passion for the unsaved and He granted that request. My zeal can wane, so I consistently petition God to increase my passion for the lost.

A Call for a Renewed Spirit of Sacrifice

History records that legions of Christians made great sacrifices for their faith in the first few centuries after Christ's resurrection, and later during the reformation. Today, millions of Christians are suffering for their faith in Muslim countries, China, and North Korea. Western Christians have become soft. If we are honest, we would admit that we tend to have a greater passion for the internet and television than we do for the lost. We are all guilty of this. Too often our lives revolve around our fun fixes and pleasure seeking. Life and its blessings are wonderful gifts from a good God. Those of us that have so much, should be even more willing to sacrifice our time, money, and heart for reaching the lost. It will take sacrifice and labor.

I am convicted by these words:

I am God's wheat.
May I be ground by the teeth of the wild beasts,
Until I become the fine white bread that
belongs to Christ (Ignatious of Antioch).

We should strive to grow in an attitude of sacrifice. Yes, pray for and work for godly prosperity for the family and the church. But one must want to increase the size of one's own heart. The desire to be willing to give up wants and needs for the expansion of the Church and God's glory is a must. We have a great Jesus! A Lord who gave it all up for us. A Savior who says in His word, "Come and follow me." A young pastor in Zimbabwe said, "I won't give up, shut up, let up, until I have stayed up, stored up, prayed up, paid up, and preached up the cause of Christ. I am a disciple of Jesus. I must go till He comes, give till I drop, preach till all know, and work till He stops me." He spoke this shortly before his martyrdom for his faith in Jesus. We in the West have so much. Most of all, we Christians have Jesus and He has us. Let us fall on our faces in gratitude and conviction and rise up with a new passion for sacrifice to win the lost.

Simple Steps to Be a Witness

1. Pray: Ask God for a holy zeal for the lost.

2. Plan: Scratch out a specific time on your calendar to go out and evangelize.

3. Prepare: Pickup some tracts, a note pad, and a pen.

4. Partner: Call a friend in advance to go out with you.

5. Preach: Step out and go hand out tracts in the marketplace.

6. Pray: Pray for the lost to come to Christ. Pray daily for a passion to witness to your neighbors, coworkers, store clerks, and everyone you see in your personal routine.

Go therefore and make disciples of all the nations, baptizing them in the name of the Father and of the Son and of the Holy Spirit, teaching them to observe all things that I have commanded you; and lo, I am with you always, even to the end of the age. Amen (Matt 28:19-20).

CHAPTER NINE

CONCLUSION: THE WHOLE KIT AND CABOODLE

It has been well for me to remember, when speaking to others, that I am a dying man speaking to dying souls (T.J. Bach).

He is no fool who gives up what he cannot keep to gain what he cannot lose (martyred missionary Jim Elliot).

He who offers to God a second place offers Him no place (John Ruskin).

God give me a deep humility, a well guided zeal, a burning love, and a single eye (George Whitefield).

All is in a man's hands and he lets it all slip from cowardice, that's an axiom. It would be interesting to know what it is men are most afraid of. Taking a new step, uttering a new word is what they fear the most. [1]

[1]. Fyodor Dostoevsky, *Crime and Punishment* (NY: Heinemann), p. 1.

> Forbid it that we should ever consider the holding of a commission from the King of Kings a sacrifice, so long as other men esteem the service of an earthly government an honor… I am a missionary heart and soul… God had an only son, and he was a missionary… in this service I hope to live; in it I wish to die (David Livingston quoted by Stott). [2]

> Ideas must be put into action. [3]

> One who believes that… his Redeemer liveth, is disposed presumably to respond in the affirmative when asked whether… his Redeemer liveth; but lip service, again, is subject to discount. Actions… speak louder that words. One way of testing belief… is by calling upon the professed believer to put his money where his mouth is (W.V. Quine). [4]

> Christians who will not share their faith with unbelievers lack fruit; they are all cob and no corn (Christian graffiti).

> The credit belongs to the person who is actually in the arena, whose face is marred by dust and sweat and blood; who strives valiantly; who errs, and comes short because there is no effort without error and shortcoming; but who does actually strive to do the deeds; who knows the great enthusiasms, the great devotions; who spends himself in a worthy cause; who at the best knows in the end the triumph of high achievement (Theodore Roosevelt).

> For "whoever calls on the name of the LORD shall be saved." How then shall they call on Him in whom, they

---

2. John Stott, *Contemporary Christianity* (Madison, WI: Inter-Varsity Press, 1992), p. 328.
3. P. Andrew Sandlin, *We Must Create A New King of Christian* (Vallecito, CA: Chalcedon Publication, 2000), p. 14.
4. W.V. Quine, *Quiddities* (Cambridge, MA: Belknap Press), p. 19.

have not believed? And how shall they believe in Him of whom they have not heard? And how shall they hear without a preacher? And how shall they preach unless they are sent? As it is written: "How beautiful are the feet of those who preach the gospel of peace, who bring glad tidings of good things!" But they have not all obeyed the gospel. For Isaiah says, "Lord, who has believed our report?" So then faith comes by hearing, and hearing by the word of God (Romans 10:13-17).

And the Lord said, to what then shall I compare the men of this generation? And to what are they like? They are like children sitting in a market, and calling to one another, and saying, we have played the flute to you, and you have not danced; we have mourned to you, and you did not weep (Luke 7:31-33).

That you may become blameless and harmless, children of God without fault in the midst of a crooked and perverse generation, among whom you shine as lights in the world, holding fast the word of life (Philippians 2:15,16).

He who wins souls is wise (Proverbs 11:30).

Also, I heard the voice of the Lord, saying: "Whom shall I send, and who will go for Us?" Then I said, "Here am I! Send me" (Isaiah 6:8).

The righteous are bold as a lion (Proverbs 28:1).

Our heavenly Father wants people who are consumed with love for Him, whose desires are one with His, and who won't be content until the earth is filled with the knowledge of the glory of the Lord, as the waters cover the sea. [5]

In this union, that Christ is so glorious and precious to believers. No heart can conceive, or tongue express the

---

[5]. Danny Lehmann, *Bringing Them Back Alive* (Springdale, Penn.: Whitaker House, 1987), p. 159.

> glory of Christ in this union. This union of Christ and His church shines forth in the exaltation of the righteousness of God in the forgiveness of sins. [6]
>
> Give me one path to follow supreme good. [7]
>
> The Bible isn't filled with stories of God making people happy. It's filled with Him making them holy. [8]
>
> It is Christ as King, not as Savior, who commands His victorious militia. And every member of that army must be obedient, just as the Commander before him was obedient even unto death. [9]
>
> When John the Baptist wielded his axe in Matthew, he made chips fly. That rough-looking man… who ate no dainties… produced trembling in the hearts of people and a confessing of their sins. This is the need of the times: men of God, skilled in the use of the axe of the word… not just playing in the woods… We need men who… willingly suffer loss of all things for the Master. There is a widespread outcry nowadays against hard strokes. But… the blows of a man of God are worth their weight in gold (Franklin Ferguson).

I have titled the conclusion of this book *The Whole Kit and Caboodle* because it is a summary that is simple and all encompassing. The expression uses two words, kit and caboodle. In early America, both words were defined as: things, property, and people. So the whole of the Christian faith can be summed up in one word: Christ. The whole purpose of man can be expressed in the simple words "to glorify God and enjoy Him forever"

---

6. John Owen, *The Glory of Christ* (Carlisle, Penn.: Banner of Truth. 1994, original 1683), p. 80.
7. Eknath Easwaran, *The Bhagavad Gita* (Petaluma, CA: Nilgiri Press 1985), p. 75.
8. Keith Green, *A Cry in the Wilderness* (Nashville, TN: Sparrow Press, 1993), p. 13.
9. John Gerstner, *The Early Writings: Volume 1* (Morgan, PA: Soli Deo Gloria, 1997), p. 83.

as taught in the Westminster Catechism. The doctrine of justification is a major Christian truth, yet it is simple, a legal term that means to be declared righteous. Sanctification is easy to understand through the teaching grace of God's Spirit. The whole of this book is to know God and make Him known. The goal is for you to delight in the truth of God's glorious word; then step out in faith and obedience by preaching the gospel to the lost. That duty is ours. And it should be obeyed as a joyful opportunity. The "whole kit and caboodle" is to rejoice in the law and gospel, and share those truths with others.

I have never considered myself an evangelist. I have a tendency to lack boldness and passion for witnessing. I tend to be self-absorbed. Yet the scriptures that call me to be a witness, stir my soul for the lost. The past ministry of fiery Christians propelled me to go and follow Christ and openly share my faith. I still can get self-focused, uncaring, and lazy. That is the reason I pray, memorize evangelism scriptures, and plan specific days to go out witnessing. I try to keep it simple and consistent. The more I step out and evangelize the lost, the more my journey is filled with alacrity and passion. The main reason I witness is Jesus loved me and gave Himself for me. I must share the excellencies of Christ. When I have stepped out in boldness and shared my faith, I have seen things that no man deserves to see. I have seen six young adults come to faith in Christ in the back of a bar; then with joy they (they were not drunk) gave testimonies to their unsaved friends.

If you pray and answer the call to evangelize, you too will see God's mighty hand move. You will fall on your face, with thanksgiving, for the privilege of your God using you to bring a lost soul to Jesus. The lost remain lost, unless we preach the gospel to them. With every fiber in my being, I pray that you will go and be a witness for Christ.

Slothfulness in Evangelism

> That for three years I did not cease to warn everyone night and day with tears (Acts 20:31).

An elderly scholar once asked a bright and promising student, "What's the difference between ignorance and indifference?" The indolent student answered, "I don't know and I don't care." That attitude has come into many churches. What does God require of all saved men and women? Obedience. This includes the command to preach the gospel. The Bible teaches us that God has gifted some to be evangelists (Ephesians 4:11). This does not mean that they are the only people who should evangelize. Paul exhorted Timothy, who was not an evangelist, to do "the work of an evangelist." Thus all true believers must be a witness for Christ. The gifted evangelist will witness more often and more effective than those who do not have that spiritual gift. They usually do not need to be exhorted and motivated. Others need to be exhorted and motivated to consistently reach out to the unsaved. We must pray for a heart on fire for the unbelievers. We need to ask God, over and over again, to give us a heart of compassion for those on their way to hell. The great English Puritan, John Rogers, one time stirred up his congregation for the lost by imitating the screams of the souls in hell. Hell should prompt your mouth to open and trumpet the truth of God. Your love for Jesus should enkindle your heart to urge Christ upon the pagan; your glorious union with Christ should prompt you to yearn for the salvation of those God has providentially set in your path. It is no longer you who live, but Christ lives in you, the one who loved you and died for you. As a Christian, Jesus lives in your heart by faith. Jesus said, "I came to seek and save that which was lost" (Luke 19:10). Since that was one of His goals, and He dwells in our hearts; we must follow Him as a seeker of the lost. To arouse your heart for the unsaved: ponder the cross, consider the love and excellencies of Jesus, look to the glories of heaven, and the eternal pangs of hell. As one old preacher said, "I want the stench of hell in my nostrils and the splendor of heaven in my eyes."

The Intent

Our life is so short. We land on this spinning blue ball and pass through like withering grass. We should glorify God and enjoy Him each day. A self-centered life is just a dash, between our birth and death dates, on our tomb stone. Our joyful duty is to start our day in worship; move into prayer, and launch into daily evangelism. Today, make a prayerful commitment to habitually reach-out in your town to the "least, the last, and the lost." Purchase a notebook or a journal. Record your prayers for the lost, your missed witnessing opportunities, and those times you stepped out in faith and handed out a tract, invited someone to church, or engaged a non-Christian in a conversation about Jesus. Remember, witnessing is simple. Not necessarily easy, but simple. Just pray and give the lost the law and the gospel. Our job isn't to record a bunch of "decisions for Christ." The intent is to see all men, everywhere, repent and believe the good news. Our prayerful goal is to see the lost come to Christ as Savior and Lord. We must demonstrate the sinner's need of a Savior by using the law in our witnessing. We should be determined to break up the fallow ground of the unbelievers heart by employing the threats of the law, then let them hear the groan of the sacrifice on Calvary. The law must be preached before the nonbeliever will appreciate propitiation. One must know why he is under the wrath of God that was turned away at the cross. All have sinned and broken God's law. That warrants the wrath of God abiding on the non-Christian. Jesus Christ is the only propitiation for the wrath and judgment of the thrice Holy God.

> Whom God set forth as a propitiation by His blood, through faith, to demonstrate His righteousness because in His forbearance God had passed over the sins that were previously committed (Romans 3:25).

The ministry that has motivated me more than any other is the ministry of the late Keith Green. Though there are some difficulties with elements of his theology, Green's passion and his "no compromise" attitude has fired me up for the lost for over twenty years. I would recommend that you purchase all his albums. The heart God gave him for the unsaved is the type of heart that I desire. Green's zeal is displayed in the following quote, "Lord Jesus, I repent for my sin of not caring for the lost souls… for bearing children of my desire and not your desires."[10] Musing on the famous lyrics by Green brought me to intense sobbing for those that do not know Jesus, and the Christians who will not go witnessing. May these words inflame your heart for the souls of your neighbors, coworkers, family, friends, and fellow citizens who do not know Jesus.

Make my life a prayer to you.
I wanna do what you want me to.
No empty words
And no white lies,
No token prayers,
No compromise. [11]

---

[10]. Melody Green, *No Compromise: The Life Story of Keith Green* (Eugene, Oregon: Harvest House, 2000), p. 218-219.

[11]. Ibid., p. 210.

Missionary David Livingston preached the gospel in Africa, and opposed slavery with all his might. He died in Africa, and his body was wrapped and sent back to England. But his African disciples cut his heart out and buried it so that his heart would always be in African soil. Is your heart so inflamed for the lost that your heart should be buried in the land that you now reside? Evangelism is a matter of truth and a matter of the heart. Christ poured His heart out for us on the cross, and we must put our whole heart into winning the lost. Paul said because of the "terror of the Lord, he persuaded men." Our hearts on fire can keep others from going to the eternal fire, if we preach the good news, and God changes the heart of the unsaved. Our goal must be to see a fire rising in our soul, boiling over onto the streets and the marketplace to win the pagan from the flames of Hades. We should do this through preaching the unpopular and mighty gospel with power. We must be gentle, yet move in the strength of God. Van Til, who witnessed on the streets for many decades, exhorted us to be gentle in the "how" and strong in the "what" in our approach to witnessing.

I have a friend, Titus, who was so hot-blooded for God, he reminded me of the eighteenth century Presbyterian preacher Robert Smith. Smith was described as a man who "never knew the fear of man." One time, I watched Titus chase a kid on a skateboard. He ran after him as fast as he could. The kid on the skateboard didn't stop and kept on going. Titus ran as fast as he could, but could not catch the kid. When he stopped, he noticed a lost man standing in front of Him. Almost out of breath, he shared the bad news of his fate without Christ. He then shared with him the gospel. At that point, the man right on the spot, was convicted, touched and changed. He professed Jesus Christ as Lord and Savior right on the side walk. That may seem surprising, but we must always remember: Every salvation is a miracle from God. The lost man's heart must be changed, and only God can do that. He sovereignly works when we urge the law on people's hearts and offer the saving gospel. We obey. And God, according to His will and His timing, will save the souls by transforming their hearts.

> After these things I looked, and behold, a great multitude which no one could number, of all nations, tribes, peoples, and tongues, standing before the throne and before the Lamb, clothed with white robes, with palm branches in their hands, and crying out with a loud voice, saying, "Salvation belongs to our God who sits on the throne, and to the Lamb!" (Revelation 7:9,10).

We must shake the non-Christian religionists out of their self-righteous stupor by preaching the law of God. We should disrupt the naval gazing of the Newagers (those who try to save Cedars by hugging trees, yet they kill babies through abortion) by warning them that they will not find the keys of the universe in the lint of their belly button. Pondering Tarot cards and running into the woods ripping their clothes off, screaming, and running naked trying to rediscover the "primal man" will only leave them empty, depressed, and sunburned. They must be told to repent of their lawlessness and come to Christ.

The Fiery Call

> And they said to one another, "Did not our heart burn within us while He talked with us on the road, and while He opened the Scriptures to us?" (Luke 24:32).

The call is to be fervent for God and His mission. If you are like most American Christians, you are indifferent and slothful when it comes to evangelism. I get my motivation through God's word and the examples of zealous and godly saints, like Wally Tope. Most of you have never heard of him. He was a veteran counter-cult evangelist and street minister; who died while preaching the gospel during the Los Angeles riots in 1992. He went out and preached to the looters, and was knocked into a coma by two miscreants. He died nineteen months later. He gave his life for the Lord Jesus because he preached to the lost. He did not fear any man or any situation. What mattered to him was saving lost sinners. Most of us do not have the gift of evangelism like Wally. But we can look to his life and other consecrated men, and stir-up a passion for the unsaved in our own souls. The same Holy Spirit of God has you and dwells in your heart that had Tope, Paul, John Rogers, Baxter, Whitefield, Carey, Camp, and Lehmann. It was said of Baxter (comparing him to a complacent minister): "Baxter would have set the world on fire while Orton was lighting a match." Ask God for a holy passion for the lost and doomed. I have often bemoaned the fact of the small size of the most theologically faithful churches. I believe the lack of passionate commitment for evangelism has be-dwarfed many doctrinally pure churches and denominations. To be like William Grimshaw, whom it was said, "a few such as him would make a nation tremble; he carries fire wherever he goes." Spurgeon said of Christians, "...they do not burn down, they burn up and keep on burning when the fire is of the right sort. When a bush is nothing but a bush, it is soon consumed when it is on fire. But, when it is a bush that burns on and is not consumed, we know that God is there. So is it with a church that is flaming with holy zeal." [12] Dear reader, ask the Most High, right now, for that "holy zeal."

The problem isn't that most of us lack zeal. The real hindrance: A lack of zeal does not trouble us. The parable, told by Kierkegaard, appropriately demonstrates our indolence toward the supernatural resources that God endows every believer. The story takes place in a make believe land in which ducks live all by themselves. When the Lord's Day comes all the ducks wake up, comb their feathers, and waddle down to the church. They waddle down the church aisle and sit in their duck pews. They sit down to hear their duck pastor open his duck Bible, and preach of God's great and grand gift to ducks: wings. The preacher exhorts his duck flock with the stirring words, "You ducks can fly. You can mount up like eagles and soar into the sky. You can break away and fly into the heavens and escape the pens and fences that restrict and confine. You can experience the euphoria of complete freedom and liberation. You can have power and victory in your wings. Fly, fly, fly away through God's power. Step out and soar every day." All the ducks in the congregation affirmed and shouted, "Amen, yes, come on." And then, they all slipped out of the their pews and waddled home. Not one of them used their wings. The impassioned sermon calling them to fly did not change them. And far too often this is the life of the average Christian. God has blessed us with the Holy Spirit, His holy word, and the gospel. But far too often, we live like Kierkegaard's ducks. When we hear a fervent sermon or read a stirring book on evangelism, we shout, "Amen." And then just waddle home. Jesus said in Acts 1:8, "But you shall receive power when the Holy Spirit has come upon you; and you shall be my witnesses." Christians have the power and the resources to spread the faith. Let us embrace God's word and stop waddling through life.

Ruin, Redemption, and Regeneration

Unbelief is the shield of every sin (William Jenkyn).

The Puritan dogma of "ruin, redemption, and regeneration" is the Bible message we need to recover and preach. A message of the law and the gospel. That before the holy law of God: All men are devoid of righteousness. The nonbeliever needs to hear how he has specially broken

---

[12]. C.H. Spurgeon, *The Soul Winner* (Springdale, Penn.: Whitaker House, 1995), p. 120.

God's law. Lost people are wandering around the world asleep and they need to be woke up. The story of the blacksmith who brought home a new dog illustrates this point: The first day the blacksmith was working in his shop; he would pound and pound the metal with his hammer. Immediately, his new dog would bark loudly. Day after day, as he worked the hammer, his dog would jump up and bark. After a few days, the barking got softer and softer. Then a couple weeks later, the dog stopped barking when the smith started hammering. He became dull toward the hammer. That is part of the problem with the lost. They have suppressed the truth of their sins so long that they have become dull towards the hammer of the law written on their hearts. They need a wake-up call through the preaching of the holy law of God. The Ten Commandments must be preached to strip the deceived sinner of "every shred and piece of self-righteousness" and leave him naked before the holy gaze of God Almighty. We cannot just offer them the grace of God without first calling the law of God on their conscience.

Get Serious

The time for all Christians to get serious about God is now. The time for you to step out in faith, to trust and obey, is now. Stott has rightly said, "The Christian faith is a missionary faith." We have a mission and a commission to be His witnesses. The Christian Church is the biggest and most powerful army in the history of the world. It is to be an army with Christ as our banner. We must hoist-up our banner and proclaim liberation in Christ. We must go beyond just affirming the truth, we must start embracing the truth, every day. The King of the universe has saved you, delivered you from death, hell, and the grave. Surely, as we ponder those truths, our souls get thrilled. We are to petition God to give us a heart for those who do not know Jesus. We should step into the world and really care. To care more about the state of an unbeliever's soul than we care about possible negative reactions we might receive for sharing our faith. I want to be part of a world wide reformation and revival. I want to strive to see every person saved. All men, in every nation, bowing the knee to Jesus as Lord. Most people would say that is too big of a goal. It will never happen. It can't happen. I don't have any delusions of grandeur, but I want to aim at perfection and righteousness. My evangelism goals are for Christians to preach the gospel, loving the lost, as God's grace brings them into the kingdom. God is the King, and He may not share my goals in my lifetime. That is a strong possibility, but I must pray and fight with all my might that the whole world would repent and trust in Christ.

A renewed passion for evangelism in the Church Universal must start with individuals and individual churches. Some of our best and purest churches have relaxed into a tentative normalcy that seldom reaches out to the pagan. Many sleep in a suffocating sameness that makes one long for Whitefield, Edwards, Spurgeon, and Brainerd. Jesus and the Apostles preached a fiery law and gospel that were at odds with the "zeitgeist" and religionists of their day. They taught and lived that the graces of the church were given for the glory of God, and to be fuel for witnessing. "Glory to God in the highest, and on earth; peace and goodwill toward men." Let us receive the word and delight in the sacraments. May we rejoice in prayer and praise to please God, and win men to Jesus Christ. Let the church become a launching pad for the gospel, as we preach it from the West to the East. This is what the godly and Reformed churches need. This is what I need, and you need. This is what God commands in His holy word by the power of the Holy Spirit, in the name of Jesus Christ, for the glory of God the Father.

Be Respectful

> We're coming out with guns blazing (Al Pacino in: *And Justice For All*).

> And suddenly, one of those who were with Jesus stretched out his hand and drew his sword, struck the servant of the high priest, and cut off his ear. But Jesus said to him, "Put your sword in its place, for all who take the sword will perish by the sword. Or do you think that I cannot now pray to My Father, and He will provide Me with more than twelve legions of angels?" (Matthew 26:50-53).

Peter, on the night that Jesus was arrested, was very zealous about swinging his sword against an enemy. He cut off an ear, and then Jesus healed it. Followers of Jesus need to be less zealous in chopping off ears and more willing to be meek and kind. In the western part of the United States, I have noticed that the main problem with the Christian witness is not too much zeal, but almost the complete lack of zeal. Most of this book has addressed this issue. But that small and passionate minority within the Christian community, can be too zealous at swinging their sword at unbelievers. The Bible does not give us license to be mean, cruel, and impatient. We should follow our Lord and have a zeal and even an anger that is controlled by God. The Bible tells us that one of the fruit of the Spirit is self-control. Let us be aggressive, yet kind, longsuffering, and joyful.

Excuses, Excuses, Excuses

> Men cannot but feel that if religion is worth anything, it's worth everything. [13]

I tire of seeing men of letters and simple followers of Christ search for ingenious reasons why believers don't have to preach the gospel to the world. While we are playing games and ignoring the clear scriptural mandate to be a witness, the cults are devouring the lost, and the watered down churches are entertaining the goats. Let the redeemed say so! Let us follow the zealous men of church history into the battle for the salvation of souls. So much of the modern church is made up of men who blushingly give weak reasons why they are not called to share their faith. Our prayer must be: God forgive me, give me a fresh boldness to speak your word to the people that you have providentially placed around me. Yes, we must affirm, profess, and stand on the sovereignty of God. But that same sovereign God, commands all believers to speak the truth in love and to preach the gospel to all nations. You may be gifted as a teacher, administrator, worker of mercy, or another spiritual gift that is not evangelism. This will not get you off the hook; you also must do the work of an evangelist.

> In light of such blessed hope and such deliverance from the troubles and sin and guilt of this life, it may be said even today: "My yoke is easy and my burden is light." Woe to those who play with these words and act as if it is meant that Christ's cause is an easy cause. The person who recoils in horror from the seriousness and the frightfulness of this cause of Christ, understands much more about these words. [14]

---

[13]. Horatius Bonar, *Words to Winners of Souls* (Pensacola, FL: Chapel Library, 2001), p. 6.

[14]. Dietrich Bonhoeffer, *A Testament to Freedom* (San Francisco, CA: Harper Collins, 1990), p. 237.

> Go therefore and make disciples of all the nations (Matthew 28:19,20).

Let us pray for and work toward the rectification of all evil and the implantation of all good, around the globe. The gospelization of all nations must be our plan. The old canards from the "last days" of the 1970's ("God didn't call me to clean the fishbowl, but to fish in it" and "you shouldn't polish the brass on a sinking ship") must be tossed. These can no longer be our mantras. The peaceful conquest of the world for Christ must be our prayerful goal. To not only confound and stagger the infidel, but to win him to Christ. Regeneration of the unsaved is the starting point and the foundation for righteousness in our culture and nation. Jesus said, "Every good tree bears good fruit, and every bad tree bears bad fruit." Through the preaching of the gospel, God changes hearts. To have a transformed nation, we must first have transformed hearts. Our job doesn't end at preaching the gospel, and standing in awe of God saving a soul. The mandate is not to make converts, but Jesus commands us to make disciples.

Breaking out the balloons and cake, rejoicing with the angels over the repentance of the sinner is a great time to jump for joy. But after the streamers come down, the cake is eaten, and the party is over, we must get down to serious discipleship with all new converts. A disciple is a student, a life long learner and follower of Jesus. We are called to instruct them in righteousness, as we model godliness. The Lord issued a command that we teach the newly saved "all that He commanded." Our duty is to preach the gospel, and pray for disciples. We should nurture new Christians. We must mentor them and spend time with them. We are instructed to catechize them in doctrine and the commandments, loving them as Paul loved Timothy. Our privilege is to follow our Lord in making disciples of all nations. Many of the most astute and talented in the church have pale faces that bespeak of those who rarely venture out beyond the dim illumination of their library lamp. Let our faces be glowing in the midst of disciples, as we impart to them that which we have learned in our study. We are not to simply be containers of God's word; we should be dispensers of His holy word.

Zeno believed that the world is just an illusion. If our world is an illusion, then the problem with that assertion, if true, is the statement is an illusion. Hence that statement is not true. Thus the world cannot be an illusion. God has revealed that this world is real. It is not an illusion, and the next world is not an illusion either. The life beyond this life has only two destinies: heaven or hell. We must be about trying to populate heaven by preaching the truth of Christ to all creatures. Let us be real. Let us be serious. And let us be biblical. Get alone with God and pray the way Baxter did when he cried out: "Truly this is that peal of conscience doth ring in my ears, and yet my drowsy soul will not be awakened. Oh, what a thing is an insensible, hardened heart! Oh, Lord, save us from the plague of the infidelity and hardheartedness ourselves."

> There is no other God besides Me, a just God and a Savior; there is none besides Me. Look to Me, and be saved, all you ends of the earth! For I am God, and there is no other. I have sworn by Myself; the word has gone out of My mouth in righteousness, and shall not return that to Me every knee shall bow, every tongue shall take an oath. He shall say, "Surely in the LORD I have righteousness and strength" (Isaiah 45:21-24).

The Fear Factor

> Golf is a game made up of errors. Learning to cope with feelings of failure and imperfections is one of the keys to freeing the mind and allowing oneself to play the best... Free the mind of the fear of failure, and the game can be played in an uninhibited, fully productive way. The mastery of the art of playing golf well undoubtedly rests upon the mastery of the art of playing poorly. Only by learning to accept imperfection and to play without fear can one perfect both the golf swing and the art of scoring. [15]

I do not play golf, but the quote listed above relates well with evangelism. Witnessing can be challenging and we can make mistakes. The "art" of successful evangelism is like golf, it rests on the mastery of doing it poorly. Nobody, except Jesus, ever witnessed perfectly every time. The two truths that can assist you in mastering evangelism are God's sovereignty and God's love. The Bible reveals a God who is completely sovereign. We need not fret when we fail or flop in a witnessing appointment. God is God, and He is in control of every soul on the earth, and everyone's eternal

---

[15]. Jim and Wally Armstrong, *Playing the Game: Inspiration for Life and Golf* (Nashville, TN: J. Countryman, 1998), p. 61

destination. This truth should help you learn to accept your witnessing imperfections. Step out and speak the gospel and if you fail, focus on God's sovereignty. The Bible also tells us that "perfect love casts out all fear." This is good news. I can step out in a relaxed and confident manner because I know, no matter what happens, God loves me. I am in God's covenant, and He loves me because I am accepted now and forever in the "beloved." If I decide to trust in my abilities, I can quickly become fearful. If I resolve to focus on Christ: His love, His covenant and His power; I can go out in the market place and share my faith with confidence. I must put my faith in God Almighty, not my ability. I then move out uninhibited, free, and productive.

A Small Thing Can Lead To Big Things

The Scottish missionary Robert Moffat came home to England from his mission in South Africa. He came home to help recruit more missionaries. He arrived at the small church to teach, and he noticed only a few people showed up to hear him speak. Most of these were women, and he was very disappointed in the turnout. He tried not to let this bother him, and he preached his text, Proverbs 8:4, "Unto you, O men, I call." In his disappointment, he almost failed to notice a little boy in the back. Moffat felt hopeless as he preached his sermon because he figured the jungles would be too challenging for any of the ladies to join up as missionaries. But God is God; He frequently works in ways we do not understand. No one signed up that night, but that little boy in the back was thrilled by the call and the challenge. And he decided to follow that pioneer missionary when he finished school. After graduation, the boy became the man David Livingston. He was one of the most successful missionaries in the history of African missions. We may never know, in this world, all the people God used us to touch and radically change. They may be the next successful missionary or preacher.

There are three main reasons Christians fail to witness. The first is blindness: "Do you not say, 'There are still four months and then comes the harvest'? Behold, I say to you, open your eyes and look at the fields, for they are already white for harvest" (John 4:35). This picture must be met with prayer. Ask God to open your eyes to the plight of the lost. Fear is the second reason we fail to preach the gospel. God says, "Fear not, for I have redeemed you; I have called you by your name; you are mine" (Isaiah 43:1). Apathy is the third overarching reason Christians fail to evangelize. The Bible calls us to a life of passion and zeal (Romans 12:11;

1 Corinthians 15:58). My hope is that the reader will aggressively confront those three reasons that inhibit one's evangelism zeal, through prayer.

The main purpose of this book was to glorify the triune God as I persuade Christians to share their faith. I really know I'm not much. I discover this truth more each day. I identify with the Dostoyevshy, when he wrote these rallying words: "Sometimes, even if he has to do it alone and his conduct seems crazy, a man must set out an example and so draw men's souls out of their solitude, and spur them to some great act of brotherly love, that the great idea may not die." May we become part of the kingdom of God that embraces brotherly love and the grand idea of the great commission.

Made in the USA
Lexington, KY
08 December 2012